MARTIN EDMOND is a prizewinning screenwriter and the
author of *The Resurrection of Philip Clairmont* (1999), shortlisted
for the Montana New Zealand Book Award for Non-Fiction,
and *The Autobiography of My Father* (1992), which took third
prize in the Wattie Book Award. His childhood was spent in
Ohakune, but as this book reveals, he has travelled widely;
he now lives north of Sydney with his partner and two sons.
He is the 2004 Literary Fellow at the University of Auckland.

CHRONICLE OF THE
UNSUNG
MARTIN
EDMOND

AUCKLAND UNIVERSITY PRESS

First published 2004

Auckland University Press
University of Auckland
Private Bag 92019
Auckland
New Zealand
www.auckland.ac.nz/aup

© Martin Edmond, 2004

ISBN 1 86940 311 8

Publication is kindly assisted by ⑤creative*nz*
ARTS COUNCIL OF NEW ZEALAND TOI AOTEAROA

National Library of New Zealand Cataloguing-in-Publication Data
Edmond, Martin.
Chronicle of the unsung / by Martin Edmond.
ISBN 1-86940-311-8
1. Edmond, Martin. 2. Authors, New Zealand—New Zealand—20th
century—Biography. 3. Biographers—New Zealand—Biography.
I. Title.
NZ823.2—B—DC 21

Cover design by Sarah Maxey
Printed by Astra Print Ltd, Wellington

This book is for Col

Soul history emerges as one dies to the world as an arena of projection. Soul history is a living obituary, recording life from the point of view of death. As one builds one's death, so one writes one's own obituary in one's own soul history.
— JAMES HILLMAN

I

MIRRORS

IN AMSTERDAM, AT ELEVEN ON A SUMMER EVENING, WHEN LIGHT still lingers in the sky and you see reflected in the canals the most delicate shades of pink and green and blue, together with faint diamonds of stars, I stopped, almost involuntarily, in front of a shop window down a narrow street in the Zeedijk. It was the display: a human skull sitting on a plinth covered in velvet or chenille of a colour I could not make out in the deceptive combination of the last light from the sky and the streetlamps which had just come on – was it red, or a faded threadbare purple, or even green? Like a rucked and crenellated sea, the cloth fell away from the plinth in such a way as to cover the entire visible surface of the display area in folds, and as I stood trying to elucidate that fugitive colour, the uncertain light produced a curious and unsettling illusion: my own face reflected in the glass over the bones of the skull, like a premonition of my death.

If I had not spent the day wandering the streets, I might not have lingered so long before this spectre; as it was, tired, abstracted, with the whole night still before me, I stood and stared until image and skull, skull and image, changed places before my eyes like a figure/ ground ambiguity. Feeling vaguely alarmed, I dragged myself away at last and was about to continue on down the skinny street lined with raised, glassed-in, protruding bedrooms where prostitutes waited in the vagrant light, when suddenly the door of the shop opened and a woman appeared. She was thin-faced, stooped, about fifty, with the exasperated, vengeful look of one who has lived a life of constant frustration and is on the lookout for someone to blame for it. In her hands was a cardboard box full of papers, and behind her, amidst the devastation of what had evidently once been a book or an antiquarian shop, stood a man in shirt-sleeves with a look of the most abject misery on his face, literally wringing his hands. I saw all of this, like a snapshot of my parents, in the moment before the woman let loose a guttural Dutch oath and threw the lot into the street. Perhaps she didn't see me, but I turned away anyway, right into the path of two sailors walking by. One of them caught me by the shoulders, steadied me, turned me round so I was facing the shop again and gave me a little push, while the other swayed gracefully out of the way in time with his mate's deft manoeuvre. I caught a whiff of beer and Gauloise cigarettes on their breath as they laughed and went on. The door of the shop was already shut again and stood, as blank as before, beside that creepy window. The contents of the cardboard box lay strewn all over the footpath and in the gutter between the wheels of parked cars. I felt oddly guilty, as if I were somehow responsible for the mess; then picked my way through the debris and went on.

I lost my enthusiasm for walking the streets of Amsterdam. The high from the joint smoked earlier had faded. I felt tired, lonely, miserable and somehow affronted by the plump, barely dressed hookers in their strangely elevated pink and blue rooms, smiling falsely towards the ubiquitous, meticulously made, overstuffed single divan beds at the backs of their tiny cages. It was as if both women and beds were upholstered so as to give no soft yielding of mattress or flesh, but a hard pneumatic bounce, like a tractor tyre. I decided to end my trawl of night streets and go straight to the railway station, where it would be warm and there would be a place I could sit down and rest, or perhaps even sleep. With my arm pressing against the now almost completely flattened plastic-wrapped oblong of marijuana I carried in the lining of my jacket, I turned and went back east under a rapidly darkening sky.

I had been sent over to Amsterdam to look for work. At that time I was part of a troupe of actors and musicians more or less stranded

4

in London; as the only non-performing member, I could always be spared. In truth, there wasn't much for me to do beyond lugging gear, helping set up and break down the gigs, and lighting the bigger shows. Apart from the lighting, which I enjoyed, the work struck me as sterile and demeaning. That passionate, self-obliterating loyalty, bordering on arrogance, which all the best roadies have, was not part of my character. But what was I to do? My wife, Gemma, was the composer of most of the music for the shows: I was, through her, as if married to the troupe as well.

Things were complicated by a kind of guerrilla war going on between the action and the music, a war in which my loyalties were irretrievably divided. I had previously acted with the troupe and was passionate about the shows we did: music was integral to them. At the same time, even though I thought she was better at theatre than rock music, I felt an obscure obligation to support Gemma's desire to turn the musicians she led into a successful, independent, rock 'n' roll band. I couldn't, however, go along with her mad attempt, every time we set up a new show, to place the music as close to centre stage as she could get it: we were, after all, doing theatre. Then there were my own ambitions as a writer, which, apart from minor contributions to the shows or to lyrics for the band's songs, languished almost entirely unfulfilled.

There had been some interest in booking our group in Amsterdam – for instance, at that famous club the Melkveg, or Milky Way, which you reach by crossing a high bridge over a canal – but the dates that had been offered were for the autumn, several months hence, and thus no solution to our immediate problems. So I was returning empty handed into the simmering internecine strife between actors and musicians and the refractory longueurs of my marriage.

That morning, I had slept past the hour set aside for the cleaning of the scrubbed, bare room at the pension, and for my slothfulness was evicted. In a mood of sluggish irritation, I decided that rather than find somewhere else to go, I would spend my last night in the city on the streets. I checked my baggage at the railway station, where I was due to catch a train in twenty-four hours, and set off. Amongst the drifting, transient crowds which gathered in those days around the fountains in the great squares of Amsterdam, talking, smoking, drinking, flirting and fighting, I fell in with a Sydneysider who offered to take me to one of the cafés in which drugs were bought and sold. I was elated: for weeks, all we had been able to find in London was a poor, expensive, pale brown, friable Lebanese hash which gave you nothing but a headache.

Under a white sky, the Sydneysider and I walked out west, past the end of the rings of the canals which reminded Albert Camus of the circles of hell, to an anonymous street where, down some stairs beneath a coffee bar, there was a basement room which at eleven o'clock in the morning was almost totally dark; only the soft-drink machine in the corner glowed dimly, its subaqueous light seeming to fail within a few feet of the source. At first I thought we were alone down there, but as my eyes got used to the gloom I saw that the walls of the room were lined with blurred shapes like our own, awaiting the imminent arrival of the dealer.

As the minutes passed, the agitation among this clientele grew palpable; we murmured and shuffled impatiently in our shadowy corners. When, a full twenty minutes after the hour, a man in a high-collared, buttoned-up leather jacket and a peaked fisherman's cap came down the stairs, he was surrounded by a throng of people three or four deep, most of them young men, offering money and calling out their orders in strained whispers rustling like the voices of the dead. The Sydneysider pressed forward with the rest, but I hung back, admiring the dealer's efficiency as, magician-like, he took the proffered wads of notes and at the same time produced from his sleeves or his pockets the requisite small packet of white powder, sachet of tablets or plastic bag of herb. In that weak light all that was visible between his hat brim and his collar was the profile of his nose; his voice was as soft as or even softer than those of his clients, and he radiated a casual menace: when the press of people around him became too great, a word that he would cease trading and leave was enough to still everyone. Each customer disappeared the moment their purchase was completed, up the stairs into the street, or else into the recesses of the basement, there to smoke or swallow or inject in peace.

The Sydneysider secured our bag of dope, we took the stairs and, over coffee in the barely functional bar upstairs, divided it surreptitiously between us. This man, whose face and name I no longer remember, accepted without rancour when I declined to go back to his hotel room for sex and, after telling me, with the somewhat tremulous braggadocio typical of Sydneysiders, that his home town would undoubtedly become the world capital in the next decade and that I could do worse than move there, left. As for me, I bought some cigarette papers, went to a nearby park and had a smoke – my first since leaving London a week before. Afterwards, with my head billowing like a sea or a travelling sky, I escaped into the nearby Rijksmuseum Vincent van Gogh.

The Rijksmuseum, opened in 1973, and home to more than 1,000 works painted, drawn or written by van Gogh in his brief career, as well as some which are the known or unknown work of others, remains in my memory a tower of light. The galleries around the open, central, airy core of the building were full that day of a silver-grey sky falling from high above through a roof made entirely of glass, and in that soft, northern light the colours of the paintings glowed like things encountered before only in dreams. And yet of all the many works I looked at that afternoon as I climbed from gallery to gallery, higher and higher, as if towards some heaven, I really only remember one wall. It was about halfway up, facing into the well of descending light, and showed the paintings of orchards in blossom van Gogh did not long after he first arrived in Arles in the winter of 1888.

They are candelabra of light, shadowless, blazing, lit from within, like a virtuous life. Their white fire burned images on my eye with such intensity that twenty years later they are still there. The apricot trees, the peach trees, the pear trees, the almonds, the plums and the apples are pictures of moments in eternity. They somehow resolve the paradox of now and forever. The former teacher, preacher and dealer in prints, who had bought and sold on the Rue des Images in Antwerp, and later, calamitously, took his life for art, for a brief time in Arles closed the gap between the two and would, for the rest of that year, live and work in a state of rapture.

I can still remember vividly how excited I became that winter when travelling from Paris to Arles, he wrote. *How I was constantly on the lookout to see if we had reached Japan yet.* Having recently sold a picture for five francs, which he immediately gave to an old prostitute who smiled at him in the street, van Gogh said goodbye to his brother Theo at the Gare de Lyon and took the train south, looking out the window all the way until he saw a place he wanted to paint. It was February and Arles was covered with snow, as you can see in his painting of the elm trees by the road he walked down from the railway station. One of the first things he did was pick a sprig off an almond tree just coming into bud; placed in a glass of water on a window sill in the room he took over the Restaurant Carrel, it became the subject of the first of the sixteen paintings of blossom from those early spring months in the south.

The simplicity of this painting – *Blossoming Almond Branch in a Glass* – is radiant. It has nothing to recommend it but its integrity. All the messy contradictions of self and other, reality and representation, consciousness and world, dissolve in a plain view. You feel that it is after all possible to look with someone else's eyes, to see what the painter has seen. A whole way of living is evoked: how many of the unsung have picked flowers like this and put them in glasses on their window sills? The painting speaks to a future which lacks all ceremony but the ceremony of daily life. That sill, that tumbler and that blossom – though not the painting of them – could belong to any of us now.

'Japan', then, was the place image and reality, art and life, became one, and in his nine months there, van Gogh painted his joyous masterpieces: the orchards, the Langlois bridges, the fishing boats and seascapes at Saintes-Marie, the wheat harvests, the *café de nuit*, the sunflowers, the Zouaves, the Postman Joseph Roulin and his family, the lost Road to Tarascon, his bedroom, and the pair of shoes which has saved some from madness. He knew what he was after:

8

when, in the high summer of this season of beatitude, he posts to his brother in Paris the drawing for his *Portrait of Patience Escalier*, he writes as if it were the actual person he is sending, this *man of the hoe*. Sometimes it is possible to capture in paint the soul of a person, a place or an object and send it down the centuries.

The painting of Patience Escalier, a former cowherd who was then gardener at a house in the Crau, is not at the Rijksmuseum Vincent van Gogh, but it hung on a wall in the house where I grew up, along with one of the sunflower paintings and *Harvest at La Crau, with Montmajour in the Background*, which the Rijksmuseum does own, although I have no memory of seeing it there. How little I remember, living as I did then, inauthentically, in that blur of anxiety for the next moment which clouds vision and poisons recall.

We also owned a couple of Gauguins – *Te Matete* and *Landscape with Peacocks, Matamoe*. I say 'owned'; they were of course reproductions. Yet it never occurred to me that they were not 'real'. Rather, I thought they were of places and people nearby. Such naivety is not necessarily absurd. Van Gogh valued copies, as if the soul of a person, a place or a thing might also survive the process of reproduction, whether by hand or by machine. Did he anticipate the proliferation of his works, which now hang on the walls of houses all over the world? He who famously wanted the peasants, the postmen, the café owners, the children and the soldiers he painted to own the pictures he did of them, as if they might thereby possess a little more of themselves?

1888, the wonderful year, ended in mayhem two months to the day after Paul Gauguin arrived at the end of autumn. The two painters had met in Paris; now Gauguin, starving in Pont-Aven, wrote to van Gogh asking him to ask Theo to sell some pictures for him. Vincent had already made plans for an *atelier du Midi*; now he enlisted his brother to the cause and was relentless in his persuasions until Gauguin agreed to come. Money was the root of it for Gauguin, loneliness for van Gogh. Gauguin arrived on 23 October and set about establishing his primacy with all the force of his avowedly savage nature. His mission, which he did not doubt was successful, was to bring order to the disorderly life and work of van Gogh.

He reviewed the domestic arrangements at the Yellow House, where they both lived and painted, establishing a kitty system for expenses and proposing they eat in sometimes to make the cash Theo sent from Paris last longer. Gauguin, who thought van Gogh made soup the way he mixed his paints, did the cooking while van Gogh did the shopping. For the sake of 'hygiene', they visited a local brothel regularly. Every day they painted, and in the evenings drank and talked; about art, said van Gogh, they had *terribly electric* arguments which left them exhausted. Gauguin liked Ingres, Degas and Cézanne, whereas van Gogh idolised Meissonier and wept to think of Monticelli. In those epochal two months, some of Vincent's work – like *The Red Vineyard*, which Theo sold in Brussels for 400 francs – did come to resemble Paul's, but Paul's did not ever look like Vincent's. In the end, it became a matter of life and death for van Gogh, who could neither assimilate nor resist the power of Gauguin.

Gauguin said that when it became clear the experiment was failing and he had already decided to abandon the stillborn colony, he would wake suddenly in the night to find van Gogh standing over his bed. He would say in a certain tone of voice: *What's the matter, Vincent?* and Vincent would go back to bed and fall immediately into a heavy sleep. The day after their quarrel over Gauguin's portrait of van Gogh painting sunflowers – van Gogh said, *That's me alright, but me gone mad* – and a night drinking absinthe, during which van Gogh threw a full glass at Gauguin's head, Gauguin told van Gogh he was leaving. That evening, while crossing the square on his after-dinner walk, he heard a quick step behind him and turned to find van Gogh coming for him with an open razor in his hand. Gauguin said he cowed him with a look, whereupon van Gogh turned and fled home, there to commit the famous insult to his ear, the piece of which, in its turn, was put in an envelope and left at the brothel door for a *fille de joie* whose working name was Rachel.

Van Gogh never wrote an account of this incident, so we have only Gauguin's version of what happened. It is not contradicted by official records; nor does his account of the aftermath conflict with those of others; but a sole witness has enormous power and

Gauguin was an incorrigible myth-maker. This is why the odour of the charlatan hangs around him, if not his work, whereas no one ever doubts van Gogh's terrible sincerity. And yet it is van Gogh's work which is forged on an unprecedented scale.

Gauguin's friend, fellow stockbroker and painter Emile Schuffenecker, painted van Goghs which his younger brother, the dealer Amédée Schuffenecker, sold. Dr Gachet, who signed his own works 'van Ryssel' and was meant to be looking after van Gogh when he died at Auvers in July of 1890, probably did some too – including the version of his own portrait in the Musée d'Orsay. Gachet's daughter Marguerite and son Paul lived on the sale of their father's paintings – Dr Gachet painted Cézannes too – for the rest of their lives, which did not end until 1949 and 1962 respectively.

In January 1928, three years after the death of Jo Bonger, Theo's widow, a German dealer named Otto Wacker opened a major exhibition at the Paul Cassirer Gallery in Berlin. The van Goghs were, he said, the property of a Russian aristocrat who had fled Paris for Switzerland and could not be named for fear of endangering his family in communist Russia. Although authenticated by eminent scholar Baart de la Faille, they were fakes, and Wacker went to jail for fraud. It isn't clear who painted the Wacker forgeries, nor what happened to them; perhaps they are among the unknown number of pictures falsely attributed to van Gogh in museum and private collections, whose owners are sometimes forced to defend their investments by pleading the authenticity of forgeries.

It seems inexcusable that this most genuine of artists should be faked. No one else put so much of himself into his work; no one else identified self and art so intensely. There are reasons. It is relatively easy to invent a false provenance for a van Gogh. He often made copies of his own works; he gave a lot away; and he didn't always do a painting from every drawing, or a drawing for every painting. Because he sold so little – though more than the legendary one – while he was alive, there are few sales records. Theo died within six months of Vincent, leaving everything to Jo Bonger who, while she faithfully kept the name alive, and has by some been credited as the architect of van Gogh's fame, simply didn't know all that Theo knew.

Even so, it is hard to resist the fearful thought that it is the man who is most himself who is most easily faked: the illusion of integrity is the very quality forgers rely upon to deceive the *cognoscenti*. The most famous forgery is the sunflower painting owned by the Yasuda Fire and Marine Insurance Company, held at the Yasuda Kasai Museum of Art in Tokyo. Yasuda, who, before the authenticity of their painting was questioned, donated £11 million towards the recently completed extensions to the Rijksmuseum Vincent van Gogh, have not yet allowed their acquisition to be examined – and may never do so. It is probably by Emile Schuffenecker, a copy of either the one in the National Gallery in London (August 1888) or of van Gogh's own copy of the earlier picture in the Rijksmuseum (January 1889). All three paintings have the same title: *Still Life: Vase with Fourteen Sunflowers*. It was a reproduction of one of these we had on our wall at home – but which one? There is no way of knowing now, so why do I feel in my bones it was the Yasuda sunflowers I grew up looking at? Is it because fakery is an integral part of my heritage?

The irony of Japanese ending up with expensive fakes is as poignant as their refusal to admit it; and perhaps Yasuda's denial they spent a then (1987) record £24.75 million on a forgery gives them a strange dignity. The response of another Japanese corporate owner of a questionable painting is as enigmatic: they have threatened that if speculation does not cease, they will burn the picture, bury the ashes and pour sake on its grave. And after all, the copies by Schuffenecker and van Ryssel may be other than they seem: not deliberate fakes but homages, attempts by lesser men to discover the magic of van Gogh with their own hands. If so, they may be forgiven in the same way as the inauthenticity of our younger selves is sometimes forgiven by the passing of time.

At one of the railway station entrances, I fell in with half a dozen young Arab boys who hung out there, lounging comfortably against the stone pillars or sitting on benches set into the flanking alcoves. They had bright, darting brown eyes and lithe smooth bodies and found everything funny, especially the plight of a stolid, dough-faced

Dane who sat disconsolately among us, sighing heavily and saying periodically, with profound melancholy, the name of his native city, Copenhagen. He was stranded, it seemed, without the wherewithal to go home.

More than that it was impossible to know, since he spoke Danish and the Arab boys only French. They were from North Africa – Algeria, Morocco, Egypt; what they were doing in Amsterdam wasn't clear either, since my schoolboy French could barely sustain a conversation. Sign language, the rolling of eyes and flicking of eyebrows, together with the odd word from each other's language, was the most we could manage as we swapped cigarettes and waited for morning. As the night wore on, their utterly unmalicious amusement at the sadness of the Dane became the leitmotif of our interplay: every time the poor kid let out another sigh, they would shout with laughter and chorus in anticipation: *Copenhagen!* Soon the mere mention of the word was enough to set us all roaring. The Dane gave us wounded looks and once even stood up and made to go away. One of the boys took him by the arm and gently pulled him back to his seat, either out of genuine concern or in order that the game might continue.

When I took the book I carried out of the pocket of my jacket – *The Life and Loves of Frank Harris* – meaning to read for a bit, one of the young Arabs pointed to it and asked what it was: *Qu'est-ce que c'est?* I shrugged and gave it to him; he opened it, letting the pages flutter by under his fingers until he came to one of the vaguely risqué drawings it contained, and paused. A top-hatted gentleman, his breeches undone, was ravishing a bare-breasted streetwalker; her skirts foamed around her waist and you could see what might have been a curl of pubic hair. The boy stared for a long time, then laughed and passed it on. The book did the rounds and came back to me. I tried to say something about it, but we ended up once more smiling at each other in mutual incomprehension. Then one of them, an Egyptian, as if returning the favour, reached into a small cloth bag he had slung over his shoulder, pulled out a book and gave it to me. It was a small, paperback edition of the *Poèmes* of Arthur Rimbaud. In French, of course.

Rimbaud! I said. *Je connais!* The Arab boys were delighted.

As I leafed through the book, looking at the titles, the boy who had given it to me spoke. *Rimbaud*, he said, *il est un africain. Comme nous.*

I looked at him. *Mais non*, I said, *il était français.*

He smiled. *Africain*, he said.

I smiled back and shook my head. He went to Africa, I said (or tried to say), but he was French. He died in Marseille.

The boy's grin widened. *Africain*. He put out his hand for the book, turned to one of the pages and pointed at some words: *Europe, Asie, Amérique, disparaissez.* He repeated the line softly, his smiling face right next to mine. *Vous voyez?*

What to do? For the first time there was tension in the air. All of the Arab boys, very still and quiet, were watching me. There was no way I could carry on an argument like this in French, and anyway, what did it matter? I shrugged, nodded my head. *Oui, africain*, I said.

The Egyptian boy grinned, closed the book and dropped it back into his bag. *Qu'est-ce pour nous?* he said enigmatically.

The Dane sighed again. *Copenhagen!* we cried out, all together.

Qu'est-ce pour nous?, sometimes rendered as *What does it matter?*, are in fact the title and the first words of the poem he had shown me, which may be translated: *What are they to us, my heart, the sheets of blood/And cinders, and a thousand murders, and the long cries/Of rage, sobs from every hell overturning/Every order; and the wind still blowing over the debris . . .* Written during or just after the Siege of Paris, Rimbaud's Zutiste period, the poem is a spell meant to sweep everything – justice, history, colonists, peoples – away. Its absinthe-inspired, incantatory holocaust obliterates not just the poet and his *romanesques amis* but the continents of the old earth as well – except, perhaps, as the Egyptian had pointed out, Africa. The spell fails; the poem has a footnote: *Ce n'est rien; j'y suis; j'y suis toujours. It's nothing. I am here. I am still here.* In this it perhaps anticipates those passages in *Une Saison en Enfer* in which Rimbaud excoriates himself for thinking that words alone could change the world; but that does not invalidate the prophecy.

How apposite that I encountered both van Gogh and Rimbaud during that day and night in limboland. They were twin poles between which my frustration and yearning oscillated: van Gogh, the man who willed himself into being as an artist and turned what was perhaps no more than an awkward facility with pencil or paint into the lineaments of genius; Rimbaud, the marvellous boy whose immense capability had devoured, rewritten, then abandoned the whole Western literary tradition before he reached his majority. The one seemed an exemplar of the perseverance I could not muster, the other of the natural ability I did not have. Which is why, I suppose, like so many other avatars of fame, I mined their biographies, hopelessly, for clues to my own fate.

I was actually more interested then in the lives of artists than I was in their works. I would read biographies meticulously, as if by tracing the life I could, like van Ryssel or Schuffenecker copying van Gogh's works, find out who I might be. The reading of biography requires that you imagine being the person it is about, which is impossible but no more impossible than the same imaginative act with respect to a character in fiction – yet wholly different for the very reason that in a biography you suppose yourself to be imagining the real. Is this also why you sometimes feel compelled to imagine not just being that person, but being, as they are, the subject of a biography yourself? Or is it a recognition of the fictional nature of any life told retrospectively and from the outside; and, following upon that recognition, a desire to imagine a similar retrospective fictionalisation of your own day-to-day existence? To read a life knowing how it ends is to read absolutely outside the consciousness of the person whose life it was, who, even if they knew the hour and manner of their death, still lived open-endedly. Radical misunderstanding of how people live may be consequent upon the passionate reading of biography. The most dangerous error is to attempt to live like the subject of a biography yourself.

One of my younger sisters once said that she grew up thinking she was going to be famous. When I heard this I realised, with a shock, that I had too. Then I thought, but did not say: I still do. Where does this come from? In our case, out of the family nexus. Both our parents were ambitious, but in different ways and to different ends. My father wanted to be known and praised for his good works while my mother wanted the purer fame that is admiration for your very essence: she would be loved for the quality of soul unveiled in her poetry. Their ends were likewise opposite. Though my father was, and among some people still is, esteemed for his good works, he lived the last twenty years of his life in the unshakeable conviction of his failure as a person; my mother achieved all the worldly ambitions she could have hoped for, yet never satisfied her yearning to be loved for herself alone. Perhaps the hypothesis that fame would redeem the inauthenticity of my self was inherited from them. Was this why I spent so much of my time in the toils of self-examination?

To begin with the presumption of fame is to acquire the habit of reading others' lives as clues to your own. You study the anatomy of fame in order to construct a simulacrum of yourself as a 'famous person', the way a person with Asperger's syndrome learns to read the facial expressions of others for evidence of their own emotions. Curiously, my habit of inserting myself into others' lives was accompanied by a belief that the proper expression of this projection was the kind of lyric poetry which places the observing self at the centre of the poem: this self would become famous, even though it was posited at the outset as inauthentic, a fiction or, more precisely, an imitation. The verse could thus only be a thing of rags and patches, made out of indiscriminate, unacknowledged, perhaps envious borrowings. I was fascinated by van Gogh's example not because he had, in 'Japan', achieved that sublime conjunction of art and life but because, even so, his manifest authenticity was still vulnerable to forgery. As for Rimbaud, it was not so much his poetry as the following silence which obsessed me. The ordinariness of their lives interested me most of all, as if in the quotidian of genius my own humdrum days might find their apotheosis.

Morning came, and with it the hour for my train. I said goodbye to the Arab boys, and to the melancholy Dane, and went off to catch it. As it cleared the station and the city, heading south through Utrecht and past Rotterdam to the Hook of Holland, the flat fields passed by outside the window, green, marshy, squared into lots, with neat paths between them. There were windmills, and tulips. I returned to van Gogh, fleeing Amsterdam with his burning hand.

In the summer of 1881, at his parents' house in Etten, he fell in love with his recently widowed cousin, Cornelia Adriana Vos-Stricker, the daughter of Reverend Stricker of Amsterdam. It was only the second time they had met. Kee, as she was known, was holidaying at the van Gogh vicarage with her four-year-old son Jan, and the three of them went out together walking and talking on drawing expeditions into the countryside. Van Gogh, who loved children, seems to have imagined them as a family, and thought that, by making friends with the boy, he might win over the mother. She was still mourning her husband and never once considered her strange cousin as a replacement for him. His declaration of love was rejected with an emphatic no, and she returned immediately to her father's house in Amsterdam. Later she remembered: *He fancied he loved me . . . he was so kind to my little boy.*

Van Gogh was unable to believe she did not want him, even when his letters to her went unanswered, and persuaded himself that it was her parents who were the problem. In the autumn of that year he went to Amsterdam to propose marriage, but Kee would not see him. To convince the Strickers of his seriousness, in their presence he held his left hand open over a candle flame until the flesh of the palm bubbled and charred. He had the previous year decided, after nearly a decade's agonising, to become an artist and perhaps this is why it was not his painting hand that he held in the flame. The Strickers were appalled rather than impressed; they remained intransigent, and van Gogh left Amsterdam alone and still obsessed. At the end of that year, after a violent religious argument with his father, who was disturbed at his son's passionate unortho-doxy, he moved to The Hague and began taking lessons from the painter Anton Mauve – the same Mauve to whom he would dedicate *Pink Peach Tree in Blossom* after he heard news of his death in the miraculous spring at Arles seven years later. It was under Mauve's tuition that he completed his first ever paintings in December 1881:

dark, muddy still lifes, one with cabbages and clogs, the other with beer mugs and fruit.

There was a portrait of Kee, now lost, but a photograph of her at that time survives. She looks austere, bereft, sitting in profile with the boy on her lap, wearing a high-collared, buttoned-up black dress with a metallic sheen to it, making it seem like armour against her grief. The fringe of white lace showing at the neck only emphasises the deep shadowy fold of skin over the cheekbone beneath her left eye; her left hand holds open the book in her lap; her other, unseen, is clasped around the boy's waist. He, in contrast to her desolate gaze, looks full at the camera, stalwart, erect, perhaps already in his own mind taking the place of his dead father at his mother's side.

During his subsequent two years in The Hague, van Gogh for the only time in his life lived with a woman, the prostitute Christine Clasina Maria Hoornik, called Sien, along with her five-year-old daughter. Sien was pregnant when van Gogh met her, and he took her for the birth to Leiden, where he tried to find a flat for the four of them to live in. He wanted to marry her too, but his family were horrified by the idea and did everything they could to talk him out of it. The affair also alienated Mauve and his other mentor in The Hague, H. G. Tersteeg. In fact, everyone except Theo abandoned van Gogh at this time. His attempts to find work as an illustrator came to nothing and, since he insisted Sien give up working, the money he got from his family was all they had. Sien thought he spent so much on paint there was not enough left over for the children, and conspired with her mother to go back on the streets. After twenty months with her, during which he produced some of his eeriest drawings, van Gogh allowed that family life was irreconcilable with the demands of his further development as an artist, and, with great reluctance, left Sien, her daughter and her young son (she had two other children he never knew about) and went north to Drente to live in the dark, peaty marshlands at Hoogeven. He took a barge to Nieuw Amsterdam and visited Zweeloo, where the painter Max Liebermann had been spending his summers since the 1870s, though he did not see him. It was another of his many failed meetings with artists whom he admired and thought might help him.

Before leaving The Hague, he wrote to Theo: . . . *a single word made me feel that nothing was changed in me about it, that it is and remains a wound, which I carry with me, but it lies deep and will never heal, it will remain in after years just as it was the first day.* He was talking not about Sien but about Kee; it was her rejection of him that caused the recoil that hurled him across Europe into the maelstrom of the sun of Arles, the dark flames of cypresses at Saint-Rémy and the devastating wheatfields of Auvers.

Van Gogh and Rimbaud were almost exact contemporaries: van Gogh was born and died one year earlier than Rimbaud; they were both only thirty-seven years old. They were alike, too, in that the theatre for their artistic activities was the same north-west corner of Europe. Both spent crucial parts of their lives in Brussels and in London; both found in Paris the incontrovertible truth of their vocation; and both wandered far from their homes without ever being able finally to escape from home. But the trajectories of their lives were opposite. Rimbaud's brief, startling efflorescence was over before van Gogh's had even begun, and his silence at the end of his life is in absolute contrast to van Gogh's prodigious output, which was ended only by his sudden death.

Both plumbed the abyss of cities, but for both the countryside they loved was still pristine, making them absolutely of another era: the age of gasoline is also the age of plastic, and now none of us expects to go anywhere without encountering some kind of rubbish left behind by others, making a certain kind of disappointment a central experience of all our travels. Both were of another age, but both were aware they stood at the cusp of the new, van Gogh looking back to the reapers and sowers, the peasants and artisans of the dying century, while Rimbaud looked forward, speaking to and for the dispossessed of every continent and culture. Van Gogh, with his implicit or explicit egotism, is the exaltation of the individual self as creator and possessor of value, while Rimbaud stands for its absolute negation or extinction.

We can't think of Rimbaud without Verlaine; in the same way van Gogh's name always evokes Gauguin's. Each *ménage drole* crystallises in the image of one man standing over the other's bed. Just as Gauguin would wake in the night in the Yellow House at Arles to find van Gogh at his bedside, so too did Rimbaud, in London, wake to Verlaine loomed over his: *After this vaguely hygienic diversion, I would lie down on my pallet and, no sooner asleep than, almost every night, the poor brother would rise, his mouth foul, eyes starting from his head – just as he dreamed he looked! – and drag me into the room, howling his dream of imbecilic sorrow.* What did they each want, van Gogh and Verlaine? What was it the other had in such great measure they would never give? Certainty, authenticity, power, indifference? Each must have known they could never possess what the other had, but that did not stop them wanting it.

The figure of a man standing over the bed of another man sleeping might be an image of the estrangement of the dreamer from the dream, the soul from the body, the poet from the poem. Or it might be a sign of their coming rapprochement. To me, the figure standing over the bed is in a sickness of desire, but desire for what? The other's sleep? His dreams? Or his very self? I was haunted by the image because it perfectly expressed my own predicament: there was no doubt that I was the bereft one standing over, while the sleeper could have been any of those I admired, whether in books and museums, or among the members of the troupe with whom I travelled and worked. It could also be, like the skull in the window, an image of my death.

If van Gogh wanted Gauguin's insouciance, if Verlaine would almost have died to possess Rimbaud's audacity, that does not mean the quality was felt by its actual owner as a gift. It could just as well be a curse, as Rimbaud's dromomania or van Gogh's deliriums must have been. In a drama such as this – artistic envy as a consequence of ontological uncertainty – we always misunderstand the true feelings of the other, for if we knew them what would we still desire to possess? Or is it that to desire possession we must misunderstand?

Here is another contrast: if it was failure in love which flung van Gogh irretrievably into his romance with art, then that same failure seems to have been what silenced Rimbaud. Most of what he wrote was given to other people, and most of that was given to

Verlaine – including, at their last meeting, in Stuttgart in 1875, the manuscript of *Illuminations*. Although some of these poems may have been written – they were certainly written out – while Rimbaud was in London with Germain Nouveau in 1874, that only strengthens the case for Rimbaud as a poet of intimacy. He needed to address an other in order to write; that is why most of his *oeuvres complètes* consist of letters. He held the highest of hopes for his liaison with Verlaine and for a while was indeed the infernal bridegroom to Verlaine's foolish virgin: *Une Saison en Enfer*, too, is unimaginable without the debacle of their affair as its immediate precursor.

Yet neither Rimbaud nor van Gogh had any talent for intimacy. Van Gogh's impetuosity, his intensity, his strangeness made most recoil. He knew this about himself: . . . *it is painful for me to speak to people. I am not afraid to do so, but I know I make a disagreeable impression; I am so much afraid that my efforts to introduce myself will do me more harm than good.* This rueful, confessional tone is completely at odds with the depthless irony or snarling scorn of Rimbaud, but it is possible that the same perception of the strangeness of the self is behind both the one's abnegation and the other's self-loathing.

Rimbaud would pick up beggars in the street and give them money, just as van Gogh was always inclined to give away what little he had to those with less. This open-hearted generosity was, in both men, allied to an abstemious nature which could not bear for money to go to waste. Van Gogh, who was for the whole of his life dependent on the charity of his family, considered his paintings and drawings to be that charity transformed into marketable goods – never mind that no one wanted them now, there would come a time when they would. It has even been said that his suicide was an act of generosity to his family, freeing Theo to look after his newborn son (also Vincent) and putting an end to the production at least of genuine van Goghs, which might then begin to find the value that accrues to finite *oeuvres*. Rimbaud's letters from Africa to his mother and sister are those of a man whose anxiety that income outweigh expenses is cosmic, the very ground of his being. To what end? Mere profit? Or something else, some kind of transcendence arising out of the absorption in day-to-day transactions? What is the connection between kindness to beggars and exactitude in financial dealings?

Van Gogh never doubted the supremacy of art, but what of literature? We search Rimbaud's later biography for any fragment which might suggest an ultimate value for writing, but there is none. Literariness is absolutely denied; even a relative merit is questionable. His abandonment was so complete there is nothing sensible to say about it. He had decided to devote his life to action, to 'real things' as opposed to 'imaginary things', and that was it. The revolutionary and anarchist returned to the ordinariness of the world where doing would replace being. In the letter to Ernest Delahaye of 14 October 1875, which contained the last poem, *Dream*, a rhyme about soldiers in a barracks comparing the smells of their farts to different cheeses, he says: *Je tiens surtout à des choses précises – I am only interested in precise things.*

What things? The *tej* (mead) pitcher he designed and had made? The *khat* he chewed? The immensely long lists of trade goods he bought or had for sale: ivory, hides, coffee, gold (rings or ingots), incense, musk of civet purchased in exchange for Indian cotton, Massachusetts shirting, knitted skirts and tunics, goatskin bags, string necklaces, flannel, merino, velvet, silk, damask, gold braid, novelty buttons, pearls, rice, butter, sugar, salt, flour, tobacco, quinine, oil, candles, scissors, rope, socks, sandals, saucepans, goblets, the *birillis* or mead pitchers of his own design, baking sheets, rosaries, crucifixes, Christs, bales of ruled notepads . . .

Perhaps he was always a literalist. Delahaye said he never made anything up, only recalled things he had seen. He told his mother *A Season in Hell* meant exactly what it said, no more and no less. But in it he also mentioned that visions were things he really saw. Is it the case that he saw 'visions' all his life, but at some point decided not to write them down any more? When he was dying in Marseille, these visions came back. His sister, Isabelle, was entranced by the word pictures he painted on his death bed. Over a day and a night, the entire past of the race, and its future, passed before her uncomprehending eyes. In Africa, in the Afar Triangle, the place where human beings may have originated, Rimbaud would fill his pockets with millet and walk out into the desert for days or weeks on end. What did he see? The things not said, the visions not told, haunt us, along with the possibility that they do not exist, but are simply a figment of our literary imagination. The strangest thing about Rimbaud's post-literary life is that it seems already to have been described in his writings. Like some of his poems, it is a hieroglyph which has not yet been deciphered.

Some say poets pass on an ancient truth, they have no other cause. Further, that there is a secret history only the poet comes to know. Rimbaud's life is an image of the secret history which he found but did not tell. Even though it may not exist, we know it to be more than a name and a fate. *Misfortune is endless*, he said in his last letter to the world. *Ask any dog in the street*. Perhaps in that corner of Africa where he was, there are still reverberations going on we know nothing about. There, where he disputed the Koran with Arab scholars; only Sufis would take the time to argue with a French trader. Harar is the fourth holiest city in Islam. Ethiopia was the fabled medieval kingdom of Prester John which Italian priests sought, as is related in the *Ethiopian Itineraries*, *ca*.1400–1524. These intricate traditions overlay the original, the African. If the poet will not tell us, how will we find out the secret history of the world?

I remember nothing of that railway trip between the first glimpse of the fields of Holland and our arrival on the outskirts of Rotterdam, where Rimbaud first left Europe behind. Perhaps I slept; it was more than twenty-four hours since I had. The convoluted piping of oil refineries is what I saw as I came back to consciousness – cylindrical tanks surrounded by ladders and derricks, the dark water of the Waal, where tankers waited to discharge their fuel, spread out under a grey sky everywhere shrouded in smoky, dirty air.

Past Rotterdam the railway terminates at Vlaardingen, and there I caught the trans-Channel ferry to Sheerness. I had been in some kind of trance the whole way from Amsterdam, but the moment I went on board the ship, whose name I have forgotten – it was a roll-on, roll-off car ferry like the ones which cross Cook Strait – I started getting anxious about the bag of dope hidden in the lining of my jacket. The enormity of what I was doing struck me: international drug smuggling, even on this petty level, is not easily forgiven or forgotten. What to do? Throw it over the side? Too obvious. Flush it down the loo? Yes, but what if it jammed in the works; what if the toilet backed up and flooded? I would become even more conspicuous than I already was.

Most of the passengers on the ferry were part of a large touring group of Australians and New Zealanders. There were about sixty of them; they had just completed a bus tour of Europe – seven countries in fourteen days – and were, like me, returning to London. It was a long time, more than a year, since I had been around a group of Anzacs and it quickly became clear that I was as unlike them as they were distinct from the few ordinary passengers on the ferry. They wore jeans and T shirts if they were men, and skirts and tops if they were women, and to an outsider were nearly indistinguishable from each other. They talked loudly and laughed a lot and were oblivious of the effect they had on others.

Feeling gauche myself in my double-breasted pinstripe suit jacket, tight black jeans and suede boots, I nevertheless hung around the edges, hoping to talk with someone. After a while a girl did come over for a chat. She was plain, sensible, matter-of-fact as she told me who the group was and where they had been. We compared backgrounds: she was from a small town in the Waikato not far from one I had lived in for a few years, and for a moment it seemed we might find friends in common. But there was no way I could tell her what was going on and anyway what would be the point? I was on my own. Then I saw in her eyes a fear that too long talking to a stranger might be seen as either a desertion or a rebuke and she rejoined her group.

I went below to try to sort myself out, and in a locked booth in the toilets transferred the dope from the lining of my jacket into my right boot, where it sat under the instep of my foot. As if there it might be less likely to be found. Those boots, of ankle-high yellow-green suede, came off the streets of New York. One of the actors had found them in an alley in the East Village and handed them on to me when they didn't fit him. I never liked them, but I wore them; they ended up in a second-hand shop in Albuquerque, where I left them in mute exchange for a pair of hand-tooled, calf-high tan cowboy boots which I did like. Now all I had to lose was in them.

Soon we had crossed the grey unquiet sea and were docking at Sheerness. I hung back while everyone else disembarked, looking for my 'friend', still hoping somehow to mingle with the Anzacs. She waved goodbye and passed with the rest into Customs ahead of me. When I stepped through the door, I found myself in a vast, almost empty shed. An enormous distance away and off to one side, the Anzacs were being marshalled. In the instant, I understood there was no way I could pass as one of them. The Customs Men themselves – *Enfer aux Deliquants que sa paume a frolés!* – were about halfway down the cavernous shed, at a tiny station towards which I walked, heart racing, palms sweaty, breathless, before stopping at a small desk and putting my bag down on the low table next to it.

There were two of them. One, who never spoke, searched my bag while the other did the talking. He was watchful, sceptical, not unfriendly, and would have me in a flash if he saw how agitated I was. The first item that came out of the bag was Frank Harris, and as soon as I saw it I started yapping: *Oh yeah that's by this guy who just spent his whole life, you know, he had a lot of women and this is the story of all of them, how he met them, what they did, you know, and he doesn't leave anything out, he's not leaving anything to the imagination, you know, so what you're reading is, mostly what you're getting is these descriptions of this guy who just roots just about every woman he meets . . .*

It's too long ago to remember exactly what I said, but my intention was to let the Customs Men know that it was a dirty book so that they might lose interest in my things and let me go. I also thought that no matter how crazy I sounded, talking would hide my anxiety. And it helped me to forget the lump under my instep. So I talked, and the guy listened and the other guy went meticulously through my clothes. The Customs Man went from bored to suspicious, then – and I remember this clearly – a flicker of interest crossed his face as he got what I was on about. *Yeah?* he said. The other guy finished going through my bag. *Take off your jacket*, said the first guy. There was a lurch in my gut; my boots would be next; I was gone. The silent guy silently, thoroughly, patted the linings of my inelegant pinstripe, then handed it back. I was silent now too. We looked at each other. *Okay*, said the first guy. *You can go.*

The distance to the great lighted rectangle that was the door to England was as far as or further than I had come to the Customs Men, but I was across it in a thought and out into the warm, wan air and flat industrial wasteland of that coast. All the adrenaline blew by in exhilaration. I was full of myself and the tale I would have to tell the troupe. Never mind that I had no gigs, only the vaguest of offers from the Melkveg for September – I had dope and a story. The high kept me going all the way up the south bank of the Thames on the train to Victoria Station and thence via the Underground to the Elephant and Castle.

I was on my way to Intergalactic Art. When we were in New York, planning our trip to London, one of the troupe noticed in a listings mag an advertisement for a place of that name which offered bed and board to travelling artists and also had rehearsal studios for bands. We got in touch and made a booking, and that was how the band and I ended up staying for a few weeks in an old hotel in Morecambe Street, just two blocks back from the Walworth Road in the Elephant and Castle.

Intergalactic Art was a co-operative of four people – Roland, Mandy, Steve and Nick. Whether they owned, leased, rented or squatted in the hotel was never clear – it could have been any of them – but they lived in it as if it was a squat. Six storeys tall, with a reception area and rehearsal studios on the ground floor, kitchen and living space on the first, and the remaining floors given over to a warren of rooms with gerry-built bunks, old mattresses, camp stretchers and sagging wire-woves in them, the hotel stood alone and crumbling along a half-demolished street that had been that way since the Blitz. The four had their own apartments on the top floor but none of us ever went up there.

Roland and Mandy were a couple. Roland was a big, ineffectual, red-headed and red-bearded man with a stammer which seemed sometimes an affliction, at others an affectation. His long-term project was building a light synthesiser in the basement of the hotel. Mandy was a palely beautiful, intensely neurotic woman who spent her time in bed or in tears or both; Roland spent most of his days hovering over her, which was why his synthesiser languished half-built down there like an obsolescent spaceship. Mandy's parents had money, and sometimes she went back home to be hovered over by them; on these occasions Roland mooched about the hotel complaining how hard life was for artists.

Of the other two guys, we saw most of Steve, a Liverpudlian, the son of a Scouse woman and a black American serviceman he'd never met. Steve had oily dark hair and sallow skin, and a manner both ingratiating and sly. Even the offer of a cup of tea from him made you wonder. Steve at least got out and about: he was a dealer, it was him who sold us the headache-inducing Lebanese hash. The other guy, Nick, had a proper job; an underwater cameraman, he worked high-paid shoots in places like the Caribbean or the Red Sea. Nick was polite, friendly and, in that English way, utterly unapproachable beyond a certain point. He had a green Bedford van he never wanted to lend but could occasionally be shamed into letting us borrow to take the band's gear to a gig.

This fab four, with nothing in common but their shared enter-prise, pursued it with an estimable tenacity and guile: no chinks in their armour, even though it was clear they didn't see eye to eye on much else. The tariff we paid included our meals, which our hosts were to cook; all they ever served up was porridge for breakfast and stew with bread for lunch and dinner. This mess of meat and vegetables was cooked in a big pot on the kitchen stove, and then reheated and added to as the days went by. In time, it became a thin grey gruel which none of us could stomach: Steve would pour the uneaten portions back into the pot and spoon them out onto the table again next meal. Only under extreme pressure would a new stew, identical to the last, be made. The bread was baked on the premises too – a dark, crumbly, sour loaf that never varied. As the stew thinned, so too did the bread dry. Any protest was answered with dismal agreement, followed by the observation that we were all in it together.

The band, comfort bunnies like all rock musicians, were appalled. They liked warm places, good food, good drink, good drugs, good music. Good sex. There was none of that here, apart, perhaps, from the sex. We'd paid in advance, so there was nothing much else we could do but snarl and bear it. It got so bad that, though we couldn't really afford to, we took to eating out. When a gig at a Commonwealth Youth Festival of the Arts in Sheffield came up, we decided to leave and find new places to stay on our return to London. By the time I came back from Amsterdam, everyone else had already gone north; my suitcase, packed and ready, was waiting at Intergalactic Art.

I climbed the multitudinous stairs out of the dark underground at the Elephant and Castle station and set off south along the Walworth Road. On the other side were streets and streets of boarded-up Victorian terrace houses with their floors torn up and their toilets smashed to discourage squatters. The Walworth Road was a clot of traffic. Chip packets and grit blew in the slipstream of the endless roar. Grey pedestrians huddled against the orange sun. I turned off and walked the two blocks to Morecambe Street, where the hotel stood tall among the empty sections of the blitzed street.

The door was never locked unless no one was in, and there was never no one in. I pushed it open and walked through the reception area where I had made more than a hundred calls seeking work for the troupe or the band; each of them had been logged and paid for. I could hear voices on the first floor, falling silent as I climbed the stairs. At the wide kitchen table where we had eaten our gruel, Roland and Mandy and Steve and Nick sat before a feast of epic proportions: chicken, cold cuts, cheeses, salads, olives, breads, fruits, a raft of condiments, bottles of wine . . . Their faces, stiff with embarrassment, floated uncertainly above the heaped table. All had stopped in mid-chew. Clearly I was not expected.

W-w-w-would you like to join us? said Roland, unconvincingly.

No, thanks, I said. *I've just come to get my suitcase.*

Bland Nick, Shifty Steve, Mad Mandy and Ro-ro-ro-Roland. They were as unhinged as many hippies, with an ideology wildly at variance with their practice and an impeccable line in rationalisation. This was just after Maggie Thatcher was elected; nuclear-armed Pershing and cruise missiles were to be installed in Germany and the world remade by the gospel according to Milton Friedman. They abhorred the Tories, and would never admit they were already practising the economic fashion on the way in: squeeze your paying customers and pig out on the proceeds. They were mean and tricky and hopeless, and what I can't forget is that they put themselves through the desolation of that Dickensian stew and sour bread so that we wouldn't suspect they were ripping us off. There was some desperate truth in their subterfuge which almost made them pitiable, as if they were only the dumb inheritors of the miserable greed of generations.

I dismissed them from my mind and, that afternoon, caught another train north, passing the time with Frank Harris – a not unlikely ally in my near debacle at Customs, I decided. Despite his rapaciousness and egotism, he was an inveterate defender of outsiders, and one of the few who stuck by fellow Irishman Oscar Wilde to the end, buying the plot for a play off Wilde when he was living in Paris, even though he knew he was paying too much for it. He did, however, object when Wilde tried to sell it again elsewhere. Earlier, after Wilde had been bailed following his first trial in May 1895, Harris kept a steam yacht at Erith on the Thames waiting to take him to France. *She has steam up now*, he said, *one hundred pounds pressure to the square inch in her boilers, her captain's waiting, her crew's ready* . . . Wilde refused. He could not, he said, *go about France feeling that the policeman's hand might fall upon my shoulder at any moment. I could not live a life of fear and doubt, it would kill me in a month.*

Oscar Wilde was exactly four days older than Arthur Rimbaud, and outlived him by nearly ten years. It's a curious though probably meaningless fact that both men had their twentieth birthdays in England – Wilde at Oxford, the day before he matriculated at

Magdalen College on 17 October 1874, Rimbaud (probably) at his lodgings at 165 Kings Road, Reading, not far from the jail where Wilde would be incarcerated when his twenty-year triumph, just beginning, was over. Rimbaud was teaching French at a language school run by a Camille Le Clair, while Wilde was continuing the study of Classics he had begun at Trinity College, Dublin. Wilde, like others of his generation, sometimes wrote poems in the manner of Verlaine, and once, in 1883, drank absinthe with him at the Café Vachette in Paris; he thought him ugly and therefore contemptible. It seems unlikely that, if he and Rimbaud had ever met, they would have had anything to say to each other, unless Wilde was attracted by such a peerless piece of rough trade. They were so different: Wilde was delighted when hundreds of American college students came to his lectures dressed as him, whereas Rimbaud was both solitary and truly inimitable.

At Reading, Rimbaud put the finishing touches to *Illuminations*, the last literary work he ever did. Much of this consisted in the anglicisation of his French prose; specifically, the literal translation of common English phrases into French. These phrases came perhaps from some of the lost among the enigmatic word lists he made, detailing such subjects as pigeon-fancying, rugby and cricket, dressmaking and the terminology of pet shops, as well as those seeking the meaning of idiomatic phrases: *The mind cannot advert to two things at once. Help yourself to anything you like.*

No more importance should be attached to the intelligence that Vincent van Gogh was also in England during that October, working unhappily at the London office in Southhampton Street of the Paris art dealers Goupil & Cie. His uncle, another Vincent, had previously established a branch of the firm in The Hague, where, from 1869, van Gogh assisted in the sale of paintings, photographs, copper engravings, lithographs, etchings and reproductions, mainly of works by the French Barbizon School and the Dutch Hague School.

In May 1873 van Gogh was transferred to London and remained there until October 1874, meaning he was resident in the city when, in March of that year, Rimbaud and Germain Nouveau took a room with the Stephens family between a pub and a dramatic agent's office in Stamford Street, Waterloo. They worked in a factory in Holborn, making hat boxes out of cardboard, and advertised for pupils who wanted to learn French. Van Gogh, meanwhile, was at a boarding house run by Mrs Ursula Loyer, the widow of a curate from the south of France, and falling in love for the first time in his life with her daughter Eugénie. Eugénie was, however, already secretly engaged to someone else – a previous lodger – and her rejection of van Gogh led to his first great emotional crisis. After a holiday at home in the summer of 1874, during which his family found him thin, silent, dejected (but noted that he drew a lot), he returned to London with his sister Anna and took new rooms at Ivy Cottage, 374 Kensington High Street. Here he lived a solitary life, neglecting his work, reading religious tracts and translating the Bible from Dutch into other languages.

Nouveau made copies of the *Illuminations* in his own hand before going back to France for good; Rimbaud, alone again, returned to the neighbourhood of his first sojourn in the metropolis, moving to 40 London Street just behind the Howland Street house he had shared with Verlaine two years previously. Here he fell ill, and became so reduced he sent his mother a piteous letter asking her to come. He found a clean and quiet boarding house near St Pancras in Argyll Square, next to a girls' school, and was already living there when his mother and his sister Vitalie arrived. The next three weeks are meticulously documented in Vitalie's diary of the visit, which Graham Robb described as *one of the most heavily censored documents in the history of Rimbaud biography*. The reason for this is that the family holiday of July 1874 was *almost obscene in its normality*. Rimbaud took his mother and sister shopping and to the parks with their preachers and sheep; to the Tower, St Paul's, the Bank of England, the Underground, the Metropolitan Railway, the Albert Memorial, to the Horse Guards, even to the docks and the Antwerp ferry. He bought his sister ice creams and tried to teach her English. When he went off to read at the British Museum, Vitalie wrote: *How slowly time passes when Arthur isn't there!* His amazing energy soon exhausted mother and sister, who began to long for home; but

Rimbaud insisted they stay until he had found a situation. They were not allowed to leave until the job in Reading came up.

London is the monstrous city of the *Illuminations*, the encyclopedia of Empire where all things from all parts of the world are collected and inventoried, along with the uncollected chaos of the city's slow accretion over time: subways, viaducts, raised canals, steam engines passing over streets, mastheads appearing behind chimney pots. Rimbaud shopped for images at the Crystal Palace but, indefatigable walker that he was, he also soaked up whatever he came across in the streets. At least once on these peregrinations, his tall, rangy, forward-leaning figure must have passed in the thick London crowds the sturdy, stocky, red-headed Vincent van Gogh – not the open, entertaining, liberal-minded man who was loved by his family and loved Eugénie, but the eccentric, taciturn loner rejected by her.

As for Wilde, there is no evidence that he ever heard of either man, although he and van Gogh shared the distinction of being painted by Toulouse Lautrec; nevertheless, all three died before their time and are buried in France: at Auvers, in Marseille and the Père Lachaise cemetery in Paris. The other thing they have in common is the way their lives were shaped by disastrous love affairs. In a letter which eerily prefigures the disquieted prose of Portuguese writer Fernando Pessoa, Wilde wrote to Henry Marillier: *There is no such thing as romantic experience; there are romantic memories, and there is the desire for romance – that is all. Our most fiery moments of ecstasy are merely shadows of what somewhere else we have felt, or of what we long some day to feel . . . what comes of all this is a curious mixture of ardour and indifference. I myself would sacrifice everything for a new experience, and I know there is no such thing as a new experience.*

Wilde, like Rimbaud, like van Gogh, was a man of prodigious talent who somehow could not negotiate the world. Or so, with hindsight, we like to think. As examples for a young man of aspiration, it is hard to imagine worse: wrecked, lonely, loveless lives, leaving behind them a freight of exceptional work. The disastrous idea that suffering is the *sine qua non* of art, whether it precedes, coincides with or postdates the art, infects their biographies, if not their actual existences. Nothing of value could be expected from my imitations, in London and New York, of Rimbaud's prose poems. Nor from my yearning for the presumed solitude of van Gogh's frenzies. Wilde's *ardour and indifference* were perhaps more serviceable and more real, but less interesting to me then. I wanted to be footloose in Afar, or mad in a wheatfield, not negotiating daily accommodations between the action and the music, trying to keep alive some sense of myself as an independent being amongst the turmoil of dependencies which made up our then fractious troupe.

Nor was my marriage any consolation. I had entered the relationship half unwillingly, being otherwise engaged at the time we met. What dragged me away from the easy sensuality of the woman I was with was, essentially, a feeling of admiration towards Gemma's accomplishments as an artist: she was a classical pianist. It seemed to give her an authority I wanted but did not have, and so I was flattered when I learned she desired me. In this I was, like Verlaine to Rimbaud, or van Gogh to Gauguin, pledging my identity to the other in return for – what? Certainty? Or the fulfilment of ambition? That it can't be done doesn't stop us trying. Anyway, as I soon found out, Gemma's gift did not, for her, translate into existential assurance; far from it. She was as timid as I in some areas of living, more so in others; she needed my support most crucially for her music, at which she was extremely talented, but with which she was extremely insecure – especially once she decided to stop playing Schubert and Stravinsky and to try to make it in rock 'n' roll.

Did we not love each other? Yes, in a way. I remember us clinging together in the bed in our hotel room on 49th Street in Manhattan when, in the aftermath of the near meltdown at Three Mile Island, the power failed in New York. Rather than two independent persons sharing a life, we were like two ill-fitting halves trying to make a whole. Or perhaps like two quarters trying to make a half; for our relationship with each other was echoed, bizarrely, in our relationship with the troupe, which was itself a reflection of our need for some outside authority to direct us towards the goals we could not reach by ourselves. It is not strange that we were constantly resenting this authority, and attempting to free ourselves from it: who is more aware of the need for freedom than someone who has voluntarily relinquished it to others in the service of ambition? These complexities were amplified by the fact that our troupe was committed, as a matter of principle, to an equality which was contradicted, we thought, by the actual hierarchy of power through which it operated.

Impossible now to recall the strenuous strategies self-alienation demands of the sufferer. The anxious scanning of others' behaviour for clues to what your own should be; the hopeless imitations passed off as work of your own devising; the constant need for vigilance constant fraud requires . . . all these are bad enough. Worse is the corrosive sense that the image of yourself seen by those who know you, perhaps the only true one, will always elude you. It is actually easier to be on your own, a stranger to others as you are to yourself.

It was a relief, then, when I was asked, not long after our return to London from Sheffield, to go on ahead of the rest of the troupe to New York to secure our next season of work. We had a commitment from The Theatre for the New City, where we had performed previously, but we didn't have dates; it was my job to lock them in. The plane flew so far north on its arc that I could see a wall of green ice towards the pole, while in the next seat a Professor of Greek explained that, although we can read Homer, we can't scan him, so no one alive now knows what his verses sounded like. I remember wondering then if the faint whistle of thin air past the fuselage of the jet contained within itself all the lost songs of human kind.

In Manhattan I stayed, alone, in the apartment of a friend of the troupe on West 73rd Street; the first thing I did was go down to the East Village to see about our dates. The aging couple with impeccable left-wing credentials who ran the theatre, knowing I was inexperienced, vulnerable and chronically addicted to appeasement as a way of getting by, refused the promised season. When I couldn't accept this, they relented and said we could have the dates after all, but only if we agreed to re-carpet the foyer. It was a set-up, but after returning empty-handed from Amsterdam, after the single gig I managed to book in London ended in a brawl when one of our fans was beaten senseless with a fire-extinguisher by the management's thugs, there was no way I was going to turn it down. The fury of the troupe when they found out what I had committed them to was a better risk than their vexation at having no dates, I thought. So it proved. After the initial howl of disbelief, they laid the carpet with good grace, and subsequently we sold out the season too.

During our previous stay in New York I had spent a couple of months working as a writer of adult fiction at a place on Third Avenue. Now, at a loose end after concluding the theatre deal, I returned there to pick up copies of the six books I had written in that time. The business, whose name I have forgotten, occupied a suite of four rooms on the top floor of a six-storey building in the east 30s: a reception area, two small writing rooms, and a larger rear room where the books and magazines were laid out at big tables. It was run by two enormous dykes, Florence and Eunice, and employed about twenty writers, most of them gay men moonlighting from other jobs. The product was, of course, pornography.

The first time I went in there I was nearly knocked out by the odour of cat. Florence and Eunice, a couple, kept half a dozen moggies on the premises, which ran twenty-four hours. Florence, who was their public face, suggested I write a sample twenty pages so they could assess my potential. On my way back to the hotel I bought at random from one of the shops selling sex aids, magazines, lingerie and so on a book of the kind I would be writing, read half of it, then threw it out the hotel window, where for the rest of our time there it lay open, face down, on the roof of the building next door, swelling in the rain, fading in the sun, amongst all the other rubbish – smashed bottles, a broken TV set, a single shoe, a Pink Panther, a dead pigeon. Having got myself in the mood, I wrote my sample. Florence was impressed enough to offer me a job and I started immediately.

I walked to work each day past the peep shows, the porno theatres, the hookers and the pimps on 42nd Street, and took my place among the gay boys and the cat smell and the heat. We writers sat at looming, antiquated word processors, typing our lubricious prose onto a perforating tape which, when full, was taken out and across town and inserted in another machine, from which it emerged set in ranks of type exactly as it would appear on the printed page. The proofs came back in a big roll, and any mistakes were stripped out with a scalpel and corrections pasted in; then they disappeared again. The final product, depending on the typing skill and manual dexterity of the author in question, would be more or less scarred with tilting lines of type, rank smears, uncorrected misspellings and simple mistakes, irresistibly recalling Rimbaud's *livres érotiques sans orthographe* in *Délires II*.

This was how it worked. Each time I began a new book, Florence would heave herself down next to me at my work station and give a brief sketch of the kind of person the fantasy was for. For example: *This is for men who want to fuck little girls, only it's against the law to publish fantasies about minors, so what you do is say that the age of the girl is sixteen, but write as if she were only seven. OK?* If it was to be an illustrated book, like the S & M fantasy I wrote, there was no need for this perfunctory brief; you were given a set of images and constructed a narrative linking them together.

At first, as if supplying myself with what was so conspicuously missing from the marriage bed, I wrote with a strong sense of sexual excitement; but it soon faded. There is only so much variation in the possible conjunctions of human (or animal) bodies, and my repertoire was quickly exhausted. Because we were paid by the book, everything was done at high speed, so there wasn't time to explore nuances of character, twists and turns of narrative, the beauties of language. Anyway, these qualities are not considered vital to a successful piece of pulp fiction, whose minimum requirement, Florence said, was a full-on sexual encounter every half dozen pages. Any longer without it and the reader's concentration, or perhaps his erection, would flag. I had a facility, it turned out. If I'd stuck at it, I might even, in time, have graduated to the writing of lewd stories for the glossy magazines – not only a far less onerous labour, but much better paid.

The business also produced a gay listings magazine, which was laid out on the big tables down the back where we did our corrections. This - access to real sex - was what everyone was actually there for: the fantasy just paid the rent. I used to wonder if the fact that almost everyone there was homosexual, while the pornography we produced was almost exclusively heterosexual, operated as a kind of guarantee of the detachment needed to write these works of violence and yearning. Yet in some odd way I enjoyed the job. There was a freedom in it. So long as I wrote, and kept the sex coming, I could say anything I liked. I used to describe people or incidents I'd seen on the way to work, inserting them into the narrative; or I'd plunder the far past and long-ago green island I came from, reviving depraved copies of my school friends or university lecturers. One book was a science fiction in which the characters went through a warp in space-time and became mirror images of themselves. Another was set among tribal people in the highlands of New Guinea. A third took place in ancient Rome.

What happened was, my mind drifted. One part of me would be constructing grammatically correct, if anatomically impossible and psychologically implausible, interactions, while the rest would wander in the landscapes of my youth. Lucid, brilliant images of beautiful uninhabited places I had once known and long forgotten floated in front of my eyes, so that I viewed the words processing behind the smeared plastic screen through a mist of paradisiacal scapes. The melancholy of these scenes, evoked in that seamy, steamy interior crowded with phantoms of lust, cruelty, rage and disappointment, is my strongest memory of that time.

Florence was pleased to see me. She thought perhaps I had come to accept the offer she had made me when I left the job at the beginning of summer: to 'agent' a 'real' novel for me and, in this way, raise both of us above the mire of promiscuous satisfaction of the random desires of anonymous readers into that other, fabled realm where a name is a guarantee of a certain quality and that quality – or is it that name? – itself guarantees a certain income, a certain lifestyle. She was disappointed but not surprised at my second refusal, and went to get the books. With their lurid covers and improbable pseudonyms, their scenes from daily life in the red-light district, their loveless couplings and clumsy attempts at morality (morality!), their aura of masturbatory sadness . . . I thought there might be something in there I could rescue, something I could later turn to deathless prose. Not so.

Florence's suggestion that I stay in New York and become a real writer was echoed, later, by the troupe's proposal that Gemma and I stick around and await their return from a tour of the home country. In retrospect, our decision not to stay was a major turning point in both our lives, but my recollection is that I treated the choice with extreme nonchalance: I don't think I seriously considered either suggestion and perhaps did not even realise they were mutually compatible. Why not? Why didn't I, like my friend David, the only other het boy pornographer, commit myself to writing a real novel and slug it out for the duration? Was it that I doubted my ability to survive in the Big Apple, or for some other reason?

Plenty of people have been chewed up and spat out in New York, but this was not why I did not choose to stay. My reasons were sentimental: I missed, or thought I missed, not so much my home country as the things which could be had for nothing there – the paradisiacal scapes which had lightened my time as a pornographer. I remember once looking down while walking one of the great avenues of Manhattan and seeing through a grille a tree growing in the rubbish that had fallen through the grating set into the pavement. This tree, which was perhaps a metre tall, was one of several flourishing underground along that stretch of street, and it filled me with longing for places where trees grew wild on hillsides and swayed in the wind. Somehow the battle in my mind between the licentious and the bucolic, fought out to the smell of cat over those primitive word processors, had been won by the bucolic: but why that battle?

To say I was homesick does not answer the question. I did not have any real home to be sick for and, anyway, I was quite happy living in Manhattan. If it was a disinclination to commit myself to any course of action beyond that of moving on to the next town, the next gig, the next whatever, then, by misunderstanding the nature of my feeling, calling restlessness homesickness, I actually made a commitment to a course of action which was the opposite of what I wanted: a strange paradox but not unprecedented. One of the problems of being young and confused is that you sometimes end up doing the exact opposite of what you want, or think you want, to be doing. Further, it is possible that this disinclination to end the itinerant life we led might have had more to do with an unwillingness to quit the troupe than with any true restlessness.

Perhaps Gemma and I did not want to be alone together in New York, preferring, as we soon were, to be alone together in Auckland, and then Sydney. Our situation was complicated by my conjecture, probably unfounded, that she had had a fling with a bass player when I went ahead of the troupe to New York, and the rather more definite suspicion that, in Manhattan, she had been raced off by a yippie guy from Tennessee called Moonshine. Maybe she was feeling contrite, or maybe the risks she'd been taking made her want to hang on to what she had. On the other hand, it wasn't like her to put the personal ahead of the professional – in this she resembled my mother – so it could just have been that she'd figured out it would be easier to hitchhike back home with the troupe and put her next band together there instead of on the road, where things fell apart much more quickly than they came together.

As for me, even though I was, as the only non-performing member, the most menial, harassed, unfree, more or less idle and of dubious use to anyone, I still loved being part of the shows. It was better to be a barely functional part than a dysfunctional whole. Perhaps, too, I already knew my theatrical days were numbered and for that reason wanted to prolong them. When we first performed the show we later took across America and through New Zealand, it was in an old church on a street in the west 20s. The roof of this sacerdotal theatre was extraordinarily high and we had to work around another show already set up there. I was not allowed to shift any lights, although I could change the gels and alter the way they were pointed. I chose colours of the darkest, most intense hues and spent a few hours up the tallest ladder I'd ever seen, poking at lamps with a stick. The show that night was a revelation, as the god-like beams of super-saturated light fell across the two car wrecks we had hauled off the streets of Manhattan as the basis of the set, while the troupe, masked and lunatic, struck post-apocalyptic poses and mouthed dystopic incantations; there was even a crucifixion. The lighting was a triumph of unwitting improvisation.

Lighting was possible because I could do it without risk to my identity. I would sit in the dark, unseen, and let there be light. I had failed previously as an actor with the troupe not because I lacked skill or empathy or audience appeal, but because I was unable to distinguish my self from the parts I played. Every character was me, yet I was no one. Thus, if I played a hero, I was that hero, and, knowing my own lack of heroism, felt fraudulent. Yet if I played a villain or a fool, I would feel that those foolish or villainous characteristics impinged upon, if they were not an intrinsic part of, my vagrant self. So no performance was whole hearted. I justified my acting failure by pretending the poet in me required a unitary voice, yet concealed from myself the knowledge that a single voice was exactly what I didn't have.

I never suspected that fictional identities could be truer than the self which imagines them. Instead, I continued searching for the chimerical one. Along with mirroring of the famous and description of the pristine in landscape, my main sources of inspiration were the ruin of history and the loss of the primitive . . . these were where I would find poetry. But the quest was impossible because it required, on the one hand, the unitary identity implied in the lyric 'I', and, on the other, the absence of an observer. My preferred landscapes were uninhabited, my savages unchanged by scrutiny, my ruins unexcavated, my idols unworshipped. I desired an unobstructed point of view without realising such a view cancels the observer. Despite my examples – and however different their strategies might appear, both Rimbaud and van Gogh ended up having to kill themselves in order to stop making art – I was yet to understand that the quest for a unitary self was really a quest for silence.

In his book *The Origin of Consciousness in the Breakdown of the Bicameral Mind* (1976), Julian Jaynes suggests that consciousness as we now understand the term – the assumption of mind-space, possession of an analogue 'I', narratisation, among other qualities – is a recent innovation, post-Homeric, only about 3,000 years old. Prior to that, humans acted on instructions understood to be the voice(s) of god(s), though in fact emanating from the right hemisphere of the brain. Schizophrenics, those under hypnosis, religious maniacs and others who hear voices are, in this theory, reverting to an earlier stage of development. Jaynes's hypothesis is congruent with Rimbaud's famous insight: *Je est un autre*. His analogue 'I' is not singular but double – consciousness narrating its own thoughts or actions, an 'I' which thinks and another which is. Thus Jaynes corrects Bertrand Russell's proof of consciousness – *I see a table* – to: *I see myself, seeing a table*. We are both self and other in the same sentence, and our consciousness is a construct of the language we use to assuage the tragic sense of abandonment by the gods who once instructed us.

By analogy, if not in fact, my consciousness of membership of the troupe was of a similar order to Jaynes's bicamerals and throwbacks: their collective voice was the source of my guidance, issuing instructions which, however much I may have resented them, I always obeyed. Sometimes, as in the church, I was even inspired. As Jaynes points out, the word 'obey' comes from Latin *obedire*, a composite of *ob* + *audire*, to hear facing someone. To hear is (or was) to obey. However fanciful it may sound, in some sense the troupe was my god, and my reluctance to leave was the reluctance of any mortal to abandon his or her divinity. (Jaynes says that in bicameral cultures each individual had their own god, often domiciled within a small figurine they carried with them, like a mobile phone, at all times.) My distressing lack of memory of almost all of the time I spent with the troupe might then be the result of existing mostly in a passively receptive state to external commands, while those few fragments narrated here, all from brief periods I spent away from the troupe, represent faltering steps towards independence, action in the world, and full possession of a functioning consciousness of my own.

2

Ruins

W E WERE WOKEN BY A BRICK SMASHING THE GLASS PANEL in the back door of the house. It was about 3 a.m. on a hot January night. Telling Gemma to stay where she was, I got up, wrapped my lava-lava round my waist, went downstairs and picked up the axe left under the kitchen cabinet for just this eventuality. The cracked and faded linoleum by the door was scattered with jagged splinters of heavy frosted glass. I picked my way through this sea of knives and went to the outside bathroom to turn on the garden light. There, crouched in the open door of the fridge, was a man. He was big and seemed frightened: when he saw the axe he shrank further into the fridge. A purple and yellow bruise stained the flesh around one eye and blood dripped from a cut on his hand, making little wet red stars on the concrete floor. The brick in the towel lay forgotten beside him.

Taking the advice of a friend, in a voice as steady as I could manage, I started to swear at him. *Get out of here you fucking bastard, just fuck off out of here and leave us alone . . .* He stood up and backed out of the bathroom and then down the garden path towards the gate into the laneway; it was as if he was being hosed away by a stream of foul language. By now every dog in the neighbourhood was yammering. A wave of baying and howling rippled outwards as dogs in other, more distant streets joined in the clamour. He kept going until he reached the far edge of the circle of light cast by the naked bulb hanging from the clothesline, where, as if taking courage from the shadow he was now in, he stopped. From just inside the same circle, I faced him across the nasturtiums. The back gate was standing open and two shadowy accomplices waited in the alley. I hefted the axe across my thighs so they could see it. What happened next was as ludicrous as it was unexpected.

He held out his hand. *Shake*, he said. As if under some weird compulsion, I took it. He had a big, warm, dry grip, both gentle and strong. *My name's George. You got any dope, brother?*

It was the 'brother' that did it. I wrenched my hand free. *What's this brother shit?* I yelled. *If we're brothers, how come you just put a brick through my door? Go on, fuck off, George, just fuck off and leave us alone!*

He stood irresolute, watching his move fail.

A shadow spoke from the alley. *Just a few joints.* Then the other. *Yeah, just a few joints, mister. Five joints.*

George looked over his shoulder, jerked his head towards the end of the alley. *Get out of it*, he said. They faded into the night.

He turned back to me, but it was too late. Gemma's voice came from the house, saying she'd rung the cops. (When they came they asked: *Were they Aboriginal or Australian?* before driving off importantly in the wrong direction.) George had a look on his face like you see on a steer about to bolt. A sort of foolish fear. He turned towards the lighted kitchen, seeking Gemma's eyes. I saw his own wounded one, garishly lit as he swayed into the light. Then he turned to go, shambling back up the path to the back gate. *I go now*, he said, *but I come back. Tomorrow, I come back to the front door.* He didn't, not to the front door anyway; but it was probably him who returned the next night and left a big soft turd on the back lawn. I stood in it on my way, barefoot, to the dunny to pee.

In the aftermath of this latest invasion, one of a dozen or so over the previous eighteen months, I came to know the bitterness and sorrow living only a couple of streets away. It was as if the broken door now looked directly into that narrow street of dust and shattered glass, where the poisonous fumes of the city lay lowest and heaviest, between the railway line and the ring road, the brewery and the station. The remnant of the hunting and gathering nation crowded into that street, and a few others – Caroline, Hugo, Louis, Everleigh, Lawson, Vine – had reached out their thought and trapped me. I became part of their vortex of destroyed dreams of a time when animals talked to men, and men to the stars and the stones, and all that was ever said was the spell that kept creation whole. The dreamtime had turned to nightmare and I was in its grip. Or so, in the hysteria of paranoia, I thought.

George was the third and eldest of three brothers I had met over the previous week or two. The youngest, along with half a dozen of his eleven- and twelve-year-old mates, had discovered the dope I was growing in an old bath next to the dunny and come for it one hot sultry afternoon while I was watering. It was bushfire weather, the sky orange and grey, the thick air full of black filaments of ash. They climbed whooping into the trees of the yard two away from ours and started swinging through the branches towards me. I pulled up the plants and took them inside, then came back out to face them. It was extremely tense and then suddenly it wasn't. They asked me for some *yaani*, which is what they call marijuana, and I stupidly gave them some. Only I made them come round to the front door to get it.

The next day a boy of about fifteen came to that same door and berated me for supplying drugs to his kid brother, who'd been picked up stoned and wandering the streets by the police. *Sorry*, I said, *but they shouldn't have tried to steal from me.*

He said, *Yes, but you shouldn't be giving dope to young kids.*

Maybe not, I said, *but they shouldn't have been in our yard . . .*

There was a pause and then, in the softest of voices he said: *You got any more?*

Of course I did, but why would I give him any? What if he got into strife? *Naaa*, he drawled, his brilliant eyes on mine, his teeth glinting in the sun. *I just like to lie on my bed and dreeeam.*

So I compounded my initial error and gave him some too. No surprise, then, that they came back next day when we were out, breaking into the house through a back window – they didn't smash it, they took it out of its frame – and stealing whatever they could find: jewellery, herbal teas, a radio cassette player. George was, I think, the older brother of Bob Murray – or *Murri* – as the second boy, the dreamer, called himself. In those days the younger kids used to patrol the back lanes of Redfern and Chippendale and Golden Grove, literally sniffing out the plants the hippies grew in their back gardens, stealing them and then selling the *yaani* to their older brothers for cash. My refusal to stop growing the precious herb had left us ruinously exposed to this familial corner of the black economy and now we were paying the price. Even so, rather than stop cultivating, we decided instead to move.

There was also the question of Gemma's expensive and valuable musical equipment stored in the house – keyboards, amplifiers, tape recorders, speakers, which she used for making music at home and abroad. She soon found another place, and we went down from the terrace house built on reclaimed sand dunes behind what had been the beach, to a headland overlooking the bizarrely ruined foreshores of Blackwattle Bay. It was a flat in a building perched on the old sea cliffs at the bottom of Darghan Street in The Glebe.

The windows of the flat looked out over a forgotten corner of the industrial sea port of Sydney Town. Stray diesels pulling empty freight trucks sometimes paused on the almost disused railway line out the front. You could see beyond the tracks, next to the Carnival and Toy Warehouse, the roof of the Kauri Hotel, a memory of the time when sawmills crowded the foreshore and thousands of superfeet of New Zealand's best timber rotted there for lack of anyone to buy it. A superannuated steam tugboat, the *Lyttelton II*, rode at anchor at an otherwise derelict wharf, its black painted sides burnished in the setting sun, while identical freighters, the *Camira* and the *Conara*, came and went through the turnstile of the Glebe Island bridge to unload coal at the depot next to the cement yard.

Not long after we moved in, Gemma and I were standing in the small bedroom which was my study, looking out at the sword grass, the straggly gums and the banana trees in the overgrown yard across the road, when, out of the blue and with some asperity, she said, *If you can't write poetry here, where can you?* It was less a question than a statement, so I didn't answer. But it was strange how, at that moment, I knew that in order to write anything at all, whether poetry, prose or film scripts, I would have to leave her. I didn't put it like that at the time, however; rather, I saw the remark as a provocation, and secretly decided that my next project would be a poetic investigation of the totality of that view out the window, an excavation of its history and an attempt to draw the map of its hidden co-ordinates.

Blackwattle Bay is flanked on its eastern end by the sandstone peninsula called by us Pyrmont, because of the many springs that rose there, and by the indigenes, Pirrama. According to a local history (*Pyrmont and Ultimo – A History* by Michael R. Matthews, 1982), there was one spring called Tinkers Well: a hermit who lived in a cave nearby had scratched that legend in the rocks above the fount. The book was folksy, sketchy, but it contained many handsome black and white photographs of the old peninsula and its present ruin, including, on the back cover, one of a residential hotel called the Caledonian. When I decided, as part of my research project, to try to find Tinkers Well again, I did not realise the quest would lead me to live in a room in that very hotel, nor what near disastrous consequences that residence would have.

I was particularly intrigued by two monumental, derelict buildings visible on the western cliffs of the peninsula, between which, I thought, the spring probably rose. One, high on the headland, of barnyard red, with a single round chimney stack and rows of unglassed empty black windows, was part of the Colonial Sugar Refining Company which had by degrees taken over most of the peninsula and was thus responsible for the demolition of many splendid buildings, including the majestic Smooges Terrace. The other, in the lee of the CSR facility, slightly nearer and lower down the cliffs, was the remains of the former municipal incinerator designed by architect Walter Burley Griffin and his wife and partner, Marion Mahony, who drew the plan upon which the city of Canberra was built. On earthworks supported by retaining walls made of great roughcut blocks of the local sandstone, surrounded by palm trees, chimneyless, it looked less a utility than a temple, especially when, on late afternoons, the rays of the setting sun moved slowly across its intricate ornament, bathing its hieroglyphs in a golden light.

On the sands that once lay below these two strangely foreboding buildings there had been, in the nineteenth century, a classic Pacific beachcomber community known as Tinpot Town. Here itinerant sailors and their women, urban refugees from the metropolis of Sydney Town one bay to the east, homeless indigenes and heterogeneous others lived out their obscure lives at the margins of the great sea port. They got their water from Tinkers Well and fish from the blue bay before them, where now water rats the size of small cats clambered over slimy rocks below the unpaved car park, the concrete depot and the fish markets.

At that time I worked three days a week, teaching English to migrants in western Sydney, and had the other four to myself; once a crop was established on the small balcony outside the flat's sitting room, I would smoke and spend long hours scanning through binoculars the enigmatic facades of those derelict buildings, gazing at the monumental photographs of forgotten Pyrmont in the local history, and imagining the life that had gone on there in the days when it was the most populous borough in the state of New South Wales. Curiously, the night before I explored the peninsula itself, I had a dream.

We were walking on wide sunny wharves below the hill, looking out to where the Glebe Island bridge was then. There, across the water, stood a tall brick building with round towers, smokestacks and empty broken windows stuffed with junk – tyres, coils of rope, tarred canvas. I could feel the warm brown flesh of the bare upper arm of an island girl against my own. A wind like the wind in dreams moved dust in the splintery timber at our feet and moved in our hair as we turned to the sun. We were boarding a sandalwood boat clearing for Guam, or shipping on Captain Carpenter's *Island Trader* and sailing to Efate . . . when suddenly I was alone, walking under green trees up the path that led from Bowman Street to Tinkers Well.

I came to an old stone cottage with deep verandas shading cool worn flagstones. Along the house wall stood a glass-fronted cabinet holding a few dusty books, and as I bent to read the titles on the spines a woman's voice said, *There are springs all over the hill.* She was an old lady with white hair sitting, beyond the doors opening from the veranda, in the dimness of her parlour. *You can come back any time,* she said as, embarrassed, I turned to go. Then I was running down slab stone steps past the site of the incinerator, where, instead of the utility, there was indeed a palm-edged, pink and white sandstone temple.

Traffic was heavy on Bank Street as I crossed past a burning bus shelter where lovers waited for rain. On a bakehouse wall the peeling letters of an old sign advertising the name of a tobacco or a rum spelt out the words: BLACK AZTEC. And mysteriously, RUSSIA, twice. These cryptic signs were the last thing I saw before waking from my dream walk a little way from home. I could still hear in my head the music of water flowing from high places in the rocks.

It was nothing like that. The incinerator was a ruin, the precast concrete tiles of the walls cracked and broken, the roof fallen in, the smokestack toppled. There was a peculiar baked quality to it, as if forty years of working life, during which, on any day, there was always at least one of the four reverberatory engines going, had fired it to an eggshell thinness. Up close, the inspiration of the building and its ornament in the architecture of pre-Columbian Mesoamerica was obvious. Inside, the furnaces were rusted and broken in, and small railway trucks lay toppled among the electrics of fuse boxes, clinker and dust along the floor. I souvenired a heavy 20-amp, 500-volt porcelain fuse before going out again and round the back.

Rank grass sprouted from the stump of the tumbled smokestack; a pug of machine oil coated the ground. The yard where the rubbish trucks had pulled in and turned and backed up to the refuse-unloading bays above the garbage trough had been fenced with hurricane wire and was used by a crane hire business. Rusty derricks leaned among coils of metal rope, machine parts, fuel drums and other junk. The incinerator office, a superb miniature of chunky deco, was full of debris. There was a foul chemical stink in the air, and, at the back of the yard, green ooze dripped from the cliff. Was this what was left of the spring? I looked up to the menacing red corrugated-iron end wall of the CSR building. How had this blasted place been made over the site of Tinkers Well?

The Pyrmont Incinerator was Griffin and Mahony's only explicitly anthroposophical building. Like their other twelve municipal incinerators, it was built by the Reverberatory Incinerator & Engineering Company (RIECo), incorporated by Nisson Leonard-Kanevsky, John Boadle and Vaselie Trunof in Victoria in 1929. Boadle, an inventor from Moonee Ponds who became Melbourne City Council's chief sanitary engineer, created the reverberatory incinerator. Trunof was a business partner of Leonard-Kanevsky, the principal, a Ukrainian Jew who fled the pogroms in Kiev for Australia in the early years of the twentieth century. A brilliant entrepreneur, Leonard-Kanevsky made his money in the Flinders Street rag trade, and in 1921 engaged Griffin as an architect, first to refurbish his current premises and then to build a new multi-storey office block in Elizabeth Street. Griffin was himself a tenant at Leonard House, and his Melbourne office there remained the base for the third partner in incinerator design, Eric Nicholls, when Griffin and Mahony moved to Sydney. Later, Leonard-Kanevsky lived in the Griffin and Mahony-designed Fyshwick House in the ideal community they planned and partly built at Castlecrag.

At that time, city waste was buried, dumped in the sea or burned in 'destructors'. The blackened brick ruins of one of these crumbled below the Pyrmont Incinerator; on a sunny day, you could stand inside the burnt-out fireplace, look up and see stars in the circle of black sky at the top of the chimney. They were simple furnaces into which men shovelled the rubbish by hand; they were cleaned out by hand too; and the smoke and ashes spewed indiscriminately over nearby streets and houses. The new reverberatory incinerators were gravity fed, and ingeniously made so that the hot gases from the furnace below blew across the waiting garbage, drying it out before it was burned in its turn. This deflecting or 'reverberating' of the hot gases of combustion under the incandescent reverberatory arch consumed the noxious fumes from the fire along with the green gases rising from the drying garbage: all that remained was a thin film of clear vapour discharged from the flue tower. Meanwhile, metal doors below the furnace were opened periodically to allow the clinker to drop through into a metal skip, by which means it was railed to an overhead gantry, raised up to the top of the building, tipped via a hopper into a truck and later used as ballast for municipal roads or to fertilise council gardens.

The incinerator building was long and low, resembling two enormous interlocking square brackets, like a reactor made from the clamping together of massive magnets. Built of reinforced concrete, it was monumental, sinister, grand; a facade of precast concrete tiles sculpted into low relief within plain geometric bands was what made it look inscribed by metamorphic hieroglyphs. I never saw it with the stack in place; that, too, was decorated in reliefs: an enormous art deco chimney which could be seen from all over the city, a visible sign of the conversion of matter into energy. It must, too, in the years after World War II, have resonated with the grim associations accrued to furnaces by the Nazi experiment.

This ominous building was conceived after a long period of turmoil in Griffin and Mahony's personal life. He was five years younger than her, a shy man whose only previous romantic attempt ended in derision. She, mannish and eccentric, became devoted to him. They remained childless but prolific in architectural collaboration. He could visualise brilliantly but could not draw well; she was a superb draughtswoman: together they were formidable. Much of what they built has been destroyed and much they proposed was never made, surviving only in Mahony's superb drawings. Her decision, taken much later in life, to black out her dead husband's name where she herself had written it on these otherwise unsigned drawings shows there must have been other strains. Now, in the late 1920s, at Castlecrag, when Griffin began an affair with the wife of a client, Mahony constructed a ouija board and started talking to the Masters.

The couple's interest in Theosophy was sparked by a window display in a shopfront near Roseville Station: copies of a Dutch architectural magazine, *Wendigen*, featuring the work of their mentor, Frank Lloyd Wright. The shop's owner, Ula Maddocks, was a member of the Kuring-gai Lodge of the Theosophical Society, and the magazines had been brought to Australia by Dutch philosopher J. J. van der Leeuw, then resident in Sydney; he was a member of the family which controlled the Van Nelle Company, tea, coffee and tobacco merchants in Rotterdam. The manager, his brother C. H. van der Leeuw, was one of the grand patrons of modern architecture in the 1920s and 1930s. When Griffin's attorney, Edward Beeby, saw the display he arranged an introduction; soon after, a party of Theosophists, including the philosopher, visited Castlecrag.

The group of committed Theosophists in Sydney in the early years of the twentieth century included Charles Webster Leadbetter who had, five years previously, identified a young Indian boy, J. Krishnamurti, as the vehicle for the coming return of Christ to earth. Leadbetter was a former Anglican curate, a clairvoyant and an occultist, who proclaimed himself by Apostolic succession Regionary Bishop of Australasia in the Liberal Catholic Church. He was conservative, hierarchical and authoritarian – anathema to the liberal, unitarian and democratic Griffin and Mahony. It was probably because of his influence that they never actually joined the Theosophical Society, though Griffin was on the foundation committee of Walter Cromer's New Renascence Society, which espoused a related form of Christian mysticism.

They had more affinity with the anthroposophical project, which its founder, Rudolf Steiner, described as *a path of Knowledge, to guide the Spiritual in the human to the Spiritual in the universe.* Anthroposophists believe in the transmigration of souls: *Learn to picture the soul's life since conception. Empty your mind of all images from the past. Into consciousness will flow intimations of the further life of the soul, beyond death, before birth: the unity of all things manifest in mind.* In 1930, two months before she returned alone to her home town, Chicago, Mahony joined the Sydney Anthroposophical Society. While she was away, Griffin also became a member, and in 1932 travelled to the United States himself, to investigate large-scale incinerator projects in American cities, and to see his wife again.

Reconciled in anthroposophy, they steamed back to Australia on the SS *Monowai*, working together again for the first time in two years – their only break in thirty years of collaboration. It was a month before tenders closed for the new Sydney destructor. They had with them on the *Monowai* (*incantatory waters*) the recently published English translation of Guenther Wachsmuth's *The etheric formative forces in Cosmos, Earth and Man*, a treatise on anthroposophical cosmology by one of Rudolf Steiner's successors. Geometric symbolism representing the *etheric formative forces* was to be the basis of the ornament on the incinerator, designed to express the utility's inner purpose: the destruction of matter. In *Magic of America* (1949) Marion Mahony wrote that the building *records the basic fact of 19th Century civilisation later emphasised by the smashing of the atom.*

A primary source for the incinerator was Mitla, the Mixtec and Zapotec city near Oaxaca in southern Mexico. Mitla, a contraction of Mictlan, the Nahuatl word for the place of the dead, was where shamans were trained in magic and healing. It was in a room off the Hall of Columns (the name is Spanish, not Nahuatl), a wide shallow gallery with six monoliths of volcanic stone along it – the supports for a vanished timber roof – that initiation is said to have taken place. A darkened doorway led through a low, narrow passageway to the interior of another enclosure, now roofless too, but covered in ancient times. This chamber, which must have been very dark unless artificially lit, has walls covered with panels of inlaid cut-stone mosaic in a stepped-fret design, a stylised representation of the pan-regional Mesoamerican deity, Quetzalcoatl. Probably it moved as light was passed across it, just as shadowy zig-zags representing the feathered serpent climb the steps of some Mayan temples on the summer solstice. In this room the neophyte ate the crushed leaves of *Salvia divinorum*, diviners sage, which is still used today by the Mazatec Indians of Oaxaca. Diviners sage is productive of intense hallucinations, out-of-body experiences, travel through time and space, the assumption of the identity of others and even the experience of merging with inanimate objects: all grist to the shamanic mill.

Mitla, with its geometric motifs on the white facades of the palaces, its huge rooms, patios, interior colonnades, the great quadrilaterals enclosing vast squares, is incomparable. The long modernistic horizontals of the massive structures, set solidly in the bare earth of the high brown plains, are a sombre, potent image of chthonian death. There are mosaics both within and without. Their motifs – meanders, key patterns, lozenges – are made of small blocks of tufa stone arranged in horizontal panels. Assembled with intricate precision, in relief they perfectly reflect the tropical light. The language of these stones receives textual support from the sacred books of the Mixtec, and turns out to be another variation upon the same prolific system of calendrical, astronomical, philosophical and shamanic signs used, in different forms, by all the Mesoamerican cultures.

A shamanic origin for the glyphs is proposed by Anglo-Peruvian writer Richard Luxton in his book, co-authored with Mayan *h-men* Pablo Balam, *Mayan Dream Walk* (1981). Luxton's adventure begins when he is arrested by Mexican police in Merida, the city the Spanish built adjacent to ancient T-Ho in Yucatan. In the local jail, as if by prearrangement, he meets Miguel Caamal, who asks why the police have allowed him to keep the books he carries: illustrated volumes on the Maya full of hieroglyphs and photographs. Their conversations during his incarceration, which don Miguel accurately predicts will last eleven days, mark out the philosophical ground for Luxton's later education in reading the glyphs. When he is released, he goes up to the city of Tulum in Quintana Roo. There, walking down the beach from the ruins to the local village, again as if by prearrangement, he meets a fisherman, Pablo Balam, who will be his guide for the rest of his journey. The remainder of the book is a narrative of Luxton's search for meaning intercut with conversations with don Pablo. These were recorded on tape and transcribed and edited later.

A peculiar sentence of don Pablo's recurs in the book: *Only hiding his face is the reader of it*. This is an instruction for reading the glyphs, and suggests that ignorance of the meaning of the signs is analogous to ignorance of the time unfolding within and around you. Hieroglyphs are a mnemonic device to release information which you already have access to but do not yet understand. If he wants to read a Mayan glyph, don Pablo says, Luxton must first dream the sign: *There are signs which arrive in your dreams. It is shown to you so that you can think it, so that you can put your idea there. Then when you understand it you remember that is what you dreamed.* Luxton persists until he is able to see the twenty day signs of the *Uinal*, the Mayan month, telling the story of the shamanic journey in which are all other journeys.

In the elaborate calendars of the Mesoamerican peoples, time is multi-dimensional and eternally recurrent. They attempt to comprehend its movements through a complex system of intermeshing counts, the two most important being the solar calendar, comprising eighteen months of twenty days, ending with five intercalary days; and the ritual or sacred calendar of twenty signs in fixed sequence interacting with the numbers 1 to 13, giving a year of 260 days – the gestation period of a human embryo. Under such a system each day has four separate designations – two numeric and two iconic – and is unique within a fifty-two-year cycle. Fifty-two years is a fair approximation of a human lifetime; any addition repeats the days of early childhood. Sequence is less important than identity: each day has its own character, more closely connected with the similarly named days that have occurred and will occur in other fifty-two-year bundles than with those immediately before and after. Thus particular events are understood as unfolding in a dynamic process modelled by some past situation. As Inga Clendinnen says in *Aztecs: An Interpretation* (1991), this is no simple replication: *the complex character of the controlling time is capable of manifesting in various ways, so events remain problematic in their experiencing, with innovation and desperate effort neither precluded nor inhibited.* Proper study of the signs yields a body of predictive knowledge which amounts to a history of the future.

The Maya were able to project their count millions of years into the past as well as far into the future. The culture of the classic period Maya (100–900 AD) divided time into a Long Count of thirteen *baktun*s of approximately 400 years each, and, according to Luxton and Balam, abolished itself at the end of one of these periods: hence the mysterious desertion of cities throughout the Mayan lands at about 900 AD and the subsequent incursion of Nahuatl-speaking Toltecs from the north. From then until the Spanish invasion, the Long Count was superseded by a Short Count, a period of 256 and a half years constructed out of thirteen *katuns* of 7,200 days or about twenty years. Post contact, the Short Count was in its turn replaced by Codices written in the Roman alphabet. These records, on stone or on paper, are mnemonics supporting the unbroken oral tradition which keeps all the counts going.

The Long Count, which began a little over 5,000 years ago, ends in about ten years, on 24 December 2011, and with it the era of the Fifth Sun; we are already in the transitional period called by contemporary Mayan *h-men*, mordantly, The Beak of Time. Why now? The vernal equinox is passing over the bottom of the Milky Way, equivalent to a cosmic winter solstice. Five suns – five 5,000-plus-year periods – make up one of the cycles we know as a Great (or Platonic) Year. The Long Count was worked out backwards from our present station of termination and renewal: time seen in a mirror. Seeing it backwards is the best way to write it down forwards. *Only hiding his face is the reader of it* also means you find out who you are by living your days back from your death as well as from now on.

If reading is the process of recognising what is already before you after you have seen it in a dream, what then is writing? Where does it come from? Pablo Balam says from the spirits, in the same way that other peoples credit their writing to the gods. Contemporary functionalists tend towards the idea that theocratic priests invented hieroglyphs as a means of social control over the masses. Their aim, according to William Burroughs in *Ah Pook Is Here* (1979), was an immortality based on the theft of the time (= lives) of ordinary people. Julian Jaynes says early writing is a transcription of voices inside our heads which are identified as belonging to outside agencies: what is written down was first spoken in our minds as an hallucination or a dream. This explanation is congruent with that of the Mayan *h-men*, acknowledging that the same form of altered consciousness is involved in writing as in reading.

What consciousness? Studies in Andean archaeoastronomy reveal that the spatial organisation of villages, towns and cities mirrored precisely the observed arrangement of the night sky. This phenomenon is common to Oriental as well as other indigenous American cultures and is sometimes called the Quadrangular Earth. There was a centre, the ridgepole of the World House, where lines drawn from four cardinal points intersected; these cardinal points represent the path of the sun from solstice to solstice, on the one hand, and from equinox to equinox, on the other. Within this zone of sky, the sun, the moon and the planets come and go on their regular paths, while inside and outside of it – in the under and over worlds, or the zones north and south of the Tropics – the stars move on a proximate 26,000-year cycle known as the precession of the equinoxes, a consequence of a wobble in the tilt in the earth's axis which is the origin of the seasons. The precise astronomical alignments of the Mesoamerican cities, like those in the Andes, were an attempt to adjust human institutions to the largest single observable cycle accessible to us. The glyphs are thus both a record of spacetime and an instrument for the calibration of its flows. To read them is to become conscious of the dimensions in which we move: a consciousness irreducibly prospective.

A neglected branch of the study of myth proposes worldwide rules for their reading. There are three 'laws'. Animals are stars. Gods are planets. Topographic references are metaphors for locations – usually of the sun – on the celestial sphere. The source for this theory is *Hamlet's Mill* (1968), by historians of science Giorgio de Santilla and Hertha von Dechend. Von Dechend's speciality was the study of Polynesian myth, and her primary insight came when she realised similar structures on Pacific islands 3,000 miles apart might be explained by the fact that one island is on the Tropic of Capricorn and other on the Tropic of Cancer. According to de Santilla and von Dechend, the abiding obsession with myth thus decoded is the precession of the equinoxes, because in that vast, scarcely perceptible motion the gods themselves move in and out of our lives.

Perhaps the flowering of monumental, astronomically aligned architecture all over the world in the last few millennia represents the culmination and destruction of an ancient tradition of observation, orally transmitted from generation to generation for 40,000 years or longer. How many times before have we seen the night sky above us now? There have been four previous ages, according to the Mesoamericans, but these are likely to be divisions of one great year rather than great years themselves. We may have been cognisant of periodicity in the heavens for about 200,000 years. But if, like birds, our animal selves migrated with reference to the night sky, our knowledge, as the Maya suggest, stretches back millions of years.

How was this tradition lost? Is written language itself an instrument of forgetting? Why carve the knowledge in stone if it was not feared for? Did they feel, as we do, out of time? As bicameral consciousness fractures, an orgy of monument-building begins. The Incas use geomantic spells to try to stop time, priests pacing the radials to the horizon and back again in straight lines, slaughtering little children in the towns along the way to send as messengers to the stars. The Aztec enact the inexplicable brutality of their contingent god, Tezcatlipoca, the Lord of Smoke and Mirrors, whose people endlessly grow up and are cut down like corn. As the stars move out of alignment with their cities, the Maya abandon them and transform themselves back into an undifferentiated, tribal people, almost indistinguishable from the forest around them, silently counting down the years.

Jaynes sees certain forms of architecture as bicameral, specifically the pyramid and, more generally, the pattern whereby man-houses cluster around a god-house – an ancient arrangement we continued into colonial times, placing cathedrals in the middle of our towns. The prodigious effort required to build the ziggurats of Sumer, the pyramids of Egypt and the palaces of Mesoamerica was called forth from people by the voices of their 'gods'; like some schizophrenics, the nearest thing to bicamerals among us now, those engaged in the work of the gods are capable of sustained efforts of concentration or activity impossible to us with our fractured consciousness, our narratising selves: who but a Zen Buddhist could sit as long and still as a catatonic? Who but a stock exchange clerk is as busy as a hebephrenic?

On the other hand, it is not uncommon for an artist to attribute some power or beauty in their own work to the 'unconscious', as if what they thought they were doing was somehow less or other than what was in fact happening. Perhaps this is where the enormous charge possessed by the Pyrmont Incinerator when derelict came from. Is it possible that Griffin and Mahony knew they were building a ruin? What gods were they listening to? Did they realise their destructor was built on the site of an ancient spring? Their model, whether the White Palaces of Mitla in particular or Mesoamerican buildings in general, is a potent architecture of ruins. Computer simulations of these centres, painted to look as we think they did, lack the mouldering grandeur of their present state, collapsed under a load of inscrutable days. In the same way, the Pyrmont Incinerator in decay embodied the deteriorated state of our culture, a visible sign of the passing of *the vast industrial economies* choking on their own waste. So it is perhaps not inauspicious that the incinerator itself was obliterated from the landscape in the early 1990s, to be replaced by an apartment block. The palms and some of the stonework remain, and a selection of the tiles with their arcane symbols is held in the Powerhouse Museum in Sydney.

The four motifs of the tiles illustrated what remains when matter is destroyed, presumably after atomic catastrophe. They are based upon the sphere, the triangle, the crescent or wave and the rectangle, and were keyed, respectively, to warmth, light, sound and magnetism. They were further associated with the solar system, the sun, the moon and the earth, as well as differing states of matter: ether, gas, liquid and solid. The rectangle was said to be *the controlling form of the solid condition as seen in the human being's blood crystals*. This quaint map of great time can thus be glossed: whirling spheres forming worlds; triangulate gases igniting the sun; a tide of crescents pulled by the moon; the labyrinth of the blood. On the building they were enclosed one within the other, with the *koru*-like spherical forms on the outside and the zig-zag, pyramidal squares of blood at the centre.

My attitude to the Griffins was never worshipful; rather, I thought their idealism, their impracticality, their naivety, their arcane enthusiasms ridiculous. Although I admire their works, and share the distress of those who lament the way their buildings have been treated, I saw them, not as images of who or what I might be, but as exemplars of what I was not: not innocent, not a utopian, neither specious nor bizarre. Not, certainly, deluded by history. I found a kind of malicious enjoyment in the fact that the designers of the Ideal City had been reduced to making utilities for the disposal of municipal waste. Whether this casting of compromised artists as personal antagonists was any advance upon hero worship as a mode of augmentation of self is a moot point. It now seems as if the crucial element in the strategy is its determination to argue against the processes of history, to say that things, and people, should and could and might still be other than they are said to have been.

I went back and back to the incinerator, as if seeking some entry to my own shamanic journey; but the clues were already there in my dream. When our increasing estrangement and frequent arguments culminated in a stupid fight – it was about whether or not to cross busy Parramatta Road against the lights after we had been to the circus – Gemma announced she was leaving me. She went to stay with a friend; and on the night of the day she left, I met the island girl with whom I had been boarding the boat in my dream. Or so I told myself. Brial was someone I had known for a while. When we first met in Auckland, just out of our teens, I was alone but she was with someone else. The next time we ran across each other, a few years later, also in Auckland, she was by herself but I was not. Now, in Sydney, in the mid-eighties, we were both notionally free. I drove her home from the dinner party where we met and, later, went back and stayed the night.

Why did I think Brial was the girl from my dream? Though she is part Polynesian, that wasn't really why; it was because of the way her upper arm lay warm and full against mine when we met at dinner that night, just as had happened out on the splintery wharves as we were boarding the *Island Trader*. I should have remembered the rest of the dream: she disappeared and I missed the boat, or at least never got on it, drifting off into the arcana of my obsession with historical Pyrmont. Instead, when Gemma, who had left only strategically, sensed something was up and moved back in, I concealed the affair from her and, every Saturday night while she played a piano bar in western Sydney, went up to the sparse, elegant flat in Kings Cross which Brial shared with her daughter.

Does this require an explanation? Isn't it what every married man does when he has an affair? It wasn't quite what it seems. Though I saw Brial often, I hardly ever stayed with her, pretending misplaced sexual fidelity somehow made the situation less dishonest. Even though I wanted her, all the time, and she wanted me, we seemed to be postponing things until I left Gemma. I was in fact desperate to leave but did not know how. Perhaps, too, I did not want to quit one relationship only to enter another. Perhaps I was afraid: Brial had a way of being wickedly disparaging of the men previously in her life, some of whom I knew quite well. Or was I just waiting for the right moment?

In the interim, an agony which lasted some months, a strange thing happened: Brial and I began to contact each other psychically, to hold not conversation but congress with each other while each of us separately went about our day. I know this sounds mad, but it was really only a variation upon the way in which those who are infatuated think continually of the beloved until they can almost conjure them into being. We found out only by chance that those times when the other was most present while in fact absent coincided for each of us. It was not so much a comfort as a confusion: why should we have to learn to be together apart, while Gemma and I continued apart together?

This was at the time of the latest visit to our skies of Halley's Comet and although the astronomers' prediction of a spectacular apparition did not eventuate – all we ever saw was a fuzzy brownish smudge in the early morning sky above Capricorn – it did seem to bring with it a new kind of weather, sultry, carnal, heavy with foreboding, as if the earth were an egg and the comet some kind of cosmic spermatozoa. Or was I just, like people throughout history, seeing in the sky a reflection of my own predicament?

Meanwhile, I continued exploring the peninsula. To get to the red corrugated-iron building belonging to CSR was much more difficult than it was to go to the incinerator: that was just a matter of walking up the road and climbing over the gate. The CSR compound, occupying most of the tip of the western side of the peninsula, was fenced, gated and patrolled by security. In those days the rum manufactory on Distillery Hill was in operation most weekends, sending clouds of aromatic, alcoholic steam into the sky, where it mingled with the smell of hops from the Carlton United brewery on Broadway to make a heady cocktail of spirituous air. I had looked through the locked gates but I wasn't brave or silly enough to climb over: the place looked too well cared for, too inhabited, to be trespassed. The only other way in was to cross the highway just before the old Glebe Island bridge and climb the steep green hill the building was perched on top of; this, one sunny Saturday afternoon, I did.

I had not realised that the electric-green shrubbery on that hillside was made up entirely of lantana; nor had I ever tried to bush-crash lantana before. I never will again. Somehow, this day, having started through the thorny, rank, yellow- and pink- and purple-flowered, pollen-dusted thicket, I wasn't prepared to stop, even though the spines tore the skin of my arms and legs and bloodied my clothes while pollen dust stuck to the sweat running down my face and neck and inside my shirt. By the time I got to the top I was a panting, heaving, bleeding mess, incongruous on the carefully manicured lawns around the derelict building where semi-tame rabbits grazed. They paused from tearing at the grass, looked briefly up at me, then returned to their mastication.

The building itself was open and empty. I walked through the end door into a vast, semi-darkened single space, a mere shell of iron, with four identical furnaces ranged at intervals along the floor towards the back; they were as wrecked as those in the incinerator next door, and on the floor in front of each one was a man-high pile of whitening bones: jaws and thighs and pelvises, ribs and skulls and teeth heaped before the rusty furnaces as in some Auschwitz for animals. For, as I later found out, they were beef bones, boated

64

downriver from abattoirs upstream, to be burned here to make a charcoal used in the purification of sugar.

Now, as I stood appalled in that grisly place, a weird compulsion came over me, a dim, fearful voice in my head instructing me to find some piece of rope or flex or wire, noose it, tie it to one of the iron struts above my head and so hang myself there. Perhaps it was the exhaustion from climbing the lantana-infested slope, or the joint I had smoked before setting out, or maybe a sign of the severe emotional stress I lived under then, but the act of self-slaughter seemed – what? I don't know, apt to that baleful place, as if the accumulation of death there suffocated the very will to live. Always, when afterwards I looked at that building, I had to banish from my mind the image of my own body, like a burnt-out filament of the globe, shrivelling to black above the white mass of bones. Because who else ever went there? Who would find and cut me down? Nobody knew where I was going that day; nobody else, surely, ever visited the Bone Char Mill on its weedy promontory.

Below the mill is an outcrop of sandstone in which I fancied I sometimes saw a face glowering, looking west; below this, I had de-cided, was where the spring must rise. I shivered out of the blackness of the mill into the sun again, and climbed down under the massive looming head where wandering jew grew knee high. Sinking up to my knees into its lush green carpet at every step, feeling the pulpy stems crush and slide under my feet, at a slight dip in the uncertain ground I began to lose my balance. Involuntarily, I reached out my arm for support on the underside of the rock hanging over me, and it was then the voices came: a hubbub, a jabber, a tumult of words in a language I didn't know but which I knew said: *Spider! Spider!* Instantly my head snapped round to where my hand was about to go, into a nest of funnel webs in crevices on the damp, musty underside of the rock.

Soon after, I found the ancient water: a galvanised pipe ran down the hill on the CSR side of the grey corrugated-iron fence separating the Bone Char Mill from the incinerator. I followed this pipe back up the hill to the mill and found that it began in a concrete cap under the ablution block at the southern end of the building, and then followed the fence down to the road – a rather easier descent than the ascent had been. The pipe debouched on the far side of the highway, a stream of water gushing out next to a Port Jackson fig tree spread graciously over the bay. This I tasted: clear, cool, sweet water, just as it flowed in my dream.

Palm trees, water and voices: even there, in that troubled place, where the rock was carved or weathered into the shape of a man's face and furnaces built over a spring or well, they came through clear and strong. Should the ancient association between springs and vatic speech be sourced to the potential for running water to unlock the hallucinatory faculties of the human brain, or to ubiquitous *genius loci*? I don't know; but since that day I have sometimes heard again that hubbub of voices rise and chorus in my head.

Once, at dusk, walking up from a beach called Werrong or Hellhole, I left the bush track and came into a circular clearing ringed by palms – a fan palm, native to the region, which has the unflattering name of cabbage tree palm and grows always near water. As I stood in the centre of the clearing, which dipped down, like the dry bed of a small lake, and was covered in tough native grass growing among clods of earth, again that sound of voices rose up, beating against my eardrums the way the sea beats on a shore. This was a welcome, a celebration of my presence and a confirmation that what or whoever abided there endured so long as people came and heard their speech. Saying what? I understood nothing that these voices said, or rather, everything I understood is awkwardly translated here, leaving the original, untranslatable speech inviolable in that place which, next time I went there, was a perfectly round black pool with the green palms growing thickly around its marshy shores.

Another time was at a beach called Flint and Steel, when the voices rolling in brought with them an elegy for my father, whose death had already bequeathed me the voice in which I prose these sentences: it came to me in the church just before we buried him. This day I left the picnic and walked out along a line of sand where the self-narrating voice in my head was joined by others, speaking of grief and dissolution, of the travels of the soul underground and then out towards the stars, dictating, in fact, what I needed to say to release my father's spirit from its earthly trammels.

This facility, while intermittent, is still with me; and those places where I can listen turn out to be if not common, not rare either. There is one near where I live now, behind the Arboretum, another circular clearing with a fragment of an old convict road at one end, a grove of palms to the east, bush to the west and a galvanised pipe running north through the native grasses towards the remains of a failed plantation of Christmas pines. Here, I can come and sit and listen to a cacophonous silence which soothes the barest mood, the hardest thought, the most bitter fear.

For it is also the case that the other voice has not left me either, the one *low down and to the side* that I first heard in the Bone Char Mill, suggesting I throw a rope over a beam. This recurs not necessarily at times of great stress or distress but in moments of dullness, fatigue or *ennui*, or even as my eye falls idly on a hanging point. I resist its nerveless instruction, so like a bureaucratic summons, but am always reminded that among the suicides there are some who seem to have taken the irrevocable step on a whim, without warning, in lieu of all the help that might have been offered by those who loved them. *She had everything to live for*, we say of such as these; but might it not rather be that she had nothing left to lose? Who knows? A salient quality of our voices is that they can never be heard, or even overheard, by others and thus we take them, or they us, to the grave.

I have always felt my sister's suicide in 1975, at the age of twenty-one, closed off that option forever for me, while at the same time making it something I would always think about: consciousness of the provisional, often atrocious, always hazardous nature of life on earth, without the means voluntarily to end it. There's the cruelty of suicide, that it leaves the living not simply bereft, but in the grip of appalling conundrums. *If she had lived . . .* you think. Or, *What if I had persuaded her to stay that night after the play?* Or, vainly, *Why was I not nicer to her . . .* A suicide in the family is like the phantom limb an amputee sometimes feels is still there. Or so it seems to me: how many times have I felt a leap in my heart and turned my head to look at a slender, dark-haired young woman in the street, on a bus, on a train? I see her even in films or on television sometimes, stupidly forgetting that, had she lived, she would be a middle-aged woman now, only two years younger than me.

After months of frozen obsession, a whole winter in fact, I heard from a friend that there were rooms going in a squat out on Pyrmont Point, and after a mature discussion with Gemma and her sister, who was staying, we decided it would be a good idea if I found a space away from home to work in. Leaving both wife and sister-in-law ignorant of the real reason I was going, and disregarding the fact that a romantic attraction to ruins does not require that you go and live among them, one Saturday afternoon I went around and knocked on the door of the Caledonian Hotel. No answer. There was a hammer banging on the top storey of the four-floor sandstock building; when it paused, I knocked again, and again, and at last heard heavy footsteps coming down the stairs. My friend had said to ask for Johnny Bear; but the pale, blue-eyed, dark-haired, hostile young man who opened up said he was in jail. I said I was after a room. There was a long pause before Ricky grunted, turned and walked away. *You'd better ask Dave*, he said.

I followed him up the disintegrating stairs amid the rank odour of cat piss, damp clothes and rotting wood. Dave was a skinny, canny, battered New South Welshman who regarded me with suspicion: I didn't look or sound much like a squatter. With Ricky's older brother Darren, a sandy haired man with colourless eyes, he was making an illicit connection to the municipal gas supply so that they could have hot showers; there was water but no electricity to the building. They were professional squatters: Darren liked to boast he had not paid rent in eleven years. Most of the rooms in the building, he said, had some kind of claim on them already, but there was one which might be available: did I want to see it? He took me back down the dangerous stairs, past an obliterated kitchen and down another flight into the basement.

The tiny space was a metre high in stinking garbage – clothes, shoes, food, paper, junk – but I liked it. The walls were oblong rough-cut sandstone blocks, mortared together; the floor concrete; the ceiling plastered; along the long wall opposite the door was a massive fireplace with a shaped sandstone mantelpiece; next to this a barred window looked out to the sloping footpath of Herbert Street; and in the well of the window ladder ferns grew. The short back wall was uniform, but the one opposite had a sash window giving out into the old flagstoned coachyard. Beyond that was a patch of lawn, a sagging back fence and then, across a narrow stretch of deep water called Elizabeth Bay, the dark satanic mill of the sugar refinery giving off hissing steam, unearthly shrieks and foul or syrupy odours. The room, and the one opposite it across the corridor, and another on the other side, had been servants' quarters. Behind it, in the further darkness of the basement, was the original hotel kitchen with a broken floor, a ruined fireplace and the empty shaft for the bygone comings and goings of the dumb waiter. Here the local cats shat and sprayed among patches of bare earth where flagstones had lifted, leaving behind a gagging stench.

The only problem with the room was that someone from Ways Terrace, the venerable block of council flats opposite the Caledonian, wanted it too. While we were talking he turned up, a kid of about fourteen in jeans and sneakers. We looked at each other in the blank way you do when you both want the same thing, then he returned home and I went back upstairs.

Johnny Bear, I learned, was in jail voluntarily, paying off his parking fines by doing time (*They started arresting my aliases*, he said later); he'd be back in a few days and I'd have to wait until then to see if I could move in. I'd actually only met Johnny once before and doubted he remembered me. A mutual friend had introduced us in a shadowy corner of the Harold Park Hotel on one of the Tuesday nights when literary readings took place. Johnny was a small, balding man with luminous eyes, missing teeth and home-made tattoos on his face and hands. He was softly spoken and had courtly manners, but we had not really talked that night. When I went around again a few days later, Johnny was still out at Long Bay, but the kid from

Ways Terrace had not only resigned his claim to the room, he'd cleaned it out as well. I took it on the spot.

Though it was meant to be a place for me to work, of course I ended up living there. I put a divan bed down the wall opposite the fireplace, a massive oak ex-public service desk (*c.*1945) which someone had given me along the short wall under the ferny window, and a small cabinet under the other window for supplies. One afternoon on the way home from the cleaning job which had replaced the teaching, I stopped in George Street and for $80 bought a cast-iron manual Olivetti typewriter; the skittish electronic I had been using was no use in a place without power. I cooked and made tea and coffee on the open fire, and for lighting bought a couple of Chinese glass kerosene lamps from an army surplus store. They were beautiful: you could see the blue spirit through heavy glass embossed with flying birds, the thick white wick blackening where it met the flame, and the yellow and red glowing and leaping inside the fragile sooty bell of the bulb.

The Caledonian had two frontages: at 140 Bowman Street were five rooms on three levels, probably originally the residence of the hotel owner and his family then, later, a shop; at 85 Point Street was the hotel proper. The two halves of the building, like the two halves of a brain, were, apart from shared verandas at the front and back, independent of each other. By chance or unspoken agreement, all the male residents lived at 85 Point Street, while only women lived at 140 Bowman Street. One of the twenty-seven rooms in the building had been adapted as a kitchen but was now derelict, without running water, a stove or even a bench. We sometimes made a fire in the ash pit where the range had stood, but no one ever cooked there. Another, the chief glory of the Caledonian, had, we learned from an old advertisement, been built as a billiard room a few years after the hotel opened. It was long and wide, with a high leaky ceiling and big broken windows looking south and west and north. We called it the Ball Room and here, in the idealistic first months of residency, held our meetings and had our parties.

We were a floating population, with a dozen or so permanent residents and any number of blow-ins: Dave Evans, Ricky and

Darren; Johnny Bear; Johnny Muller, his girlfriend Lyn, her South African friend Lyndi; George, Shona and Rachel, the three New Zealand girls, along with Stefan and Tania, friends of theirs. After our equinox party, we woke up to find a tall, dark, strange-eyed man called Mark sleeping on the floor under the kitchen table: he stayed. Johnny Bear was the only one who did not actually live in the hotel. He, his wife Vivie and their two children rented a terrace house not far away in Little Mount Street, towards the southern end of the peninsula where Pyrmont runs into Ultimo. Johnny used his room as a workplace, building the props and puppets for a show he was writing about a man abandoned by his luck.

Although I do not believe he knew it at this time, Johnny was already infected with the virus that would, five years later, kill him; and perhaps that looming fatality informed his meditations on fate, which were drily funny, unsentimental, bleak and courageous, shot through with images of luminous strangeness and aphoristic optimisms. *If your ship doesn't come in*, he advised, *swim out to it*. Or, *It's the ones who think they're alright who do the most damage*. Johnny was a rare example of a poet whose medium was almost entirely oral. He wrote only with difficulty, using a pencil or a biro on lined foolscap pages torn from pads or books; he had never learned to spell and so put his words down phonetically. Reading aloud – or rather talking aloud – as he did one night at the Harold Park, he was as hilarious as William Burroughs, in much the same deadpan, desperate style. He was best in conversation, though, a raconteur who never let an opportunity go begging. When you made a remark to Johnny, there would be the briefest of pauses, a slight tremor around his mouth and then, with an uncanny suffusion in his lustrous eyes, he would offer a devastating reply in the softest of voices.

He came from a line of Irish stonemasons, but was himself apprenticed to a bricklayer and knew the craft incompletely. He had given up this trade to play guitar; with a mime artist he toured America on the college circuit in the late seventies, the same time I was there with the troupe. In Santa Fe he lived for a few months in the house of Denis Hopper and told anecdotes of reckless extravagance from that time. Over the next few years the cause and meaning of Johnny's physical decline would preoccupy him more and more until he was consumed, not just by the disease but by the questions the disease asked of him, the most momentous being: why is it that I am prevented from saying what is in me to say? Why must I go unheard into the dark? Or, as he put it to me on another day with fearful intensity: *How not to hate?*

Pyrmont in those days was at the nadir of its fortunes. A working-class suburb, it had been devastated by the industries which formerly supported it. Hardly anyone lived there any more, certainly not out on the point where the Caledonian was. Among the vacant weedy lots and half-demolished walls, the tumbled sandstone and the steps leading nowhere, there were only a row of terraces running south from the hotel, the council flats opposite, and the Pyrmont Squats, a square block of workers' cottages with a pub on one corner built, like both the Caledonian and the refinery, in the 1870s. While I lived there, there were hardly any dealings between the two squats, perhaps because some of them were junkies and none of us were. Even so, the mutual suspicion with which we regarded each other was nothing to the gulf which yawned between all the squatters and our neighbours who rented or owned. For whoever does not pay for their space lives beyond the law, as if the absence of a regular financial commitment were a disqualification from the protection of statutes which are, after all, mostly concerned with the preservation of property.

Perhaps it was the lawlessness of our occupation which led us to seek a means of legitimising it. The Local Government and Community Housing Programme offered government loans to properly constituted associations of squatters with which to purchase and renovate the buildings they lived in. Title would be held by the State Housing Commission, and the building leased back to the Residents Association, which would, in theory, have a say in all decisions regarding use, renovation, management and maintenance of the premises. Although we knew this initiative would probably be cancelled in the imminent change of government, we decided to give it a go anyway.

It was a daunting assignment for a bunch of no-hopers: we had to draw up floor plans specifying a communal household, separate units or a mix; arrive at a purchase price for the building; hire an architect to detail and cost renovations; constitute ourselves as a legal entity with a charter and the right to enter into binding agreements; work out maintenance costs on a weekly basis to arrive at an equitable rent; and, finally, keep accurate account of all income and expenditure.

If none of these tasks was particularly onerous in itself, we still had to come to some sort of agreement among ourselves in order to proceed with them. This was hard. We were so different. None of us, with the possible exception of Johnny Muller, who was rumoured to work in the Post Office, had a proper job. We were mostly on the dole, with the usual range of illicit stratagems for picking up extra cash. Ricky dealt; Darren played the pool competitions in pubs; Dave gambled; Mark traded in junk; I had my cleaning job; Lyn was a student; Lyndi had rich parents who sent her money; the New Zealand kids, second-generation hippies, just got by, no one really knew how, not even themselves. How were we to pay for an architect, for instance?

There was a deeper problem: Ricky and Darren. These two, it was said, had as young kids been regularly locked in a wardrobe while their parents went to the pub, or drank and fought in the room outside; they had been rescued from this desperate situation by a family friend, a single man, who raised them up himself. He was the one who gave Ricky the motivational tapes he used to pump himself up, along with his fanatical enthusiasm for Australian Rules and especially the Carlton club. The absolute authority Darren wielded over Ricky perhaps also came from this man, if it did not come out of the wardrobe with them. Their tragedy was that, emotionally, they were still in there; every space they inhabited was both jail and refuge, and their apartment on the top floor was barricaded within and without and no one, with the occasional exception of Dave, ever went in there. Even he, ultimately, like the rest of us, had to decide whether to confront or live in fear of them.

For Ricky and Darren, recourse to authority for any reason was a mistake if it was not something worse. It would inevitably lead to involvement with the police, which to them was just another step on the way to the courts and the jailhouse. Looking back, it seems remarkable that they went along with the plan at all; it must have been because for a brief time we were all seized by a miraculous faith, an airy conviction that we were some kind of elect, whose miseries and frailties would, in the context of the group we were becoming, mutate into something solid and real and so find us a place of our own in the world. When Dave saw an advertisement in the window of a real-estate agent in Bondi offering the Caledonian for sale (they were asking $220,000), we took it for a sign: I sat down and wrote a letter to the owner.

We'd already been to the Land Office and done a search of the deeds. The Caledonian was part of Lot 24 of the MacArthur Estate, the original subdivision of the peninsula. In 1876 the then vacant Lot had been leased to Thomas McCredie, joiner, for £30 per annum. The original of the Pyrmont McCredies was a Scottish stonemason brought out to work the three quarries on the peninsula called Hellhole, Purgatory and Paradise on account of the variable quality of stone to be got from them. The finest yellowblock came out of Paradise, to be used both as building blocks and decorative carvings on such Sydney eminences as the Queen Victoria Building, the Town Hall, the State Library, the Observatory and Sydney Hospital. This stone is soft and grey and easily worked when it is cut; later, it hardens to that pale gold which seems to drink the sun. The McCredie family grew rich and diversified into the building trade; in the late 1870s, they built the Caledonian.

It first appeared in Sands Register in 1880 as a private hotel; the Billiard Room, *with one of Alcock's best tables and appliances*, was added in 1883. Gentlemen engaged in business in town wanting a quiet home were offered one on very reasonable terms. There was a stable, an attic and a basement as well. A curious feature of the hotel was the incorporation of a boat hold cover in the ceiling of the top floor. You climbed a ladder and slid back this cover to get out onto the roof. A long pole bearing a red lantern, it was said, used to be hoisted out this hole to attract the attention of sailors on ships docking at Tumbalong or Darling Harbour. Perhaps the gentlemen engaged in business found more than billiards and a private bar to entertain them.

The hotel remained in the McCredie family for nearly a century; in 1923, Susan McCredie, wife of Thomas and mother of George, paid £2,500 for the freehold title. George, an architect, sold it in 1965 for £17,000 to Avoca Holdings, which was the family company of a Mrs Kearney of 20 Victory Road, Clovelly, who became sole owner of the building in 1970 and still had it when we were there. About this woman we could find almost nothing: it was rumoured she had inherited the Caledonian, along with many other properties in Sydney and Adelaide, when her husband died; and that some fatality bound her to the building, making her unwilling to sell or maintain it in a livable state. We never discovered the nature of this fatality, though it may have been that his death occurred or was caused there. Nor did we ever meet Mrs Kearney; but it was to her that I wrote, outlining our plan to buy the hotel with a government loan.

Reaction was swift and sour: we received a letter from Mrs Kearney's solicitors containing a Notice to Quit. This is the indis-pensable first step in the process of evicting squatters and, even though it was never followed up, was enough to blow our fragile community to bits. Ricky and Darren, in particular, never forgave me for jeopardising their bolt hole: the letter had my name on it.

Nevertheless, in the bitterness of our disappointment, we decided Mrs Kearney must be getting bad advice from her solicitors and tried to make a direct approach. The house at 20 Victory Street was a massive, forbidding, yellow-painted pile built on a windy corner overlooking the bare carpark on the crumbling bluff of Clovelly. We knocked on the door and waited and then went around the back to see if there were windows open or lights on; if the widow was there, she did not show herself. One day not long after, Lyn and Lyndi watched perplexed as a taxi drew up outside the Bowman Street entrance, the back door opened and an aging woman in a fur coat, with tears pouring from her eyes, sat gazing at the Caledonian. When they tried to speak to her, she shook her head, closed the door and told the cabbie to drive on. This could only have been the

Widow Kearney, but what it was that caused her grief, and why she would not talk to us, remain forever dark.

Meanwhile, when the Notice to Quit was not followed up by any action, we calmed down a bit and continued mending fences, making gardens, repairing broken stairs and so on; we got the electricity legally connected; we even had a party. But something had gone from us: the conviction of the rightness of our little group and a belief that blessings would follow right action on our part. Our idealism shattered, we returned to what we were: an atomised remnant hanging insecurely on in a place that would never be ours.

It was all so hand to mouth. Without a proper kitchen, food was always scarce. There weren't any real shops in Pyrmont then, only the sandwich bars for the daytime workers, the pubs selling pies and sausage rolls, and one poorly stocked minimarket which, like the sandwich shops, closed when it started getting dark. How can you build a community without communal meals? All of us kept food in our rooms, which might be shared piecemeal with whoever dropped by; but never once did we sit down at a table or round a fire and eat from the same pot. I have dreary memories of going to sleep with an empty stomach. Either that, or a belly full of beer and crisps to get me through until the pubs and sandwich shops opened again next morning. There were a lot of pubs: the Pyrmont Arms, the Royal Pacific, the Terminus, the Duke of Edinburgh, the New York, the Pyrmont Bridge, the Quarryman's Arms, the Dunkirk. And there were the drugs: the New Zealand kids had a constant supply of dope, augmented now and then with dashes of speed or LSD, and they were generous to a fault. Being stoned on marijuana and hungry is torture, but the other drugs are appetite suppressants, giving you a splendid sense of your own possibilities without a hint of a need for other sustenance.

I also had a couple of plants of my own, which never really flourished because there was nowhere secluded and sunny for them to sit in the garden. Tired of watching them sicken and yellow in the dankness of the brick pile, I decided to move them into one of the empty rooms on the top floor. It was perfect: looking west and with a dormer window. They cheered up immediately. On fine days

I would move them three or four times so they remained always within the lozenges of slow light traversing the splintery boards. At night they looked out to the turbid sky with its scatter of small brown stars. There was only one problem: via a mental process I didn't understand, Ricky assumed their proximity to his space gave him rights over them. He used to water and pick them. Meanwhile he and Darren were aggressively extending their hold over rooms they had no need for. Anyone who objected was either ignored or threatened. I didn't care that they were colonising empty rooms, but I minded Ricky messing with my dope plants. One day I asked him not to.

I was in my room when I heard his step on the stairs and then he was standing in the doorway, one of the plants in his hands. He gave it to me. *Where's the other one?* I asked. He laid back and punched me so hard in the chest he cracked a rib. Croaking for breath, I pushed past him and out into the coachyard, with just enough presence of mind to keep talking. *Why did you do that?* I said. *I only asked you where it was. You didn't need to punch me.* Ricky was the kind of guy who, if he hit you, expected to be hit back, but I wasn't going to do that. He would have murdered me. I kept on talking and after a while he went away. Of course he never gave back the other plant. What's more, he soon found out where I hid the one he returned, among the long grass and creepers growing over the ornate sandstone blocks out along the derelict end of Herbert Street where carved pieces of the disassembled gateway to Pyrmont Bridge were piled. He continued to pick from it – at least I assume it was him – less, perhaps, for the smoke than to show his contempt for me.

I made one other mistake before I went home for Christmas. For our solstice party we built a bonfire in the back yard and eddied drunkenly around it into the wee small hours. Somewhere on that evening, encountering Lyndi in the leaping firelight, I leant forward, unasked, and kissed her softly on the lips. I don't know why: perhaps because I knew she wanted me to. Lyndi, the South African, was an unhappy, needy, forlorn, sometimes desperate woman harbouring the common middle-class delusion that the world still owed her the happiness she had not found in life. Her expensive education had not qualified her for anything in particular beyond the poems she wrote and the photographs she took, neither of which satisfied her yearning for expression. She was attracted to me partly, I think, because of the time I spent working. It did no good to say that the film treatment I was writing was merely speculative and no evidence of greatness of soul: she had, in her own mind, already deified me. Plagued by doubt myself, the last thing I wanted was an acolyte, especially one with romantic aspirations.

Moving into the squat hadn't resolved my situation, only exacerbated it. I still felt tied by invisible bonds to Gemma, still yearned for some irrevocable consummation of the affair with Brial. If I had thought – and I had – that the Caledonian would become our love nest, I was wrong. She came round one day for a look and then didn't come back again until months later; it wasn't really her kind of place. We had always kept in touch by phone; now she couldn't call me, and though I could always go up the road and ring her from the pay phone, I hardly ever did. Even our psychic connection failed. Unaccountably, now there was no reason for us to spend our time apart, that was apparently what we preferred to do. Was it that we both wanted the other only when we could not have them? Or was it that I was still not really free?

So there I was, involved with two women, one of whom still did not know about the other, and neither of whom was getting what she wanted from me. Nor I from them. My life did not need further complication. And yet, knowing all that, I kissed Lyndi by the firelight. From the look in her eye afterwards I knew she felt in that kiss all her hopes fulfilling. How then could I tell her that all I was able to give was desolation? How could she know that adulation for my so-called powers had replaced mother-love in my childhood; that I preferred reticent, stylish, enigmatic women to any excess of ardour or devotion? That night, as I lay alone in my bed, I knew Lyndi was lying alone in her bed, longing for me; while outside the fire blazed until dawn, fed by the dark, solitary figure of Ricky silhouetted, heaping on more and more wood as if to consume the whole world in his own private inferno.

I had been reading in the State Library of New South Wales, chapter by chapter, Rutherford's exhaustive and exhausting 1961 biography of George Grey. My interest in Grey was sparked by mention, I no longer recall where, of a meeting between him and Robert Louis Stevenson on board ship in Sydney Harbour. Though I had never written a play, I wondered if their conversation might yield drama enough to make one; but I found no corroboration anywhere of the alleged meeting, which could only have taken place in the early 1890s, during Stevenson's sojourn in the South Seas and before Grey's final return to England on the SS *Gothic* in 1894. They would have talked of Samoa, in whose byzantine politics Stevenson became implicated; not long after he arrived back in London, Grey addressed Members of Parliament on the Samoan situation. Grey believed in imperial federation and colonial self-government; his plan for a Federation of the English Speaking Peoples of the World was something like what later became known as the British Commonwealth of Nations; and he wanted Australia or New Zealand or both to make an empire in the Pacific.

Grey's last hurrah in Australia, where he had begun his career as an imperialist, came during and after the Australasian Federation Conference in Sydney in 1891, at which he was hailed as one of liberalism's great contemporary thinkers and an heroic figure from the frontier era. His actual ideas were less enthusiastically received: popularly elected governors and limited federal powers lost out to Crown appointments, a strong central executive and a nominated Upper House. And New Zealand never did join the Federation. Yet, in the aftermath, when Grey toured the cities of southern and eastern Australia, he was given a delirious welcome wherever he went. At a banquet in his honour in Adelaide he delivered an oration on the nature of democracy, the rights of the working class and the need for social equality to a tumultuous audience. He visited the grave of his infant son, dead more than fifty years, and stood with the three surviving members of Sturt's 1846 expedition to farewell David Lindsay's trek to the interior. From Adelaide he travelled to Broken Hill, Goulburn (here he gave five speeches in one day), Melbourne, Newcastle and finally Sydney again, where he spoke in Centennial

Hall and at the Gaiety Theatre. How quaint it now seems to read of the old reprobate, cheered by the crowd as he made his querulous way on board ship in Sydney, pausing to advise a young lad of twelve against the perils of smoking tobacco.

My plan for a play segued into a treatment for a film, not about Stevenson but about Grey. At the end of his life the old man, immured in rooms in the London of Oscar Wilde, haunted by ghosts of empire and consumed with regret for past actions, attempts a reconciliation with his wife Eliza, whom he has not seen for nearly forty years. The source for this melodrama was the Aston Letters, a collection of correspondence held in the Auckland Public Library. Miss Isobel Aston ran a private hotel for gentlemen in West Kensington and used to visit Grey daily at his rooms at 7 Park Place, St James, to read to him, nurse him and handle his personal correspondence. She became the nexus of an extraordinary whirl of friends and relatives eddying around the rapidly decaying old man, attempting the impossible: maintenance of appearances while securing their own share of his considerable (and illusory) fortune.

Into this insipid group of schemers and hypocrites Eliza Grey lobs a letter of her own, proposing a dutiful reunification with her husband, last seen in 1860 on board ship off Rio where, incensed by her flirtation with a naval officer, Grey had her put ashore. Despite – or perhaps because of – his failing eyesight, his dementia and general decrepitude, the old man agrees, and the two ancients live together again in cheaper lodgings at 52 Stanhope Gardens. These are secured for the old man by his 'niece', Annie George, on a visit from New Zealand. She is, with Miss Aston, the only other person in the drama not actuated by self-interest, and a match for any of the scheming relatives; but Annie has nine children, the youngest newborn, and cannot stay in England. On her departure, all hell breaks loose around the old man's bowed and trembling head. He has been *blackmailed for years by a family . . . and they have had large amounts*, but nobody says who they are nor for which indiscretion they are bleeding him; under persuasion from General Horatio Robley, the artist-soldier veteran of the New Zealand Wars, he is tempted to squander what little money he has left in a dubious speculation in gold; and he and his wife find they still cannot stand the sight of each other.

In the hostilities which follow, the relatives and friends take sides, and the hitherto circumspect phrasing of the letters is abandoned in favour of calumny and vituperation. She is *a miserable wreck*, *the old cat*, *a perfect devil* with *greedy, designing, so-called friends*; he is *disturbed and unhinged*, a *bully*, perhaps *mad*. He will not wash, or open the windows in his rooms, and is apt to cast off all of his clothes without warning. His opium addiction is by now obvious to all and out of control. There is talk of having him committed under section 116 of the Lunacy Act of 1890. He gets lost wandering the streets of London looking for pastries, so his name and address have to be written on a card safety-pinned to his lapel. Eliza demands money and when it is refused starts opening his mail and driving his friends away. A Roman Catholic, and devout, she nevertheless expects to live once more in gubernatorial luxury.

The couple sunder again after not very long, and die within weeks of each other: Grey has always wanted to outlive her, and he does. His only comment on her death is enigmatic. *She liked turtle soup*, he says, *and she was inordinately fond of champagne*. Nevertheless, as old politicians will, throughout the mayhem he keeps some of his wits about him, entertaining on a regular basis a young journalist, James Milne, who wrote up the talks to make an otiose, triumphal record of Grey's memory of himself, *Romance of a Pro-consul* (1911). This book, a copy of which I also found in the State Library, was another source for the film treatment.

Grey was thus another antagonist, more durable and more culpable than the Griffins. My plan to dramatise those last derelict years was an opportunity to indict the man before some notional tribunal of history as it might have been. Everything wrong with the decrepit milieu I lived in, even my atomised, post-colonial, neo-romantic self, could be sourced to the calamities visited upon us by Grey. I don't mean to be wholly condemnatory of this impulse: anger is an energy, and historical drama does not have to pay heed to facts so much as to what facts might come to mean. And I was not so deluded that my personal crusade against Grey the man led me to ignore what actually happened. Rather, it gave me an attitude with which to gather evidence against him. After all, a dismantling of the man might be a means of deconstructing the official version so as to clear the way for a history of the unsung.

Essential to an understanding of Grey are his own *Journals of Two Expeditions of Discovery in North West and Western Australia* (1841). Following a formative tour of duty in Ireland, then brutally ruled under the Coercion and Insurrection Acts, Grey set out for the colonies hoping to discover a new land for the unfortunate Irish to live in. He was twenty-five, an ensign in the 83rd Foot. His formal brief was to familiarise the natives with the British name and character; record information on the country's natural state with an eye to possible colonisation; collect botanical and zoological specimens; and keep strict discipline at all times.

While he did all this with skill and alacrity, both expeditions – to the country in north-western Australia now known as the Kimberley and to Shark Bay further south on the same coast – were disastrous. Grey had no idea of the harshness of the land he was attempting to explore and only the vaguest notion of how to proceed with the small, ill-equipped and fractious group under his command. He did not even realise it was the rainy season. Nevertheless, he slogs on through atrocious weather and some of the most difficult country in the world, shadowed at all times by hostile natives and under increasing pressure from his sickening, waterlogged men, with their pack animals dying, resolutely recording each misadventure for posterity: despite their meticulous observations and frequent rhapsodies over the beauties of the landscape, much admired at the time, the most intriguing aspect of the *Journals* is the procreant contradiction between the man Grey thinks himself to be and what his own narration reveals about him.

On one of his sallies forward to find a path through to the fabled inland sea, he falls into a violent confrontation with a band of Aborigine. In the one previous close encounter (with this same group), the firing of a gun over their heads was enough to disperse them, but this time it does not work. When Grey fires the other barrel and shoots one in the arm, they respond with a hail of spears. He takes shelter behind a rock to reload, while one of his two companions tries frantically to free another gun from its waterproof covering and the other gibbers in fear: *O God, Sir, look at them! Look at them!* Grey rips the recalcitrant gun free and takes on the attackers single-handed. Walking doggedly towards them over open ground, he is hit by three spears, one of which lodges in his leg near the hip joint. Heroically he pulls the weapon from the wound, which he conceals from both his men and his attackers behind his haversack, then shoots and kills the leader of the Aborigine. They flee, carrying the dead man with them. Grey faints and has to be left with the still gibbering youth while the other man goes back to the main party for the doctor and a horse. Safe in camp, tossing and turning, unable to sleep for the pain, all night he hears the *piercing shrieks of wailing women and the mournful cries of native men, sorrowing over him who had that day fallen by my hand*. For the rest of his life he would be inclined towards hysterical remorse at the taking of this man's life, but it was the spear which left an indelible mark. He was able to withstand the rigours of this and the following expedition only by recourse to the laudanum in the medical kit, and the result was a lifetime use of, if not addiction to, opiates.

Not long afterward Grey became probably the first European to see in the Kimberley paintings of enigmatic beings called Wandjina, which he speculated were evidence of some previous, lost civilisation. He sketched those he found, along with what he thought was a picture of the head of his only precursor, perhaps Portuguese or Dutch. Grey's head has not been found again – it may have been a misreading of a natural feature – but the Wandjina, tall, mouthless figures with enormous eyes and haloes of cloud and lightning, are numerous and have been intensively studied. They are still sometimes said to show ancient visitors coming from the sea to the west, bringing rain; but their present-day guardians have a more complex view.

The local people remember a great punitive war between humans and Wandjina, but whether it was caused by the malice of the spirits or human transgression is debatable. Further, the Wandjina who act as spirits of place for moieties of people may be distinct from the war-makers. These individually named spirits made dreaming tracks across the country before entering the rock upon which they are said to have painted themselves; human agency is limited to the periodic repainting of the images. They are guardians of the spirits of unborn children, called forth by their fathers: *You dream them, you catch them in your hands; they say, I am waterlily, bat, stone, pandanus. They slip from your grasp and go into the womb and wait there. You know who they are, later, when they are born.* Later still, the children are taken to their tutelary Wandjina to begin learning sacred history. After death their spirit, and perhaps their bones too, will return to the Wandjina cave. Wandjina are certainly associated with water, but with some ambivalence: songs are sung to them, asking for rain to fill the rivers and provide food for all creatures, yet inadvertent touching of or otherwise disturbing the image might anger the spirit, who could then send great winds, rain and hailstorms to destroy the people, or rise from the nearby sacred standing water as a snake and swallow the intruder.

Grey's drawings of Wandjina show figures with great staring eyes and sky-blue or yellow or orange turbans, robed from the neck to the ankles; one has around its head what looks like ancient script. After Grey's book came out there was a great deal of speculation over who these paintings might represent: Macassans, Malays, Sumatrans, Moors, Japanese and Hindu were all proposed, while the script was identified by one scholar as Archaic Japanese and translated: *The number of the hopeless ones is 62.* This was supposed to be a message left by the survivors of the wreck of a Japanese ship on that coast.

By 1930, Grey's Wandjina had been found again and photographed; after World War II, curator of Anthropology and Archaeology at the Western Australian Museum, I. M. Crawford concluded the 'script' was, in fact, only markings caused by cracking and peeling of successive layers of paint. Crawford thought that Wandjina, some of whom are seven metres long, are representations of clouds in human form, occasioned by the rolling of thunder imagined as a spirit in the sky. He quotes W. Arndt's hypothesis that Aborigine *drew pictures of clouds and later added eyes and nose to these.* Of course, it is unlikely that any outside observer would be able to gain a full understanding of the complex of meanings around these paintings, and in recognition of this another theme of the film treatment was Grey's haunting by the Wandjina he inadvertently disturbed, as if a lifetime's misfortune in his personal life had been caused by this original violation.

George Grey and Eliza Spencer first met in the aftermath of his second expedition, either during the three months he spent in Perth under strict instruction from London to attempt no more exploration, or else after he was appointed temporary Resident Magistrate of Albany at St George's Sound, about 400 kilometres to the south. He replaced Eliza's father, Sir Richard Spencer, who in 1839 died leaving a widow and nine children. Eliza was sixteen; he twenty-seven; he took up his post in August and they were married in November. She had just lost her father; he had never known his. They were alike in their pride, their stubbornness and the intensity of their grievances, and in time each developed an implacable grudge towards the other; but they were happy enough at first.

It was the death of their only child, George, in Adelaide in 1841 which began the disintegration of the marriage. He was born on board ship as the young couple made their way back to Australia from England, to which Grey had no sooner returned than he was sent away again, this time to govern the cantankerous, almost bankrupt colony of South Australia. The boy lived only five months and there never was another. Rutherford says that Grey blamed his son's death on Eliza's neglect, but who can say? Perhaps she was post-natally depressed, already paling under the cold glare of his personality. Perhaps she didn't know what to do. Like many young couples who lose a child, they were probably very close for a while after the catastrophe then began to drift irretrievably away into the land of *if only* and *why not*. No one knows if Grey's numerous infidelities with indigenes began now or later, though it probably started happening with Maori women during his first governorship of New Zealand.

In Adelaide, the Greys were thought aloof, because they did not entertain as lavishly as had their predecessors, the Gawlers. In the early days, when Grey was burned in effigy by settlers protesting his unemployment policy (he cut back on public works and tried to force the workers out of the city onto farms), nobody knew that he spent part of his own salary on relief for the poor. Perhaps the Greys did not entertain as another measure of economy; or was it that they preferred their own company and that of a few close friends and family to the hurly-burly of public feasts and balls? That was certainly the case in New Zealand, where their revels, such as they were, took place mostly behind closed doors. There are only a few tantalising glimpses of social life in the Governor's household, one of which has a direct bearing both on Grey's infidelity and its consequences for future generations.

In August 1851, in Wellington, Grey fired his secretary, George Cooper, supposedly for flirting with Eliza. Not long afterwards, in November, Maria Harper, a maid in Grey's Wellington household, finding herself pregnant, fled to Nelson, to marry a carpenter named Matthews. Grey's half-brother, Godfrey Thomas, the alleged father of the child, went after Maria and managed to get her away from her husband and into a hotel, from which they were unfortunately expelled in the middle of the night. They then found refuge with a minister, Robert Cole, who, next morning, summoned a couple of other members of the local gentry and together they gave Godfrey a good talking to. Cole then sent an extraordinary letter to Grey, in which he asserted that Godfrey might support Maria financially but that she was spiritually her husband's for his lifetime. The sting is in the postscript. There was, he wrote, *a wide spoken contempt held towards the Government among the lower orders* because public offices were filled by men who *outrage unblushingly God's Holy Law & the Public Sense of delicacy & decency in the grossest Manner and to the worst Degree.* He meant that officials like New Munster's colonial secretary, the poet Alfred Domett, and the commissioner for the extinguishment of native title, Walter Mantell, cohabited openly with Maori women.

Nevertheless, Godfrey paid Matthews £130 and brought Maria back to Wellington. Eliza, perhaps out of spite at the banishment of her favourite, would not let Godfrey stay at Government House any longer. The child, a daughter named Annie, was born in July 1852. In October, Godfrey went to England where he was required by the death of his older brother to assume the Thomas baronetcy. Upon Godfrey Thomas's own death in 1861, Grey took over guardianship of the nine-year-old girl, who became, as the biographers like to say, the daughter he never had: his faithful 'niece', Annie. In 1872, Annie married Seymour Thorne George, the younger son of Colonel George Thorne George, an old military friend of Grey's. Grey made Seymour estate manager of his private fiefdom on Kawau Island in the Hauraki Gulf, and in return he conferred respectability upon the illegitimate Annie. Together they founded the New Zealand branch of the Thorne George dynasty.

The most recent account of this imbroglio, *To Be a Hero: A biography of Sir George Grey* (1998) by Edmund Bohan, leaves several questions unanswered, the most obvious being: who was Maria Harper? The Thorne George family version says she was a 'daughter' of Robert Cole, which may go some way towards explaining the Reverend's indignant letter to Grey when Godfrey arrived on his doorstep. Cole had no daughters; in this context, the word means a Maori girl given into the care of the church by local chiefs seeking political advantage in their struggle to retain their lands. She was likely of Ati Awa or Ngati Toa, Te Rauparaha's people. Perhaps Cole was himself involved in her placement at Government House. Or perhaps she was never there until later: the Thorne Georges say Annie's mother became pregnant in Nelson, but gave birth at Government House in Wellington. If Maria was seduced under his roof, no wonder Cole was outraged at Godfrey's arrival. But was he really the father? Godfrey's mission to retrieve Maria is open to other interpretations than the obvious. Godfrey Thomas had lived with the Greys in Adelaide and later followed them to New Zealand. He was quite a few years younger than his half-brother, an agreeable young man of whom Eliza was once very fond: *I am very glad to have him here*, she wrote, *for I do not feel so lonely when he is here to chat with sometimes.* Why then did she undergo a nervous collapse over the business with Maria, and insist Godfrey leave their house?

It is significant that Grey did not assume guardianship of Annie until after he and Eliza had parted; and that Annie George could not herself abide Eliza: it was she who called her *the old cat*. Members of the Thorne George family believe that George Grey was the father of Maria's child, and Godfrey Thomas merely his proxy. They trace their ancestry directly back to Grey via his illegitimate daughter, Annie.

Grey's well-documented outrage with respect to Eliza's flirtation with Admiral Keppel on board HMS *Forte*, which led to their sundering, was hypocritical in the extreme if he was himself a philanderer. Even so, the Bishop of Oxford, Samuel Wilberforce, who was consulted after the event, would *not admit that the sin of infidelity in the wife is altered by a want of chastity in the husband*. His reference was to Eliza's claim that Grey moved his African mistress into Government House in Cape Town; Eliza left and went back to England. When they set out on the *Forte* for South Africa, they had only just made up their differences. Meanwhile Keppel and Eliza fell into the flush of a shipboard romance. They passed notes to each other through a partition between their adjoining cabins, anticipating a liaison which was thwarted only when Grey found the letters. In an apoplectic rage, he threatened either suicide or the murder of his wife if the ship – which also carried the explorers John Hanning Speke and James Augustus Grant en route for Africa – did not put into Rio; there, Eliza was ordered ashore and then despatched back to England. This was in 1860; they did not see each other again until the disastrous reconciliation in 1896.

Why had I made an antagonist of this (in Canterbury settler Henry Tancred's words) *terrible and fatal man*? It couldn't just have been because the mother of one of my closest friends is a Thorne George, who, when you see her, you do not doubt has the blood of Rauparaha in her veins. Did I find in Grey's dissimulations an echo of my own? Reconciliation with Gemma remained a possibility all the time I was at the Caledonian and for a while after as well – in fact, as long as the affair with the mostly absent Brial lasted. On the other hand, I could scarcely bring myself to acknowledge, let alone contemplate, the possibility that a part of Brial's allure for me was her Polynesian ancestry. Was I, like Grey, obsessed with her because she was, in the old discredited parlance, *a native woman*? Never mind that she was born and grew up in Auckland, partly on the streets, and had never been to the islands. Never mind that one of her grandfathers was Dutch, a sailor. I remember her once showing me a photograph of him, taken in Papeete in 1908. He was a handsome, smiling man in a striped shirt, with tousled hair and that air of romantic freedom the Pacific has always evoked in the chilly European soul. When I looked at it I wanted to be him. Was that the reason I desired his granddaughter – not for who she was but for what she represented to me? Is that why I sometimes called her, but only to myself, my Gauguin girl?

Intellectually, my film treatment was based on the flawed notion that Grey could be resurrected on screen as the conscience of a century. Flawed, because he was clearly someone who, however anguished at the consequences of his actions, was never made a coward by conscience, unless his guilt or otherwise at the atrocities of empire was always kept private, a matter between himself and the Christian god he did not abandon or feel himself abandoned by. Was it a real attempt to get behind the Victorian mask which still governs our public life? Or did it arise from the aching sense I had of the wrongness of the history I seemed to have inherited in my diminished person and reduced circumstances? As if Grey were somehow personally to blame for the ruin I was and the ruins I lived among?

In fact, the figure of the Consul in the film treatment resembles not Grey so much as my own father, at that time living out his last years in the small New Zealand town named Greytown after the Governor. It was my father who was haunted by ghosts from his past, my father who drank away his days in an agony of *what if* and *why not*, my father who was paralysed by guilt and shame for what he had and had not done. Was it bad faith on my part to try to shoehorn the historical Grey into a fusty Victorian melodrama in an attempt to betray his hidden weaknesses for all to see? Perhaps my hostility towards the Grey of history was a displacement of hostility towards my own father which I could not admit. If so, it is apposite that it was in my father's company I made a trip to Kawau Island after Christmas, there to try to uncover some more visceral image of the man than I had been able to find in books, letters and libraries.

My methodology was unorthodox. I had with me a small slip of paper with a blue and red and yellow transfer of Superman on it. It was impregnated with LSD. I intended taking it once I pitched my tent in Heaven's Camping Ground (John & Mary Heaven, Props.) at Pa Farm on Bon Accord Harbour. The trip was given to me by Stefan and Tania at the Caledonian in Sydney. I concealed it in the spine of *The Marquesan Journal of Edward Robarts* and for the second and last time in my life took a prohibited substance across an international border. Towards midnight on Christmas Eve in Wellington, the Customs Men stolidly unwrapped one by one the Christmas presents I had brought for my family, but they didn't find the acid. I would have claimed ignorance if they had: Robarts' *Marquesan Journal* was on loan from the Sydney Public Library.

We took a ferry out to the island, sitting in rows as if on a bus, looking out through salt-crusted, foam-flecked windows at a choppy grey sea. My father sat next to me, his false teeth clicking as he chewed his tongue. We didn't talk much. A little blue penguin swam alongside us for a while. To the south was Mahurangi, where I used to cut scrub on rainy hills above wide estuarine waters. North, the long flat reach of Takatu peninsula lay like an arm flung across the shoulder of the gulf. The quiet bay where I lived and worked one summer fifteen years before was now a clutter of holiday homes. Kawau ranged ahead, a blue shape rising from the sea. I had often looked out at it while spraying the farmer's gorse with 24D, but this was my first visit.

Kawau means shag. The island was known as a good place for gathering seafood, especially a kind of mud shark called *muru*. A group of piratical Maori, Ngatitai and Ngatiwai, lived there during the contact period, preying on passing canoes. By 1830, the mainland tribes had had enough. They descended, slaughtered and, at Bosanquet Bay, largely ate them. The island was later 'sold' for a few muskets and some gunpowder. There is copper ore. A New South Wales company, North British Australian Loan and Investment, founded the Kawau Company and began mining in the 1840s, bringing in Cornish miners from Falmouth, Welsh smelters from Swansea. Later, Auckland lawyer and politician Frederick Whitaker and his partner Theophilus Heale deviously obtained a mining lease on land below the high-water mark and began tunnelling up towards the diggings. There was a protracted law suit which ended with the Kawau Company buying out Whitaker and Heale for £5,000; but the tunnel allowed sea water in, flooding the mines, and the whole enterprise foundered.

Grey was instrumental in settling the court action in favour of the Kawau Company during his first Governorship of New Zealand. In 1862, early in his second tour of duty, he bought it for himself. It cost £3,700, and he spent another £5,000 joining the mine manager's house and the assay house to make a mansion which is still there. The following year, 1863, was *the year New Zealand went mad*. Grey, who volunteered to return from South Africa in order to forestall the threatened war with Maori, through hubris, illness, poor judgement and plain bloody-mindedness precipitated the very war he had come to prevent. When he told his brother-in-law Ormus Biddulph that he did not think he would *ever be truly happy again*, it was perhaps to his part in the carnage in the Waikato he was referring, though others have seen it as a comment on his sundering from Eliza, which, further, is said to have contributed to his erratic judgement during the war years and so, inexorably, to his dismissal as Governor in 1868, after which he retired to Kawau.

Huge exotic gardens were established, and a menagerie as well. Magnolia, palm and rhododendron were planted round the house, while back up the valley and on the hills were jacaranda, wattle, red gum and other eucalypts, silver fir from Table Mountain, cork and walnut trees, olive and oleander, oak, elm, bay and poplar, as well as Fijian climbers, spider lily, bamboo and bougainvillea. He tried cultivating banana and pomegranate, camphor and cinnamon, breadfruit and custard apple, mulberry, cinnamon and loquat. It was on Kawau that Grey isolated the heavy-bearing New Zealand grapefruit known as the Poorman Orange, whence it spread to most gardens in North Auckland. He brought in peacock, Chinese pheasant, kookaburra, emu, guinea fowl, turkey, duck, goose and quail, along with crocodile, kangaroo, wallaby, antelope, deer, monkey, and zebra which used to pull children along in a little wooden cart. Sheep were farmed and shorn as well. Kawau was infested with wild cattle and Grey used to enjoy provoking a wild bull to charge, then wait until it was only a few metres away before shooting it. He presided over his island and the large staff who ran it like a feudal lord, leading his people in prayer every morning. He even tried to have it made a district of its own, with its own registrar, separate from the Auckland Province.

The gardens at Mansion House Bay are mostly gone now. What is left is a pleasant, park-like domain running down to the water. A pair of massive Chilean wine palm still stand. On the hills behind the bay is a pine forest, where kookaburra and wallaby flourish. You pay to go into the house, which is a colonial museum now. Heavy furniture roped off in the drawing room, dull pictures in dark wooden frames, the beds lumpy and unslept in under white covers. There was something inexpressibly melancholy about us, the celebrated history teacher turned decrepit alcoholic and his awkward, fearful son, trailing along with everyone else gazing blankly at the bric-à-brac of another age. The Victorians provided themselves with such exacting comforts. Of course they had servants to do their living for them. Afterwards, we ate sandwiches on the lawn and I went for a swim in the murky waters of the yacht-crowded bay. Soon it was time for my father to get back on the boat. He didn't tell me he was on his way to Sandspit to see his old friend Ken Lawn, who died of a heart attack only ten days later. I hadn't told him about the trip, either; it would only have worried him. We were not uneasy together, there just wasn't much to say. He had entered that silence which is broken only when you ask or offer something. As the ferry pulled away, he sat hunched in his seat, back on the lonely treadmill of thought. I shouldered my pack and headed up the path into the pines.

A couple of hours later I came down off the ridge through tall kanuka scrub mixed with second-growth bush. The track crossed a flat wooden bridge over a muddy creek where bits of nameless machinery rusted among the mangroves. The tide was out and a black ooze bubbled with iridescence. This was where Grey had kept his saurians. Nearer to the sea was a soft green mound in a grove of the ubiquitous kanuka. The camping ground was the size of a couple of football fields, flat, stony, covered with a sparse growth of stringy grass. You could see it had been cultivated previously: Pa Farm was the nursery for the various botanical experiments on the island. On its far side, huddled under the hill, stood the house of the proprietors. The sea looked grey and distant across mudflats. At the back, the field merged into ragged scrub and bush. Everywhere, wild on the hills and wild in the valleys, agapanthus flowered blue and white under mackerel skies.

I was pitching my tent near the kanuka grove when I heard voices. Two men approached, one short, round and red-faced, the other tall, lean, craggy, with grey upstanding hair and a tangled grey beard. They wore the nondescript clothes of far rural places. The little guy was John Heaven; his bony friend's name was Nott. I said who I was, that I'd rung . . . *yeah, just one night*. There didn't seem to be much else to say.

John Heaven fixed me with his beady eye. *Are you a Christian man?* he asked.

Mr Nott wore a fierce and staring mien. *We follow the Lord here*, he said.

I fumbled for some reply. *I believe in the right of every person to find their own path to salvation*, I said. *I don't myself worship the Christian god.*

Nott was leaning back on his heels, his head tilted sideways, one eye half-closed, the other wild. He harrumphed and turned away. But John Heaven seemed satisfied. *You can eat with us*, he said. *Just come over when you're done. Mary'll wait to serve until you do.*

The house smelled of dog. We sat at a round kitchen table covered with checked red and white plastic, eating corned beef, a white sauce with bits of onion in it, boiled potatoes, boiled vegetables.

Stewed fruit and yellow custard followed. Mary Heaven was lumpy, red-faced and dishevelled like her husband. She emanated a kind of stolid endurance. They had a son, Brian, sixteen and hostile. There was a girl, Sue, staying with them. She smiled at me across the table. She had curly blonde hair, baby-blue eyes, tiny delicate hands and a soft white mounded body. Nott's biblical gaze did his talking for him as he forked the floury potatoes into his beard. Outside the window, light was fading from the sky. As soon as it was decent, I excused myself, saying I wanted to take a walk in the bush before it got dark. In the subaqueous light of the tent, I took the picture of Superman from my wallet, swallowed it, then headed for the hills.

I took the track over the bridge then followed a left-hand fork I'd noticed on the way down. It seemed silly to be wearing boots, so I took them off, stashed them and went barefoot along the mossy path. Banks of bracken clustered below the hairy trunks of tree ferns. The fronds of the punga glimmered greenly beneath a kanuka canopy. The whole had the aspect of a formal garden: moss, bracken, fern, scrub. I heard the cluck and squawk of weka chasing each other through tunnels in the bracken. Fantails twittered and hung. The wavering, fluted whistle of a grey warbler came and went.

The track wound up the side of the hill for a kilometre or so before it joined the Carriage Road. I walked out of a wall of scrub onto a red-yellow, hard clay rutted surface under a vivid sky. Barred clouds in serried ranks receded into the west. The sea was silver sheet metal rucked with waves, from which the islands of the gulf stood out in black silhouette. Here and there was the blue-green stain of copper ore. Quartz pebbles glinted. When I picked one up to worry with my thumb, I realised the acid was beginning to work. That dryness in the mouth, the way your skin feels tacky and porous at once and looks all mottled.

Up on the ridge were kauri trees. I left the path to visit one of the larger ones, standing alone in a clearing shelled with its own bark. Curls of pink and orange and gold crunched underfoot as I walked up to touch the smooth grey trunk. Bright red resin oozed from a wound in the wood. Scattered on the ground were pieces of pale translucent gum, which crumbled between my fingers and gave off a clean, antiseptic smell. Through the coppery high branches of the tree, upthrust like the arms of a candelabrum, the sea continued on its kaleidoscopic tilt towards night. With a whirr of wings, a wood pigeon crossed, and I saw the impossible whiteness of its breast, the green and purple wing feathers, a bright red eye.

In places the kanuka was so thick and high it met above the path and made a gloomy tunnel of scrub, out of which stick insects fell into my hair: a harbinger of death among Maori. The Carriage Road led up to a trig station on Grey's Heights, where he used to take guests in a small trap to admire the view from the summit of the island. I was hoping to get that far, but as the climb continued and light fled the sky, I began to feel oppressed. I turned and went back down.

The drug was roaring in my head by the time I reached the bridge again. A white figure loomed from the thick dark, its face a pale oval floating past the trees. I heard embarrassed, girlish laughter. It was Sue. We walked down to the beach and sat on the sand and talked. She told me all sorts of things. John and Mary Heaven were surrogate parents. They were nice, but Brian was horrible, leering through the bedroom door when she was getting changed. She was from the small mainland town of Wellsford. She'd left school, but there were no jobs. She had a job once, in a tearoom, but it only lasted two weeks. Her friend was killed in a car crash; it was after that she became born again. Once, at a seance, her friend had spoken to her. She didn't know if god existed or not. If he did, why had he taken her friend? If he didn't, where was her friend now, that she could still talk to her? Did I believe in god? She was going to believe in him for another year and then see.

The land was dark now, the black saddle of hills across Bon Accord Harbour outlined against a still luminescent sky. Stars flared like coloured stones: Canopus, Sirius, Betelgeuse, the constellation Polynesians call *Te Manu Nui*, the Big Bird. The tide turned and an immense agitation of water rushed towards us over the mudflats. White noise resolved into an intricate, depthless music. Sand squeaked between our fingers as we played with it. The sky lightened further, and then a full moon rose sudden and yellow over Emu Point. Prismatic cirrus trailed across its craters and seas, refracting purple, blue, green. The whole bay resounded with the sound of water and from the land behind us came a stridulation of crickets, a *kree-kreeing* of frogs, the high piercing *keeeee-wiii* of kiwi. It was too much. Thinking to be by myself for a while, I told Sue I was going for a swim. She stood up, scratching in the sand with a stick. *I'll get my togs*, she said.

Thigh deep in the warm cloudy water, mud squeezing between our toes, we stood side by side for a while. She kept looking at the bulge in my swimmers and giggling. It was hard for me to ignore her soft, white body too. *Here goes*, I said, and dived. My skin felt slippery, as if soaped. The water was soft with the moonlight falling down through it. Grey shapes of fish slid away from me; when I tried to touch bottom I put my foot on a flounder and felt its spiny skin. I lay on my back and looked up. The moon was silver now, smaller, the clouds had gone and the Prussian-blue sky showed only the brightest stars: the Pleiades setting in the west, Taurus, Orion, Sirius. The lights of a few scattered dwellings shone yellow across the water.

When I got out, Sue was waiting on the beach. She had not wanted to get her hair wet. Waves broke at our feet as we sat on a log and talked some more. I was starting to feel cold, so I went to the tent to put some clothes on. *Shall I wait here for you?* she said.

If the Heavens had not sent for her, she might have stayed all night. We saw a torch beam wavering from the house, then heard Brian from the middle of the camping ground, yelling her name. *Dad says you have to come inside!* The instant she said where she was, torchlight pinned us both in its glare. Brian sniggered and went back inside. Halfway to the house we were met by John Heaven himself. He looked suspiciously at me in the gloaming. *You'd better come in for a cup of tea*, he said.

The interior seemed smaller, yellower, smellier than before. Sue had been sent to her room. Brian too. The Heavens, Mr Nott and I had our tea in the living room, sitting on sagging armchairs, a decrepit lounge. A big black Bible lay on the coffee table, the gold lettering on its spine blazing. The dog, a little brown curly-haired mongrel with fur coming out along its back, snuffled at my elbow, wanting the homemade coconut biscuit I could not eat: it (the biscuit) looked as big and hairy as the hearth rug. John Heaven began his interrogation. Had I seen a tui on my walk? A wood pigeon? Weka? Fantail? Shag? He wasn't really talking about wildlife, he was talking about Sue. Had I laid hands upon her when we were down there sifting sand? The more birds I said I'd seen, the more hostile he became. *Kiwis*, he spat out at last. *Did you see any kiwis?* I shook my head. He leaned back in his chair, satisfied. *Well*, he said, *you have to live here, don't you?* Mr Nott was looking intently at me, his eyes bulging. Mary Heaven was reaching for the biscuits again. The dog whimpered and leapt up from its rug on the hearth. I finished my tea and stood up to go.

Outside the night was silvery and calm. The camping ground was full of grazing wallaby, which thumped away as I walked slowly back to the tent. I lay on the lilo while parades of phantoms racketed through my head and the unseen kiwi screamed from the bush. When the house lights went out, I got up again and walked into the kanuka grove. Agapanthus brushed against my thighs. The moon cast clear shadows on the soft grass. The tide was running up the estuary: exhalations of swamp gas, soft bubbles collapsing into air, salty tricklings as water ran into muddy channels between the mangroves. The waves overtook each other, lapping like tongues. The stream bed sighed open, making minute adjustments of fluid earth as the sea ran up in.

It seemed to me I rambled on the flanks of an immense being. She was the river and the banks of the river. She was the bay, the surrounding hills and the hills beyond. She was the whole island. In the middle of the kanuka grove the tall heads of the agapanthus bent gracefully over the grassy mound, their thick juicy stems upstanding, their flat dark leaves cascading down. Here the hallucination was at its most intense; here I was submerged in the roar of tidal waters, the gasp and suck of the river, the heavy settling of the land into itself and the slow rotation of the planet among the stars. I lay down and floated in that immensity, that eternity.

Back in the tent again, when I closed my eyes, the welter of images returned like a cavalcade. I was tired, too tired. I didn't want any more. More, however, was coming. From the psychic distance where the river twisted in its bed and the sea slowly withdrew, another being approached. He was thin, with a grin like a rind of the waning moon, eyes vacant as the spaces between the stars. He came stepping lightly on the balls of his feet, every muscle tensed, and twirling a *taiaha*. His tongue flickered in and out, his eyes rolled. From his brow a horny crest like a tuatara's swept up and over his head and down his back. He was tattooed, the *moko* resembled lizard skin. I knew he was coming to kill me. A tightness gripped my chest, I broke out in a sweat. He was coming to kill me! I made myself breathe in, slowly, then out. I thought, this is a test. It is about courage. This is not something I can run from, this needs to be looked in the eye. He was only a metre or two away now, one *taiaha* blow distant. I could hear the hiss of his chanted breath. I found his eyes and looked in. There was nothing there but emptiness, silence, death. He did not once pause in his dance, nor cease twirling the *taiaha*, but he began to retreat. Stamping, chanting, twirling, he walked backwards to the riverside mound again.

Much later, just before dawn, I heard distantly, from up on the Carriage Road, the sound of horses. Four horses galloping and a mad old man in a rocking car whipping them to a frenzy as he drove them up to the trig station. They arrived and wheeled around and came to a panting halt, lather on their flanks. The old man stood upright in the car and stared wildly around. Islands were starting from the sea, white foam cascading down. The sky was a wound. He raised his hands above his head and cried out. His soul was sucked from his body like the pip from an overripe fruit.

When it got light I went over the hill to Bosanquet Bay, where the massacre of piratical Maori is said to have occurred. It was a wild ocean beach, with great logs tumbled above the tide line and weka scratching among the kelp. No skulls or long bones, though they must still be there somewhere. I dived into the warm clear water and swam out over a white sandy bottom. I'd had my vision, but what did it mean? The events of the night seemed as portentous and incoherent as a dream, and like a dream existed in a space which was neither wholly in the mind nor wholly outside it.

At the camping ground I started taking down the tent. Sue came over to say goodbye. She liked meeting me, she said. I liked meeting her too. It was a pure romance. When John Heaven appeared in the distance, she blushed and went away. I gave him seven dollars, he gave me a receipt. He stood, looking unhappily around. His was a mortgaged domain, at the very edge of the world. *Yeh, the place is for sale*, he said at last. *We're moving on.*

What kind of genealogy is it that begins with George Grey and arrives at a John Heaven or a Mr Nott? Who are these men with their mysterious obsessions, their inability to articulate the merest emotion, their great need? Whenever I think of that strange trip, I think of him, Nott, with his leer of complicity, his corrosive suspicion, his righteous anger. He only ever said that one sentence to me: *We follow the Lord here.* Otherwise, he chewed his beard and glared. There seemed no love in his religion, no hope, and only a vestigial, a resentful charity; and his faith was like rage. In the demonology of the kanuka grove was more wisdom than in all his false and malevolent piety.

Papa-tu-a-nuku is the name Maori give to Mother Earth. The man with the *taiaha* was Whiro, the personification of evil, darkness and death, bringer of disease, patron of thieves, whose symbol or *aria* is a lizard. James K. Baxter called him *the thin man who'll eat the stars*. Curiously, Whiro is not mentioned in Grey's pioneering *Polynesian Mythology and Traditional History of the Maori as told by their Priests and Chiefs* (1854), which is perhaps why he is still abroad on Kawau. So much is clear: but how did I, an irreligious pakeha with no particular knowledge of these gods, 'see' them? Did they come out of the right side of my brain or were they somehow existent in that place, waiting only for someone with the right degree of susceptibility to come along? Would I in fact have died if Whiro had come that one step closer? There is no answer to these questions, just as there is no way of knowing if the spirit of George Grey does really gallop his nightmare car up the Carriage Road to the summit of Kawau, there to give up his ghost to the sky.

Rutherford says that Grey was *a perfectibilist of the eighteenth century type handling nineteenth century facts and anticipating twentieth century conclusions*: a man of the enlightenment trapped in the nineteenth century, a Regency buck entrammelled in Victorian morality. As a young man he was conventionally romantic about landscape and full of anthropological zeal for the primitive. To his Aunt Julia Martin in August 1838 he wrote: *You can but little conceive the charms a savage life holds out to myself . . . there is a kind of wonderful freedom which is delightful.* This did not, however, prevent him from becoming one of the great civilisers of indigenous peoples when he gained political power over them. He was good at languages – he translated Schiller before he was twenty – and became adept in the speech and culture of Aborigine of southern and western Australia, Maori of New Zealand, and Zulu and Xhosa of South Africa. As an administrator, this sympathy almost always gave way to the demands of real politik, with devastating results for the indigenes of all three countries he governed. In South Africa he presided over the ferocious carnage of the Cattle Killing Delusion.

In his own mind he was more than a hero: *like all prophets I was without honour amongst my own* he reflects when, during his West Australian expeditions, on the only night he camps near his men, he realises from their talk that they hate him. A talent for self-dramatisation is revealed as, after his wounding, with only a demoralised lad for company, he waits for help to arrive. He expects to die and writes lugubriously of pioneers like himself: *A strange sun shines upon their lonely graves; but let us hope that when civilisation has spread so far, that their graves will be sacred spots, that the future settlers will sometimes shed a tear over the remains of the first explorer, and tell their children how much they are indebted to the enthusiasm, perseverance, and courage of him who lies buried here.* Perhaps he was too imaginative to make a good politician, too ready to dream universal solutions to common problems, and too impatient for the gradualist strategies needed to implement his vision in practice. A strange mixture of utopian and autocrat, he seems to have wanted to decree paradise into being; when that failed, he ended up in hell.

He knew Darwin, Carlyle, John Stuart Mill, with whom he was an early proponent of a uniform tax on the accruing value of land, which he attempted to pass into New Zealand law before Henry George popularised the Single Tax, later also espoused by Griffin and Mahony. Despite his own autocracy, he consistently advocated the principle of one person one vote, and like most Australians today, wanted Governors popularly elected. His favourite philosopher was the Stoic, Epictetus, who believed *we are all fragments torn from god*.

Epictetus also said: *Wherever a man is against his will, that to him is a prison*. On Kawau, Grey had a sentry box set up at Lady's Bay where he would stand, wearing a top hat several sizes too big, scanning the sea to the south for ships coming from Auckland. But when in Auckland he wanted to be on Kawau, just as he always wanted to be in England whenever he was not there. What if, despite all that has been said, he was never a philanderer but, like my father, faithful to one woman all his life? And the genteel Anglicanism he bequeathed his true religion? Because he lived with Maori in his house throughout his governorships and afterwards does not mean he was making love to the women. We can't know. Does it even matter? The lack of inwardness which makes it impossible to answer these questions is his most desperate legacy. If, as so many New Zealanders believe, he was the father of their country, then that deficit belongs to us all and is another reason why we cannot live without exploring the darkness within.

In Pyrmont, nothing much had changed. It was already night when I got off the bus and, lugging my bag down Harris Street, felt again the familiar apprehension at entering the lawless zone of the Point. On Cross Street a Volkswagen was standing with its motor running; the woman behind the wheel called out to me. She was waiting to buy a gun and thought I might be the one bringing it. *No*, I said, and walked on. Police never came down to the squats unless someone called, and no squatter was ever meant to call them: it was a point of honour that we sorted things out among ourselves, no matter how twisted the circumstances. One of the New Zealand kids, Egg, had his face cut with a razor in some bitter, trivial dispute over words said or not said – his attitude, in fact – but for his junkie slasher no legal consequence ensued.

At the Caledonian, I walked round the back and through the coach house to my room, smelling the usual smell of cat piss and tom spray. It was not exactly as I had left it, though nothing had been taken. On the desk was a poem from Lyndi, declaring her love for me. She found out where I kept my spare key and had been using both desk and bed: not to sleep in, to lie on. This was what George told me, her seal's eyes full of curiosity and dismay. She was cradling a kitten in her arms, the latest addition to the household; Mark had named it Rover. George said Dave had been beaten up again, and then fallen through a balcony rail onto the concrete a floor below; fortunately, he was so shickered he hadn't been hurt much more than he already was. Sober, Dave had the almost courtly manners of an old beat but, when drunk, an ungovernable tongue. Though he'd take anyone on, no matter how big or bad they were, I doubt he ever won a fight.

Darren had bought a ute, a battered brown Holden with no registration and a single headlight, which gave it a crazed look, like a one-eyed tomcat. He'd taken to parking in the street outside my window, which Lyndi considered a trespass against my rights and tried to prevent; Darren was predictably derisive. As for Ricky, one night he had brought back a girl from the Cross and moved her in upstairs. A skinny little hooker, George said, who, after a few days thought better of it and told Ricky she was leaving. He hit her across the head with a bit of four-by-two. The brothers had more or less successfully colonised the rest of the top floor, not including Dave's room, but everyone was too scared to say or do anything about it.

Tania was working behind the bar in the New York, the pub where Dave got belted, and she and Stefan were splitting up. George's brother, Peats, had arrived (Peats was their surname, a Maori family from Whangaroa in North Auckland), and Richard Gapes, son of David, one of the original Good Guys on the pirate station Radio Hauraki, which was moored out in the gulf south of Kawau when I used to listen to it as a teenager in the Waikato. David

Gapes managed Hello Sailor, once friends of mine, on their ill-fated attempt at America. I remembered him hectically on the phone in LA while the band lounged by the pool. Richard was stalwart and smart; he saved me from a beating, taking the blame (or credit) when I wrote at the bottom of a list of Ricky's demands, posted on the kitchen wall, that he (Ricky) was a dickhead.

What else? Jim, a friend of Johnny Bear and of Mark, had arrived from Darwin with an Indonesian woman called Dah; the celebrations when Dah discovered she was pregnant turned to lamentations when the pregnancy was found to be ectopic and Dah was rushed to hospital for an operation in which she lost her remaining ovary. As for Johnny Bear, he had attached mannequins of the *Moerae*, the Three Fates, to his pantomime piano, and was rehearsing his tale of lost luck under the sightless eyes of spinning Clotho, measuring Lachesis and Atropos who cuts the thread of life with her shears.

I settled back in, although 'settled' is not an appropriate word for that place of shadows and violence. The hard thing was exchanging the freedom to travel and spend I had in New Zealand for the harsh durance of life in the squats on the dole. I couldn't seem to get myself down to the phone box each evening to call in to see if there was cleaning work the next day. On the other hand, the temptation to huddle back into the warm domesticity of the flat in Darghan Street where Gemma still lived was something I tried to resist. Strangely, refusing the urge to call Gemma meant I didn't try to contact Brial either.

So it was a surprise when one night, out of the blue, they both showed up. We sat in the coach house on the small concreted space outside my room, had a cup of tea and chatted. About what I could not say. They knew each other, not well, from that brief period in Auckland a decade before, when Brial had taken photographic portraits of both Gemma and myself. Like all her photographs, these portraits were cool, elegant and detached, with an emotional quality arising purely from the image. Gemma's ignorance of the true situation seemed implausible, to say the least; but then, she did not think me capable of a deception as large as this. I felt for her; but at the same time could not wait for her to go. That night, as she did one other time during our affair, Brial got pregnant; and, just as she did the other time too, aborted the foetus before telling me about it.

This seems more distressing now than it did then, when I was cravenly but unmistakably relieved. I know she wanted another child; why did she not at least talk about it with me? Was it because she thought such a commitment had to be mutual or not at all? Was she declining to use a child, even the possibility of a child, as a pawn in the game? Did she know that she could have bound me to her in this way, and refuse, out of nobility, pride or some more scornful emotion, to do it? Gemma had also always wanted children, or so she said; but she was in fact as fanatical as anyone I've ever known about birth control and made absolutely sure there were no accidents. With Brial it was different, but, even now, I'm not sure what the difference truly was. The result, however, was clear: when she told me what had happened and what she had done, it was another veil added to those which already drifted between us, blurring every word, distorting every gesture.

Not so very long after this, Brial lost patience, rang Gemma and told her what had been going on. That resolved one point of the triangle: Gemma's distress at the scale and duration of the deception decided her once and for all that there was no hope for us. She stopped waiting for me to make up my mind if we were still together, and got on with her life, which soon came to include the child she had always wanted.

As for Brial and me, we tried one more time to find a way forward together, but it didn't work out. One morning I woke up, looked at her sleeping face beside me and realised I could not love her as she wanted and needed and deserved to be loved. I did not say that to her in so many words, but, being Brial, she knew instantly anyway. Why then had I dallied with her, she wanted to know? I didn't really have an answer, and still don't, unless one is contained in these pages. It would have done no good to say that our failed relationship was a casualty of my struggle to extricate myself from my marriage, that I could not make the kind of commitment she wanted until free of the trammels of the one I had so unthinkingly made ten years previously.

And so I went back to work. During the late summer months I finished the film treatment about George Grey and gave it to a director I knew to read. She had already lined up some producers and was confident they would be able to secure development finance for us. While waiting for her to get back to me, in that casual manner which is often the way to success, I began another.

Freddy Beckett, aka Blackspot, was the friend who had introduced me to Johnny Bear. He sometimes also worked for Barclay Wade, the former Olympic rowing medallist and demolition contractor who gave us the cleaning work, which was not cleaning as it is usually understood, but the clearing out in tall buildings of office suites either before or after they were made over in that process of ceaseless destruction and renewal going on in the corporate world. Blackspot, who told me that when a man has woman trouble he needs his mates around him, took to dropping around to the Caledonian at odd times. I helped him with an application he was preparing for a course in a film school; later, through a process I no longer recall, we began collaborating on an idea for a film he wanted to make. His training was in law, but he had never worked as a barrister or solicitor. Although admitted to the bar, he'd refused to purchase the required practising certificate because he no longer believed in the law as it was administered; most of his working life had been spent as a journeyman carpenter. Now he was without tools and his health was failing, he'd decided to try accruing intellectual capital from his chequered past.

The story was based on a job he'd had in Barbados in the West Indies. In Amsterdam, he and a group of drinking buddies had been recruited by a bent American psychotherapist to rebuild an old house on the island. It was going to be used as a Retreat for the psychotherapist's patients. The job turned into a farce, with Blackspot's best friend, Digby, going rum crazy and Blackspot running off with the girlfriend of another in the gang. Needless to say, the Retreat never got finished. We decided to set the film in Fiji because they have cane fields there too, and made the emotional core the story of two wild young men, best mates, sundered through love of the same woman. I think in Blackspot's mind it was also an elegy for Digby, who died young. I'm ashamed to say I wrote it in the most cynical fashion, never thinking it would be anything other than a favour for a friend, something I could easily afford to do in my present state of desultory idleness. Blackspot would come round, we'd talk and make notes, which I would then write up and give to him for his response.

He was there sitting cross-legged on the bed smoking a cigarette the day it started to end at the Caledonian. We heard heavy feet stomping down the stairs from the kitchen and then Darren appeared in the doorway, spitting. Lyndi had been onto him about the ute again: it was an intrusion on me; he should move it now and park it somewhere else. This was nonsense: I didn't care where he parked it. I'd told Lyndi this, but she took no notice, just as she took no notice when I asked her to stop using my room when I was out. Now I had to try to explain this to Darren. I thought I was getting somewhere when I saw Lyndi herself creeping around the door with half a brick in her hand, apparently intending to dent Darren's head with it. Darren didn't realise she was there, was too angry to look. Somehow I had to make her back off. I stared past Darren's shoulder, willing her away. She raised the brick in her hand; the air itself seemed to tremble with impending frenzy; then she lowered it again. I realised I'd been talking the whole time, and stopped. As she sidled away, in the silence I heard Blackspot's cigarette crackle as he drew on it. Then Darren drew back his arm, just as Ricky had done, and slammed his clenched fist so hard into the door it cracked one of the wooden panels. He went away; after a while Blackspot said helpfully he mustn't have wanted to hit me or otherwise he would have.

This was the Friday of Anzac weekend. That night Ricky and Darren's mentor, Stanley, the man who had saved them from the wardrobe, came up from Melbourne to see how they were getting on. He was an unkempt, overweight, genial, sixty-year-old man, who treated the brothers like sons. The three of them spent Saturday and most of Sunday up on the top floor, drinking beer, smoking, talking and playing Ricky's motivational tapes over and over again, until a strange muttering hum seemed to resonate out of there and into the rest of the hotel. On Sunday afternoon Stanley brought a slab of beer and we all stood around the ruined kitchen drinking before he left to go back to Melbourne. I think he'd realised there were divisions in the house and tried to heal them; unfortunately, as so often, the opposite occurred. Stanley's attempt at peace-making only exacerbated the sense of grievance Ricky and Darren felt against the rest of us, and once he'd gone they decided to settle things once and for all.

I was down in my room getting a smoke organised when I heard raised voices on the floor above. I came up into the kitchen to find the party soured beyond recall. Everyone had retreated to one side of the room, while from the other Darren, with Ricky as usual at his side, was haranguing them. He turned on me as I entered. *You!* he bellowed. *You!!* Ricky was just a thug, but Darren always seemed plausible, if devious; now he was right out of control. His eyes bulged, his body swelled as he came towards me. Spittle coagulated into a brownish foam at the corners of his mouth, something I had seen only once before, on my Third Form English teacher. What was he on about? It wasn't clear. Lyndi, me, all of us . . . were fucking arseholes. We should get the fuck out of there and leave them in peace. Peace! That was funny.

It was no use trying to reason with him. Anyone who so much as spoke risked actual violence to their person. It didn't matter if you were male or female, big or little. I remember George being marched backward across the room purely by the force of Darren's anger. She was not a timid person but she left then and didn't come back. One by one, we all followed her into the women's side of the house: eight adults huddled timorously behind locked doors while the brothers stormed and raged through the house and round the outside.

It was night now, and Johnny Bear arrived. He would not accept the situation and went out to try to talk Ricky and Darren down. Something happened, some blow was struck or insult passed and Johnny came back trembling with fury, stripped the clothes off his upper body and went out again to fight. He was only a small man, but he'd wrestled competitively in his youth and thought he could handle them. He returned a few minutes later with blood all over his face and joined us in the room while the brothers, further inflamed, hammered on the door and jeered and swore at us through the windows, uttering menaces and threats. Then we heard them stomp away and there was silence.

Their bluster had gone on for hours, it seemed, and its cessation left behind an eerie emptiness. We were all still whispering. Everyone wanted to get out, but no one dared open the door. Maybe they were waiting just outside. Who knew? We stayed there, wondering and waiting, for about twenty minutes and were just beginning to relax when, without warning, one of the windows facing the street exploded in a shower of glass and maniacal laughter. Then the next window went, then the next. They'd gone and got some pieces of four-by-two from a nearby building site and were systematically smashing the outside windows of the hotel. Big, solid, plate-glass windows, some of them 100 years old, burst to smithereens. This insult to the house was far more chilling than the threats to our persons, striking as it did at the only home most of us had. In a desperate, futile attempt to restore our security, we started heaving furniture over to the windows, crunching a heavy wardrobe across that floor of knives.

It might have been when the windows started to go that someone from the council flats across the way rang the police, or that might have happened earlier; anyway, they came. We were still locked in that one room, with the light turned off, when we heard a bull wagon pull up outside and the voice of a policeman: *What's going on here?* Darren transformed seamlessly from a raving maniac to the most reasonable of men. *It's just a domestic, mate*, he said. *It's all over now. It's under control.* The cops must have known something more was going on. They must have seen the broken glass. But this was a squat, and in those days *a domestic* was code for some private atrocity, usually within a marriage, they did not have to bother themselves with. Darren knew this, and so it was through the oddest kind of complicity, him and the law, that the cops, relieved, drove away and left us to them.

Why did one of us not cry out we were terrorised within? I don't know. Perhaps, like anyone in a domestic, we were intimidated into complicity with our tormentors. Perhaps it was that old squatters' interdiction against involving the law no matter what. Perhaps we thought it was better to let them go than have to deal afterwards with the consequences of involving them: something Ricky and Darren would neither forgive nor forget. And the visit from the cops did mark the beginning of the end of that night of terror. Ricky and Darren stayed outside for a while longer, chortling and gloating, but they never recovered the full force of their anger and, after a while, went back upstairs to smoke more dope and drink the rest of the beer, leaving us to pick up the pieces down below.

I was lucky, I guess. The only window facing onto the street from my room was barred on the outside and unbroken. Peace of mind was something else. I lay awake most of the night, listening to the mutter of voices from above: not the gods and certainly not the right side of my brain. The empty shaft of the dumb waiter began at the head of the stairs on the top floor and terminated just outside the corner of my room where the bed was. By a peculiar quirk of acoustics, which I had not noticed before, this night the shaft acted as a conduit for the voices of the brothers. I could not make out any actual words, only timbres and tones; my imagination supplied the missing sense and over the course of the night I became convinced that I was hearing the working out of a plan to murder me. This was probably as absurd as it sounds: if they wanted to kill me, why wait until morning?

The horror of the night was somehow accentuated by the fact that it was Anzac weekend: the day itself had been on Saturday, but the public holiday was the next day, Monday. Into the noxious anger and fearful pain of those voices I read the whole story of our fascination with death, our inability to house or banish the ghosts of war, our desperate flight from history into fallacious myth. I suppose in the end I did sleep, but only once I had resolved this atrocity into an image: I saw the Caledonian set on fire and burning, the incandescent pyre of every hope. As the bricks went from red to white hot and the venerable walls began to fall and tumble inwards, a great plume of smoke rose from the ruin in the black shape of a man, paused and hung there for a minute, then was blown away on the wind.

Next morning I got up early, locked my door and window, and went out for the day. By some warp of fate, I ran into an old friend in Glebe who had just received a large compensation pay-out for an injury to his thumb and was going to spend it on an overseas trip. Vic was leaving at the end of the week and vacating his flat the very next day: would I like to take it over? Would I! Coincidentally, I'd just had word that finance was available to turn *Ghosts of Empire* from a treatment into a script, so for once money was not a problem. I didn't even go round to see the flat, just to the real-estate agent to secure the lease. A huge relief: I'd escaped.

A few days after I moved out, leaving behind, as some kind of hippie spell, four concentric circles of coloured stones in the middle of the bare concrete floor of my room, my brother-in-law turned up in Sydney and asked me if I'd like to drive out to Dubbo with him on the weekend? Barry was making a documentary about a faker of postage stamps and wanted to shoot some film at Seven Seas Publishing, sellers and distributors of philatelic material. As a child I used to answer the advertisements Seven Seas placed in the backs of comics, receiving by return post envelopes containing small opaque cellophane packets of stamps, but I'd never known exactly where these stamps, which were from places all over the world, came from. Now I had the chance to go there. Odd, with such a name, that it was in such a landlocked place as Dubbo.

Barry picked me up on Friday afternoon in a rented blue Ford station wagon. We drove up to Glebe Point Road and stopped on the corner of Toxteth Road so I could call in my licence number to the rental company and share the driving. Walking along the footpath to the phone box, I saw a dance of coloured paper eddying in a small whirlwind. Banknotes! I quickly gathered them up: ones, twos, fives, tens, twenties, about $130 worth. Where had they come from? There was no one around. Perhaps some unlucky cabby's float or takings. I made my call and hurried back to the car to show Barry the windfall. It seemed like a good omen. We drove cheerfully out along the Great Western Highway and up into the Blue Mountains where, at a restaurant in Katoomba, we blew most of the cash on a swanky meal.

Afterwards we drove on through the mountains and down onto the enormous country west of the ranges, arrowing through the dark while Barry filled me in on his project. A guy he knew who sometimes used the name Bruce Henderson had, in the mid 1970s in Auckland, printed letterheads for the non-existent Consul General of the Sultanate of Ocussi Ambeno. 'Henderson' may have believed Ocussi Ambeno didn't exist. If so, he was wrong: it is a former Portuguese enclave in the Dutch East Indies on the northern coast of West Timor and constitutionally now a part of newly independent East Timor. 'Henderson' also printed extremely basic postage stamps purporting to be from Ocussi Ambeno. These were of poor quality, made individually with rubber stamps, and featured cats, fish, teddy bears and steam trains. Though not expected to be taken seriously, they were submitted anyway to an international philatelic journal, with a covering letterhead from the 'consulate', and appeared in the next issue as a curiosity, in the section devoted to Cinderellas. (Cinderellas are a diverse category of illegitimate stamps, including locals, fiscals, fakes, forgeries, phantoms, propaganda, telegraph or registration labels, strike posts or any other stamp issued by an authority to frank mail within a restricted area.)

Two months later, a major European-based engraver/publisher wrote to the 'consulate' in Auckland, expressing cordial greetings, sympathy for the position of struggling small nations, and inquiring about the diplomatic hierarchy: was the Consul in Auckland the senior man overseas? Did the consulate have any particular needs that could be addressed? Since the Consul was clearly a keen philatelist, he might be interested to learn that the publishing company printed stamps, very good ones, and specialised in international covers, large packages and long-term client relationships. Eventually, after some more correspondence, they offered to pay a fee for an exclusive contract, including the right to market commemorative sets to investors.

One day US$30,000 arrived for 'Henderson' in Auckland. He had more Ocussi Ambeno stamps made, beautifully designed and printed, featuring tropical fish and animals. Everything was done properly and quickly, and the stamps arrived in time for the Queen's silver jubilee, which was the theme they celebrated. But that was all. 'Henderson' and his friends partied most of the rest of the money away; when they sobered up and realised that, while the company probably wouldn't prosecute them, it might well take action privately to recover the cash, 'Henderson' spent the remainder purchasing a new identity and moving to Australia.

In Perth, he elaborated upon his micronation, nominating a Sultan, naming and ranking government ministers and departments and writing a short history. Although it is unclear if he had any strong political views, in Western Australia he contacted, or was contacted by, a group of exiled East Timorese and their Australian friends working to free the country from the Indonesians. The apparent existence of a government-in-exile in Australia soon attracted the notice of the Australian Security and Information Office (ASIO) and 'Henderson', badly scared, changed his name again and fled, making his way to Sydney and thence back to New Zealand. Barry, who was making the documentary without his co-operation or approval, said he was currently in hiding down on the West Coast of the South Island. There are some suggestions that he has continued to issue the lucrative Ocussi Ambeno stamps, along with other phantoms, ever since.

Strange tale! This was before the plethora of virtual states which have since appeared on the Internet: micronations like the Republic of Lomar, structured and organised as a nation-state, specifically a constitutional republic, but without a localised territorial imperium. A key focus of Lomar has been the provision of passports and other necessary documents to refugees, stateless persons and persecuted individuals. It is currently inactive, partly through lack of funds but partly also because, in another parlous confusion of reality and fiction, migration agents in Nigeria have been selling bona fide emigrants passage to Lomar.

Our mission in Dubbo was to film an interview with Seven Seas' owner and to view some of the stamps 'Henderson' produced with the money from the European – I believe they were Dutch – publishers, as well as any other phantoms they had. We drove on through the sparsening land, downhill all the way to Dubbo. At the top of a rise a few kilometres from the town, we stopped to stretch our legs and saw in the clear freezing air, under a whelming bowl of the stars, solid silver at the heart of the Milky Way, the pale orange glow of its lights on the horizon. It was late, after eleven, when we arrived and checked into a motel; next morning we drove through the flat wide town to the outskirts where, behind an acacia hedge down some nondescript street, the long, low offices of Seven Seas Publishing were.

It, too, was like something out of an old tale: dusty corridors opening into rooms full of dusty books, the brown smell of dry paper and gum and ink, a sense of antique, half-forgotten things. The owner, Bill Hornadge, founded the company in the early 1950s, along with the journal *Stamp News*, which is still printed in Dubbo. He was a writer too, and a self-publisher: his early books appeared under his own imprint, Review Publications. As well as works about stamps and stamp-collecting and a self-published manual on self-publishing, he had written volumes of local history, children's stories (*The Boy Who Talked to Bunyips*), a book about kangaroos (*If It Moves, Shoot It*), another about Australian attitudes to Asians (*The Yellow Peril*) and the hilarious *The Ugly Australian*, a compendium of unflattering observations like this one by H. G. Wells: *Australians want reality hushed up. They are fundamentally inspired by a fear of life*.

He was mild-mannered, cheerful and forthcoming as he showed us the Ocussi Ambeno stamps: highly coloured, splendidly designed large-format postage stamps. Bill was a Cinderella expert and had other phantoms: a stamp from Queen Maude Land showing walls of pink ice; a sheet from Sealand bearing pictures of navigators (Da Gama, Columbus, Raleigh, Drake, Cook, Magellan and Frobisher); issues from the Principality of Thomond, the Hutt River Province, Lundy, Capolan, Griffin, Sabine and others. Phantoms are neither fakes, which attempt to fool collectors, nor forgeries, which try to deceive postal authorities, but stamps issued by fictitious countries, illegal 'governments', would-be leaders, or organisations with genuine causes. They are extremely collectable; 'Henderson's' phantoms are now worth a lot of money.

As we drove away later that day down the backroads through Gulgong and Bylong and Kandos, heading for the Hydro Majestic in Medlow Bath, it felt as if the visit to Seven Seas had closed a circle, taking me all the way back to my childhood in a small mountain village, where the packets of stamps from faraway places arrived in the mail to be pasted onto the pages nominated for their respective countries in a red album. Looking at these stamps of imaginary places conjured into some kind of existence on little squares, oblongs or triangles of gummed and perforated coloured paper somehow banished the hurly-burly and turmoil of my nine months at the Caledonian from painful reality into a realm of fiction, just as the ideal community we attempted there was itself exiled in the capricious zone of internecine violence.

'Henderson' himself seemed a true image of the self as fake or forgery, as necessary a creation, perhaps, as the Edwin Holmes Arthur Rimbaud became in order to escape servitude as a mercenary in the Dutch Colonial Army in Java and make his way back, on the ship *The Wandering Chief*, to Europe. Some of the relief I gained from the trip to Dubbo was remission from the strenuous demand to make the self unitary, whether through imitation or through the no less exhausting process of definition via antagonism. It was too soon to say that I had found a third way, but there was at least a glimmer of hope in the possibility that I could learn to be by being other than I was; that the forging, of conscience or identity, need not take place in the smithy of a soul, it might just as well proceed via instructions delivered to a printer.

3

Others

I WAS SITTING AT MY DESK WHEN THE TELEPHONE RANG. IT WAS Blackspot. *Pack your swimmers*, he said. *We're off.* He meant that our film treatment, *Running to Paradise*, had been funded to first draft stage by the Australian Film Commission and that we were going to Fiji to scout for locations. This was not what the Film Commission thought we should be doing with their ten grand but I didn't find that out until after we bought our tickets. They wanted us to stay in Sydney and write the script. With hindsight, they were probably right; but the fact is neither Blackspot nor I considered for a moment not going.

The meeting with the AFC had been a revelation. Whereas previous encounters had been dour, tense and suspicious, this one was full of hearty laughter and a slightly forced bonhomie, as if we were all good friends already even though we had only just met. *This could be a real movie movie*, one of the assessors said. They obviously thought we were on to something, which was perplexing, because I didn't know what and I wasn't sure if Blackspot did either. But it was clear they wanted to give us the money, so I decided it must have been for other reasons: on 10 May, just as we were about to submit the treatment to the Commission, Lieutenant-Colonel Sitiveni Rabuka had led ten soldiers into the Parliament in Suva and staged a coup d'état against the recently elected Labour Government of Timoci Bavadra.

I didn't stop to consider that feature films are almost always better made after the events they deal with have happened, and hardly ever work when they concern themselves with things that have not finished happening. Besides, they take so long to complete: even if we'd encountered no problems, it wasn't likely that our film would be made in less than a year, and who knew what would have happened in Fiji in a year's time? Nobody seemed to know what was going on now. Further, the film wasn't a political thriller, didn't have a background in politics of any kind except the politics of the personal. We'd only set it in Fiji because it was a sugar-cane island nearer to home than Barbados. And anyway, as the wallies at the Film Commission pointed out, even if we did want to set it in Fiji that was no reason it could not be shot in Queensland.

On the other hand, there was a tenuous, half-hidden rhyme to my reasoning. Sam and Tony, the two mates in the story, are wild boys coming up against the realisation that wildness will not get them through their thirties the way it has through their teens and twenties. Sam is already looking for the compromise which will allow him to settle down to some kind of future, while Tony is determined to hang onto the ethic of his youth: *hope I die before I get old.* He thinks Sam is selling out, which Sam finds juvenile and offensive. This argument constructs a nice dilemma for the female lead, Anne. What is there to choose between the charismatic hell-raiser Tony and a steady-rolling man like Sam? At that time I believed that every film script, however obliquely, reflects its author(s) in its characters. Whether Blackspot was Tony and I was Sam, or vice versa, or a bit of both, we both thought it would be mad to sit in a room in Sydney and write a script when we could be living what might become one in post-coup Fiji.

I had another secret, or perhaps secretive, agenda: for years I had been obsessed by the Pacific, especially the Polynesian past as it was glimpsed – by navigators, beachcombers, traders and missionaries, more or less in that order – during the contact period. I felt some deep need to reconstitute, at least in my mind, the culture as it had existed at that time, or rather, before contact. I thought the Polynesian understanding of how to live more profound than ours, and I wanted to understand things in the way they had before their world was irretrievably changed. Never having visited the Pacific before, I thought I might find echoes of this lost primitive still abroad in Fiji, and learn something there of the secrets of sex and death. This atavistic desire was partly inherited and partly came from growing up amid the survivals and the wreckage of the process of change: at a certain point, it seems, we post-colonials want to become the thing destroyed in the name of our future. But it also came from my family: my maternal grandparents, on holiday in 1946, were seized by a desire to live in Suva and even bought a cottage there before abruptly changing their minds; and my father was beguiled in Tonga during the war and for the rest of his life was both distracted and sustained by a vision of the life he might have led if he had accepted the offer made to him there, and stayed.

We taxied to the airport on a dark and murky Sunday morning. The streets were grey under a warm heavy rain as we surfed past the misshapen, tumbledown terrace houses, the warehouses and the industrial plants in the ugly suburbs of South Sydney. Blackspot and I hardly spoke as we emplaned without incident, took off in the rain and climbed laboriously through the clouds into the blue empyrean above. The flight, too, was almost silent – we were both hungover after celebrating our impending departure with a bottle of Mescal and a few friends the night before – and uneventful, until after hours of empty ocean I saw out the window a chain of black islands in a turquoise sea.

These were the Yasawas, the westernmost archipelago in the Fiji group, a line of volcanic remnants stretching about 80 kilometres north-north-east off the coast of Viti Levu. Here William Bligh, sailing intrepidly for Timor after the mutiny in the *Bounty*'s seven-metre launch, was pursued by two Fijian *drua* or war canoes, the fastest vessels in the central Pacific. It must have taken a lot of rowing to get away. Luckily for Bligh, there was a following wind, the only one in which a *drua* can't go at top speed. Here too three of the four films based on Henry de Vere Stackpole's 1908 novel *The Blue Lagoon* were shot: the almost completely obscure 1923 original was made in Australia, but the 1949 British version starring Jean Simmons, the

Hollywood remake of 1980 with Brooke Shields and the 1990 sequel, *Return to the Blue Lagoon*, were all shot on Nanuya Levu, aka Turtle Island. Apart from the obligation to understand the country we had the temerity to write about in our treatment, another justification for the trip was our pressing need to find a coconut palm-fringed white-sand beach just like those on Turtle Island. It was to be a major location for the film. This spurious quest, with its absurdist subtext, became a constant theme of our travels.

Nadi Airport was a miniature terminal full of Indians waiting to leave. Dark-eyed women and girls in candy-coloured saris sat on plastic seats in front of light-dazzled windows. Outside, palm trees drooped amidst neat formal gardens, and beyond that were roadblocks where soldiers stood with sub-machine guns held casually in their crooked arms. The atmosphere was a strange mixture of lassitude and tension. It was like being at an airport in a small New Zealand city which had been taken over by the police – another outpost of collapsed empire trying to make its way in the larger world. Blackspot had disappeared. I saw him through the bright window talking to a handsome young Indian man. He came back and said the cabbie would drive us to Suva for F$55.

The western end of Viti Levu was dusty and brown. We rattled down dirt roads running through patchwork fields of sugar cane where vivid birds flitted in the silvery green leaves and cane flowers dangled in feathery tassels. The hills, too, looked like New Zealand hills, a profusion of fern growing amongst dark trees on volcanic slopes. Elsewhere, coconut palms with yellow and green fruit bent over tiny white mosques, and the intense orange flowers of parrot trees flared against glossy leaves. There were goats, chickens, pigs. And people everywhere: girls and boys, mostly, waving from the roadside as we passed. They wore saris or lava-lava and moved with a leisurely ambling carriage.

Fijian houses followed the design of traditional *bure*, even though they were mostly made from non-traditional material: shacks of weatherboard, corrugated iron, concrete or coral block, many of them unfinished. The cabbie said this was because the owners were away earning money to buy materials for the next stage. Indian houses were more conventionally European in design, and painted bright blue or pink or green. There were many cemeteries – by the roadside, in groves of palms back from the beach, or in gullies running up into the hills – the concrete graves decorated with plastic streamers, plastic flowers. Roadside stalls offered a few pieces of fruit. Or coral blocks. Next to the Adam and Eve Supermarket and just down the road from the St Joan of Arc Chapel, a petrol station was selling ZOOM Gasoline.

Red dirt began to show through a lusher green as we approached the eastern end of the island. We passed the Suva gaol, a grim building of grey, dirty stone, a concrete made from burnt coral. There was a uniformed man just coming out and closing the gate, a glittery look in his eye. I did not know then that an astonishingly high proportion of young Fijian men spend time in jail, apparently because marital law is based on the Wesleyan missionary belief that adultery was both an imprisonable offence and the only the grounds for divorce.

In the city, narrow dingy painted streets, blue and green and brown, led up past the La Perouse Bar in the Star of India Hotel. As we entered the predominantly Fijian northern suburbs of Suva, the cabbie became excitable to the point of hysteria. He said every Indian feared being murdered in his or her bed. Fijians were savages, cannibals. There was no knowing what they might try next. The only thing to do was leave, but where for? And with what? He had intimated several times that $55 was too little for this dangerous journey and that $80 would have been fairer. Now he asked straight out, but we refused. When we got to where we were going – Tanoa House in north Suva, near Samabula, chosen at random out of the *Lonely Planet* guide – he became afraid, leaning closer and saying: *This is a bad place!* He wouldn't go up the drive. When we gave him his money and got out, he slammed the car into reverse and screamed off down the hill backwards. It was only later that we learned the manageress of Tanoa House was a partisan of the ultra-nationalist Taukei Movement.

We had flown forwards in time, so it was now late afternoon. A brown butterfly with red lights in its wings flitted under the dark trees of a glade-like garden as we walked up the path to the door, there to be greeted by a shy, smiling Tongan-looking woman called Mrs Weeks. The long, dim, barely furnished sitting room had a wooden floor and was lined with *tapa* cloth. There was a tiny bar at one end where we sat on high stools and drank Fiji Bitter, then ate a meal of sweet potato, fish and greens cooked in coconut milk, while Mrs Weeks told us that a giant had woken from a 200-year sleep to put things to rights. There didn't seem to be much else to say. A lizard walked up a wall. A young Indian couple entered like intruders and went straight to their room.

After dinner I settled down to read, while Blackspot went looking for another drink. I had with me two books in which I hoped to find intimations of Fiji as it had been before the *kaiwalangi* – us – came. That they were both written by missionaries did not seem to me then a great obstacle. I would ignore the ideology and concentrate upon reconstructing what must have been. One was *The Diaries and Correspondence of David Cargill 1832–1843*; the other *Fiji and the Fijians: The Islands and their Inhabitants Vol. I* (1858) by Thomas Williams. I began with Cargill, because he was earlier.

A Scots convert from Presbyterianism, David Cargill, along with his colleague and enemy William Cross, was the first Wesleyan in Fiji. He was stationed at Lakeba in the Lau Islands from 1835 to 1839, and spent the following year, 1840, at Rewa on the south-east coast of Viti Levu. This after just eighteen months in Tonga, where he had witnessed ecstatic mass conversions: *We found the Chapel even at that early hour crowded with people; most of whom had been engaged in prayer the greater part of the night. Young and old – male and female – the chiefs and the lowest of the people – the robust and the infirm – all were under the influence of the Holy Spirit . . . there were few dry eyes . . . many fell prostrate on the mats of the Chapel and lay as if dead for a length of time. The first exclamation of most of these after their recovery – was 'I love Jesus.' Some vehemently struggled as if legions of devils were being cast out of them. Others incessantly cried out for mercy on their bended knees . . .*

Despite their straight-laced reputation these days, the early Wesleyans were more charismatic than either of their rival denominations – Roman Catholic and Anglican – in the missionary period in Tonga and Fiji. They were also, if you discount the failed Tongan mission of the Anglican London Missionary Society at the turn of the nineteenth century, primary. The Wesleyans held 'love feasts' in which the power of the Holy Ghost was importuned to descend upon them, and sometimes did; like John Wesley himself, they were anti-institutional and peripatetic and preferred to preach in the open air; and the early Tongan conversions they did achieve were often the result of mass hysteria induced by their proselytising fervour. This was not the case, however, in Fiji, where conversion tended to be a result of astute politicking or outright conquest; and Cargill's extraordinary year at Rewa left him a broken man and contributed to his early death.

Curiously, there was a big gathering of Pentecostals in Suva for the long weekend, and most of them seemed to be at the Assembly of God next door. Tiring of Cargill's earnest importunities to his clearly distracted Lord, which is what most of his diary consists of, I lay back listening, through the breezy falling rain, to the hymn-singing, the hand-clapping and a mad preacher roaring about the evils of prostitution. In the aftermath, the night was cut across with vivid high yelping laughter, spontaneous song, piercing cries, as if all those exorcised devils had been set free to roam the streets once more.

I was asleep by the time Blackspot returned, but his stumbling through the darkened room to his bed woke me up. Always a happy drunk, he was muttering to himself, or perhaps to me, about shipwreck, buried treasure and a map. I roused myself:

What are you talking about? I asked.

Gold, matey, gold, he slurred in a passable imitation of some piratical old sailor. Then, switching register: *There's gold in them thar hills.*

Where? I asked, with perhaps more hostility than I felt.

By now he had succeeded in getting onto, if not exactly into, his bed. I heard the wirewove creak. *Tell you tomorrow,* he said. And was instantly asleep.

Next morning after breakfast, Mrs Weeks offered us a guided tour of the city, then shouted us the bus trip into town. We waited outside a video shop displaying posters for Geoff Murphy's film *Utu*, featuring the grimacing tattooed face of Zac Wallace as Te Wheke, a character loosely based on the nineteenth-century Maori prophet and insurgent Te Kooti Rikirangi. Mrs Weeks admired the image then remarked that although there was no television in Fiji at that time, Australia's Channel 9 would begin broadcasting in just a few months. In the meantime, everyone watched videos.

Downtown Suva resembled, as an Englishman later said to me, Auckland without the pakehas. Notwithstanding, one historian has reckoned that if, in pre-1970 colonial Fiji, the city had disappeared from the face of the earth, the only thing lost to most Fijians would have been the record of their debts. Founded in 1870 by a boatload of Australian settlers hoping to make their fortune from cotton and, later, sugar, its existence is a consequence of the Melbourne-based Polynesian Company's decision to buy out the so-called American debt in exchange for land, trading and banking rights.

The debt had its origin in the accidental burning of the house and store of the American commercial agent in the former capital, Levuka, when a cannon misfired during Fourth of July celebrations in 1849, and the subsequent 'liberating' from the doomed premises of trade goods, which the local Fijians responsible declined to return to their owner, John Brown Williams. By the time Williams died of dysentery in 1860, the 200-odd English pounds the goods were worth had grown, partly by the addition of penalties for other American grievances, partly by mere chicanery, to the vast sum of US$43,000. When Cakobau, the self-proclaimed Tui Viti, or King, was forced, on board an American warship, to sign a promissory note agreeing to pay up within two years, the settling of the debt became a factor not just in the founding of Suva but in the eventual cession of the kingdom to the British. The example of the American debt was used by Leo Tolstoy in his 1886 book, *What Then Must We Do?*, as a classic model of debt enslavement, with implications still with us now.

Mrs Weeks wanted us to see the statue of Cakobau outside the Government Buildings in which is the Parliament where the epochal events of 10 May took place. A slight rain drifted from the sea as we crossed the road outside the forbidding pile. Built in the 1930s of the same grim grey burnt-coral concrete as the jail, the Government Buildings were vast, monolithic, intimidating, and I couldn't help feeling grateful that security considerations made it impossible for us to approach any closer than the lawn out the front. We wouldn't even have got this far without our guide, who appeared to know all the soldiers personally, waving to the ubiquitous Toyota utes patrolling the streets, each with three armed soldiers sitting uncomfortably in the tray, sub-machine guns raised. To those at the gates of Parliament she smiled and spoke in Fijian; they lowered their guns and waved us through.

There were actually two statues, one of Ratu Sir Lala Sukuna, *the architect of modern Fiji*, the other of the aforementioned Cakobau: a massive, imperious head with a magnificent moustache. In the fountain below it I saw a dull gleam of metal and souvenired, surreptitiously, the slug of a .22 bullet. Being in the company of a partisan of the Taukei Movement made me feel both furtive and under false pretences: I did not see myself as the automatic ally of the coup Mrs Weeks assumed that, as *kaiwalangi*, we must be, but was too polite to say so. As for Blackspot, he seemed to be having trouble focusing this early in the day; but when a scab-faced, red-eyed, tangle-haired denizen of the streets loomed up before us clutching something long and thin wrapped in newspaper and tried to give it to him, he had the wit to refuse. Mrs Weeks dragged us away, explaining that these sword-sellers, who carry badly made wooden copies of ancient Fijian artefacts, consider a purchase made once you lay hands on the package, and can get violent if you don't pay up.

She left us finally, reluctantly, at the bus station, where we waited for hours because our bus couldn't go until a boat arrived from another island where celebrations following the ordination of a Catholic priest had just concluded. At last it did and, accompanied by a celebratory group of Catholics, we got on. Still the bus didn't leave. After about ten minutes we all had to get off again. The tyre on the front left wheel was flat. This was too much for a young, aggressive, moustached Fijian in a white singlet who had been strutting around the bus station in an increasingly alarming manner as the delay lengthened. He attacked the Indian bus driver with his fists, while everyone else, incuriously, watched. The driver ran away and got the police. Four of them came in a jeep, but they couldn't seem to raise the enthusiasm to do anything much at all. While they were interviewing the singletted man, another bus arrived, with a different driver, and we all got on. Blackspot and I were the only *kaiwalangi* aboard, and the new driver the only Indian. Everyone else was *taukei*, people of the land, women in bright patterned granny frocks, and men in slacks or lava-lava and shirts.

The road wound uphill past mean little shacks among glorious trees – palm, breadfruit, paw paw, frangipani. We rattled along in great style, crossing the wide, brown River Rewa, at the mouth of which Cargill was stationed. It was then, and perhaps still is, infested by a vicious man-eating sand shark. In a little town on the other side I bought from an Indian boy a paper bag of curried peas, and ate them as we drove down a red dirt cutting through thick bush. Suddenly, at a bend in the road, instead of turning the bus ploughed straight on ahead and crashed spectacularly into the trees beyond.

All the rivets holding the bench seats to the metal floor ripped out so that the seats concertinaed hectically forward to the front of the bus, with the passengers squeezed between. There were shrieks, then silence. One woman was thrown clear out through one of the canvas flaps the bus had instead of windows, and dislocated her shoulder. Another old woman lay unconscious and moaning in the aisle for about ten minutes, then made a miraculous recovery. The man who had carefully stacked thirteen dozen eggs at the front of the bus lost every one. The mess of yolk and white dripped steadily out the front door into wet red mud. I had grazes down my spine, a ripped jacket, bruised knees, sustained when Blackspot, sitting behind me, cannoned forward into the back of my seat and I hit the one in front. He was lucky to have no one sitting behind him.

There was no panic, just a brief flare of anger at the Indian driver. He, too, ran away down the red dirt road, never to be seen again. We picked ourselves up, found our luggage, got out. The bus was nose down in a ditch, having lost a wheel when the left front axle sheared off. This was the same wheel which had caused problems in Suva, leading us to wonder if it was in fact the same bus – perhaps they had just driven round the block and come back with another driver? After about twenty minutes, two more empty buses came around the corner and we all, trustingly, got on.

We were on our way to the old imperial capital of Levuka, on the island of Ovalau off the east coast of Viti Levu. It was the middle of a sunny afternoon when we finally arrived at Natovi Landing, a concrete ramp among glittering trees on a bare shore without so much as a terminal, a kiosk or shelter of any kind. There were, however, groups of people off other buses waiting. The ferry, also called the *Ovalau*, was a small, battered, roll on/roll off job. It turned laboriously 180 degrees offshore and came in, lurching stern-first up to the concrete ramp; the freight door at the rear came down with a clang to form a bridge, and the disembarking passengers poured forth like the lost airmen from the spaceship at the start of *Close Encounters of the Third Kind*. They were, like our company, a mass of villagers carrying with them provisions and supplies.

The boat smelt of diesel and copra. Everything was sticky with salt spray. Rust bloomed along the steel plates. A video of a movie in which heroic Westerners battle a putrid, incredibly infectious plague virus blared out from screens and speakers upon every available deck, while palm-fringed islets drifted past, white water breaking over their pewter-coloured coral reefs. I found a quiet spot outside and half dozed on a bench in the sun, talking politics with Blackspot. After a couple of days in each other's company, we'd realised we didn't really know each other that well. Apart from actually writing the treatment, most of the time we'd had together we'd spent socialising and thus either drinking or drunk. I knew about his Irishness, his dyslexia, his background in the law and his fondness for alcohol, but not that he was the Catholic son of a career army officer, with whom he had violent political arguments. His relationship with his mother was, by contrast, apathetic. He rarely saw his only sibling, a twin sister who had married into the Hong Kong magistrature. Blackspot had been diagnosed in his late teens with Goodpasture's syndrome, a disease of the lungs and kidneys caused by a defect in the immune system which persuades antibodies to attack healthy tissue, and given only months to live. His persona – reckless, nonchalant, anarchist, iconoclast – had its origin in this diagnosis, for, instead of taking the drugs and bed-rest the doctors recommended, he walked out of hospital determined to spend what remained of his life in the best way he could. Twenty-odd years later, his health wasn't good, but he wasn't dead either.

Although neither of us was sympathetic to the coup, I was emotionally inclined to support one of the aims of the Taukei Movement: their nationalistic quest to restore the old ways. That the ideology of the primitive was clearly being used, along with the fomenting of racial hatred and probably with the connivance of various spooks, to restore a corrupt oligarchy, didn't deter me. Blackspot thought my romanticism kept me from seeing what was actually before us, while I found his insistent disenchantment both specious and crass. Though I didn't know it then, in this divergence of attitudes lay the seeds of disaster for our film. The very fact that we were in Fiji for me meant that the script would have to take account of the real situation, assuming we could find out what it was; but for Blackspot we were only doing what we'd told the Commission: scouting locations for a movie which wasn't about Fiji, only set there. He was too circumspect to say what he really thought about my idealistic view of the Pacific – that it was crap – because he didn't want to upset me or the project. It might have been better if he had.

As the ferry entered the reef and began to circle the island, I changed the subject and asked him what he'd been on about the night before. *Just because your nickname's Blackspot doesn't mean we're on our way to Treasure Island,* I said.

He looked pityingly at me and shook his head. *Just pisstalk, mate,* he said. *Forget about it.*

We were nearing the town now, passing a white-domed chapel on a headland, red roofs among the coconut palms. Levuka is on the eastern, further shore, looking out over the Koro Sea to the Lau Islands and Tonga. It was a glimmer of lights as we came up to it, a miniature metropolis of only 1,400 souls. A green neon cross shone out from the grey stone twin-towered Catholic church. The rattling easterly wind smelled of fish.

We had already decided to stay at the Royal, an old colonial hotel famous since the days of Bully Hayes and one of the last survivors of the forty or fifty pubs which used to crowd the narrow strip of land between 200-metre-high cliffs and the sea. There were sea shells, shark's jaws, a huge turtle carapace, spears, guns, *kava* bowls, pictures of boats and *tapa* cloths festooned around the walls. It was a family business; our host's name was Eddie, and he was *kai loma*, that is, a descendant of a nineteenth-century European man who had taken a Fijian wife. *Kai loma*, of whom there are some 12,000 in the islands, have hair which is blond but frizzy; their features are Fijian but their skin pinky-grey like ours. Albinism is common. Eddie said business wasn't so good any more, and that he was thinking of moving to Pukekohe, where he had relations.

After checking in, we went to the bar, which was full of loud, drunken Americans, and fell into desultory conversation with two bored girls from New York. Stella and Bobbie had met Rabuka at a garden party in Suva on the weekend. They thought the coup was just what Fiji needed. *The people here are not ready for democracy*, said Stella. After dinner, we played snooker on a hundred-year-old table with a couple of Aussie blokes who worked for Crawfords TV in Melbourne. Before going to bed I went outside to check the weather. The easterly gale was rattling the window glass, bending the palms, sending ragged black clouds hissing past the glittering stars. *If it blows two days*, Ron the barman said, *it'll blow for eight*. This was the third day.

David Cargill, on a visit he made to Levuka in May 1839, saw at the local temple *a bowl of singular shape and appearance, and upon inquiry found it to be the bowl from which the priest was in the habit of drinking anggona* (yaqona, or kava) *during his fits of inspiration, and that it was sacrilege for any person but the priest alone to drink out of this sacred instrument. The appearance and use of this utensil excited in me a desire to become its proprietor* . . . Cargill importunes the chief, the Tui Levuka, to let him have it; the priest is summoned and at length agrees to give up his bowl in expectation of a gift or offering in return. Instead, Cargill says, *we took this opportunity of warning them of the danger to which they were exposed while worshipping false gods.* A few days later, the missionary party is prevented from leaving when a gale blows up. The Tui Levuka says the priest has told him that their lack of a gift or offering has angered the gods, hence the contrary wind. But Cargill and his companions *suppose this to be another artifice to procure property from us,* and again refuse. At this the chief looks *serious and surprised,* but Cargill asks only if there isn't another bowl somewhere?

Cargill's unconsciousness is of a piece with his relentless, almost hysterical need to exhort his god for grace, fortitude, power and love to descend upon him and his labours, and his unwillingness to admit to any personal failing apart from the smug, standard testimony: *I have been an unprofitable servant.* When his wife, Margaret, is dying at Rewa of dysentery in the aftermath of the birth of their sixth child, Cargill is uplifted, even transported, when he is able to persuade himself that this is what with her last breath she says. It is proof that she has died *a happy death.* Yet his own perception of unworthiness in the sight of god does not preclude the gross lack of elementary manners in the taking of the *yaqona* bowl, especially considering he is a guest in a culture where exchange is a part of every communication.

Only once in the *Diaries,* in the very early days on Vavau, does Cargill admit to what must have been a constant and increasingly difficult problem for him, his self-loathing: *During the last week my mind has been given to wandering and dissipation,* he writes. Nor does he own up to habitual drunkenness – which his fellow missionaries do not mention either, or at least not until after his death. What one of these meant when he wrote, *He was a dreadful man,* we can only speculate. Hypocrisy, in Cargill and his colleagues, is of the essence, making it impossible for them to recognise it in themselves. During each of his wife's pregnancies (there are six over a period of seven years), Cargill writes only that she is ill, without once specifying the cause. The babies, when they arrive, seem to have been conjured out of thin air. His attitude to sexual matters among the Fijians and

Tongans is as obtuse: although he writes at great length and in detail about violence, illness and death in the culture, sexual mores are literally unmentionable.

Not so cannibalism, which has an enduring fascination for those who do not practise it. On Halloween 1839, Cargill wrote: *This morning . . . 20 dead bodies of men, women, and children were brought to Rewa as a present to Tui Dreketi from Tanoa. They were distributed among the people to be cooked and eaten. They were dragged about the water and on the beach. The children amused themselves by sporting with and mutilating the body of a little girl. A crowd of men and women maltreated the body of a grey-headed man and that of a young woman. Human entrails were floating down the river.* Early next morning, Cargill finds the old man's head, cooked and partly eaten, with maggots feeding on the remainder, in his garden. What his wife and four young daughters made of this horror is not recorded.

Although there is no doubt that these customs were of some antiquity among the Fijians, it is also true that the arrival of firearms had caused them to run out of control. Formerly, as in the Marquesas, warfare was ritualised and relatively orderly, most battles being concluded upon the death or capture of a known warrior; with the arrival of muskets, all hell broke loose, and slaughters and feasts of hundreds were reported, as they were from New Zealand at this time. The early missionaries probably didn't understand they were witnessing a society in the flux of accelerated change, and even if they had it might not have made any difference to them: they were deliberate agents of change themselves.

Cargill could be stubborn as well as evasive: during his four years at Lakeba, when the bulk of his learning of and translations into the Fijian language occurred, he never allowed the existence of the perhaps fifteen distinct dialects across the archipelago. He insisted instead that the one he was using – that spoken in the Lau Islands – would make a perfectly adequate *lingua franca* for the whole country. At Rewa, when it must have been as obvious to him as it was to his fellows that he was wrong, he still would not concede the point, probably because the admission would invalidate most of his work up to that time and make further progress along the same lines impossible. In fact, it was the dialect spoken on the south-east coast of Viti Levu, where the political power of both Rewa and Bau was concentrated, which prevailed.

Perhaps the accumulation of unbearable facts about himself, which he could neither admit nor any longer deny, led to Cargill's suicide. After the death of his first wife, he returned to England with their four surviving children, remarried and then, despite his request to go back to Fiji, was sent once more to Tonga. Here, in the grip of depression in the aftermath of an attack of dengue fever, faced with general backsliding, resentment and apostasy among the previously ecstatic converts of the Tongan Pentecost, and mired in a loveless marriage (Wesleyan missionaries were not allowed in the field without a wife), he lost his way. Remarkably, the document he was writing at the time of his death has survived. It is a letter to the church fathers in London detailing his progress in the few months since his return to Tonga. Rambling, incoherent, dejected and crude, especially in its contempt for the Tongan people, it comes to the bizarre conclusion that it is their enthusiasm for the study of geography that is the root of their rejection of the gospel.

During the drafting of this letter, Cargill's second wife, Augusta, castigated him, perhaps not for the first time, upon his drinking, whereupon he went in a rage to the medical supplies, poured, and drank in front of her a fatal dose of laudanum. Despite her attempts, and those of his colleague, Thomas Jaggar, to get him to take an emetic, he refused anything but brandy; nor would he agree to testify that the fatal draught was taken by accident; and died unrepentant later that night. The church for 150 years successfully managed to cover up or explain away this death, but, in retrospect, it seems the truest act in a life of strenuous falsity.

It wasn't exactly that Cargill reminded me of myself, but I couldn't escape the resemblances. Whereas the Calvinists rejected Catholic indulgences and the institutionalisation of sin in favour of the doctrine of predestination, the Wesleyans denied both confession and election as a means to grace, thereby condemning themselves to an exhaustive process of day-to-day negotiation with a personal god, relieved only by the periodic exaltations of the Pentecost. In this, they were ancestral to all the many modern revivalist churches. If you cannot sin and later be redeemed, and if you are not already one of the saved or the damned, your spiritual state becomes a matter of personal responsibility: agonies of choice, confusion between seeing and being seen, a tendency to try to seem whatever it is you want to be are among the results.

Cargill's inner voice reminded me of my own: although I didn't have to pretend that a conversation I was having with myself was actually a conversation with god, this agonising, soul-searching, essentially unconscious man's attempts to find some form of certainty where none was possible were so like my own I was alternately fascinated and repulsed. The other major virtue of his book is that it frames, in a pure form, one of the conundrums of Pacific history: how did this crazed religion, which teaches, among other things, that the Fijian people came from Nubia via Lake Tanganyika, turn out to be compatible with the largely surviving tribal law of the *taukei*?

At breakfast next morning we were joined by one of the carousers from the night before. John Porter was a big, genial, enthusiastic American from Hawaii, the Director of Project Development for Honolulu-based architects Pacific Area Design Consultants. He gave us his card. His two friends, Diane and John, were Californians he was showing around the Pacific. To avoid confusing the Johns, he suggested we call him Porter, which anyway suited him. His friends were on holiday, but he was investigating the possibility of building a resort on Wakaya Island offshore from Levuka in the Koro Sea. (There is now an exclusive resort on Wakaya, where the Hollywood elite go to audition new lovers, but whether it was designed by PADA is unclear.) Porter questioned us closely about our reasons for being in Fiji, and seemed sceptical when we said we were scouting locations for a film. We weren't sure if we believed his story either – we thought he might be one of the CIA men rumoured abroad in the islands – but that was okay: mutual suspicion gave us a basis for friendliness.

We spent the morning photographing Levuka and environs. A bit bored, on impulse, when the truck which was the local people-mover passed, Blackspot flagged it down. We had seen it coming and going several times a day, ferrying workers to and from the Japanese-owned fish packing factory, and wondered where it went. There were two wooden benches fixed to the insides of the tray of the truck, upon which everyone sat jammed together facing inwards under a blue canvas canopy which made our skins look milky and diseased. Blackspot and I were again the only *kaiwalangi*, and the driver, Lala, the only Indian. The road hugged the coast, leading around the island. It was bumpy and unsealed and probably impassable in the wet. After about forty-five minutes, and numerous stops for people to get off and on, we pulled up on a green lawn outside the village of Ruku Ruku and got down. There, as if expecting us, was Isikeli.

He was a tall, rangy guy with a bullet head and a perpetually worried look. Whatever we wanted, he would make sure we got: swim, shower, toilet . . . *yaqona*. We were dying to try some, and none of those who had previously promised it had yet delivered. In fact, Ruku Ruku seemed to subsist on the growing, drying, packaging and selling of the drug. There were the scrubby plants themselves in plantations on the hills behind, masses of the greyish-brown, twisted root drying on the corrugated-iron roofs of lean-tos, and, under a breadfruit tree at the centre of the village, the *yaqona* pounder itself. We watched as Isikeli, his friend Ben and others took turns pulverising the dried roots to a powder, using an eight-foot-long, six-inch-diameter iron shaft and an old World War II shell case. The powder was wrapped in cloth and passed through water in a preserving pan, making a thin brown liquid which, sitting in a circle on mats outside Isikeli's house, we drank from halves of coconut shells.

Tall, spindly paperback trees, used to make *tapa* cloth, bent over the lean-to kitchen. The beach was just beyond a hibiscus hedge. When the grog – *yaqona* – was offered, you clapped once, preferably with a deep, hollow sound, before accepting the shell; the whole circle clapped three times as you drank; you handed back the drained shell and clapped three times more. One of the tests seemed to be how long you could endure a bladder full to bursting. The effect was otherwise subtle, timeless: a numb tongue and gums, heavy legs, a relaxed, drifty, peaceful feeling. Palms exploded silently along a distant ridge. Roosters crowed, waves plashed on the shore, a small wind rustled in the paperbarks. Distantly, we heard children chanting their times tables in the schoolhouse.

Isikeli had a boat, but his brother sold it. He and Ben were hoping to lease fifteen acres on Vanua Levu to grow sugar cane. We asked him what he thought about the coup: *We are too far away, we don't know much about that stuff.* Later, another guy, Bose, said vehemently: *Rabuka is a bastard, like all politicians.* Much of the talk was in Fijian, and then Rabuka's name was constantly on their lips. 'Coup' they pronounced 'coop', in a locution so soft and open it sounded like the cooing of doves.

Meanwhile, inside the two-room house made of concrete block, with interior walls plastered smooth, painted pale blue and decorated with pictures of Michael Jackson, Mr. T. and an outback Australian scene, Isikeli's wife Karoline sewed at a treadle machine, making a new granny frock from island cloth. She didn't take grog, but she monitored the conversation closely and occasionally interjected: *Talk too much! Bushman!* She had gone as housemaid with the Tui Levuka and his wife to the Great Council of Chiefs in Suva after the coup. When it was time to leave – we were catching the three o'clock truck – Isikeli implored us to stay. Under heavy persuasion, we decided to go back to Levuka, get our things, then return the next day.

That evening we spent in the Ovalau Club, half-heartedly chatting up two hearty blonde Scandinavian backpackers. Well, I was half-hearted; when they left to watch a video – *Silkwood*, with Meryl Streep – Blackspot went with them, while I drank morosely on beneath photographs of the piratical World War I German sea raider, Count Felix von Luckner, and his ship, the *Seeadler*. There was a framed letter of thanks from the Count to the owner of a house on Katafaga in the Lau Group, where he and five men, arriving by lifeboat after the *Seeadler* was wrecked in the leeward Society Islands, made themselves at home: *We are very sorry that we have not meet you here. Although we had a good time on your island. I and my mates sleep in your house. We had a good meal, and are now quite fit to proceed on our sporting trip. The wonderful stroll around your island we will never forget . . . all things we took is paid for – turkey, 10 shillings, bananas, 2 shillings. Me and my men are thankful to you.*

Blackspot returned sometime after the middle of the night; again he woke me up with talk of pirates' gold; this time I ignored it. Next morning, before going to Ruku Ruku, we had to arrange our further travel. The plan was to spend the night in the village, then come back to Levuka and return by boat or plane to Suva. At the booking office, we learned there was no boat to Viti Levu the next day and no seats on the plane either. Blackspot swore and walked out of the office. I stuck around and learned that we could, however, go by ferry to another island, Taveuni, and then fly back to Suva from there. Taveuni was in precisely the opposite direction from that in which we wanted to go, but perhaps our fabled white-sand, palm-fringed beach was there? It certainly wasn't on Ovalau, everywhere hemmed by pewter-coloured coral reefs. Or so I said to Blackspot when I tracked him down in a nearby teashop. His anger seemed to have gone as quickly as it came. *Yeah, maybe*, he said. *It's just that I've got a bloke to see in Suva.*

You mean you're missing the bars, I said, but he just smiled and shook his head.

If you like.

The truck was again full of big women in bright dresses, and it just got fuller, until we were jammed up together like fish in a can. Amazingly, there was always room for one more. We carried gifts. Blackspot had a T-shirt for Isikeli, cans of meat for the household. I gave Karoline a length of cloth wrapped in newspaper, which she did not open until after we had walked off up the red dirt road with Isikeli to get cassava (tapioca) for dinner. The tall spindly plants with leaves like lupin and improbably fat roots were simply growing by the road. Keli chopped off the stems with his cane knife, pulled up the tubers, cleaned them, put them in a woven basket then deftly improvised a handle for it with a stick. On the way back to the house he gestured towards the rocky outcrops on the steep central spine of the island: *The men of olden times were bigger than us*, he said. *They had forts up there. They used to tie ropes around big stones, throw them down to split the enemy skulls, then pull them up again. Covered with blood and brains.* Was this my ancient paradise?

Afternoon tea was fried bread, margarine, bowls of tea. Then: *yaqona.* We sat outside, as before, drinking, talking, not talking. Sometimes it seemed that it was the day before. Karoline was sewing another granny frock from the material I had brought, to wear to a wedding at the next village on the weekend. Ben arrived; then his wife, very pregnant, joined us; they had four other young children. Ben, it turned out, was on probation, though I never learned what his crime was. He and Isikeli met in prison, where Keli was doing time for divorce. Now Ben was his responsibility, under a kind of buddy system sanctioned by the court. They were good mates, but there was something unpredictable about Ben – hence, perhaps, Keli's perpetually worried look. It was a bit like me and Blackspot, except I was beginning to feel as if I wouldn't mind losing him.

The *yaqona* trance seemed deeper than before, as I fell into a reverie about time and its meanings, the intricacies of our division of it into smaller and smaller increments which, paradoxically, grow vast as they proliferate; while chance, with its sudden illuminations and obfuscations, pays no attention. Do we fill time with our actions, or do our actions make time? The *yaqona* ritual is an engagement of minds over a period defined by the imbibing of the drug. It makes a ceremony of passing time in a culture that has plenty of it to pass, and is the perfect drug in a place where the finite is always about to segue into endlessness. In some strange way, the tedium of paradisiacal days is answered by the vacancy of the intoxication.

In the old days, it was a medium for prophecy. Anyone, upon the presentation of firewood, yams or a sperm whale tooth, might consult a priest as oracle, and the drinking of *yaqona* from his special bowl, like that which Cargill took from Levuka, preceded the prophetic trance. Priests placed the bowl directly on the floor and bent down on all fours to suck the *yaqona* up with their mouths: *Unbroken silence follows. The priest becomes absorbed in thought, and all eyes watch him with unblinking seriousness. In a few minutes he trembles; slight distortions are seen in his face, and twitching movements in his limbs.*

These increase to a violent muscular action, which spreads until the whole frame is strongly convulsed, and the man shivers as with a strong ague fit . . . while giving the answer, the priest's eyes stand out and roll as in a frenzy; his voice is unnatural, his face pale, his lips livid, his breathing depressed, and his entire appearance like that of a furious madman . . . as the god says 'I depart', (the priest) announces his actual departure by violently flinging himself down on the mat.

Thomas Williams, whose account this is, suborned a Tongan friend to question one of these shakers, a man called Laqu, who was famous for *tremblings of the most violent kind, bordering on fury.* The Tongan suggests first that Laqu decides beforehand what he will say, but Laqu denies it. The Tongan then says in that case he must just say the first thing that comes into his head. *I do not know what I say,* replies Laqu. *My own mind departs from me, and then, when it is truly gone, my god speaks by me.*

Along with the cassava got that afternoon, dinner was *dalo* (taro), tinned corned beef cooked with onion, then tea and more fried bread, which they called pancake – lumps of dough, dropped into hot fat for about thirty seconds, with a rubbery crust and a soft inside. After we ate, the mats came out. As well as a length of *tapa*, Karoline had woven two new mats as wedding gifts, and we had one each of these stretched out on the sitting- room floor, with a blanket and pillows, to sleep on. It was a restless night once the soporific effect of the *yaqona* wore off. The village generator ticked until midnight and there was only one switch: if any light was on, all were. I lay under a naked 100-watt globe, watching the yellow lizard that lived in the house inch along the wall and across the ceiling. There was a soft wash of waves outside, laughter and sweet low affectionate murmurs from the bedroom next door where Isikeli and Karoline were making love. Later on it rained. It was still dark when the roosters started to crow.

After a breakfast, we said goodbye to Karoline, resplendent in her new dress; she would already have left for the wedding when we returned. Isikeli took a carry pole and his cane knife, and we set off along a red dirt road past shacks where people laughed and called after us, hilariously suggesting Isikeli might be going to eat us. The path uphill beside a stream was slippery from last night's rain. Yellow, black and white, red and blue butterflies drifted by in the glades. We saw frogs and toads and skinks. The deep, soft cries of wood pigeons sounded oddly like words in the Fijian language: *Roo-rook-rook, roo-roo-rook*, they called, as if saying the name of the village over and over again.

We stopped under a mango tree about halfway up while Keli got each of us a green coconut to drink. The milk was sweet, nutty, cool, delicious. We went on, climbing more steeply now, until we reached a makeshift hut of wood and iron, built *in situ* by Isikeli, his brothers and friends the previous year. Here were the *yaqona* plantations, growing on a lease Isikeli's younger brother mortgaged for $2,000 to the Native Lands (No) Trust Board. The three brothers were also growing *dalo*, yams, cocoa, cabbage and cassava in the rich volcanic soil on the slopes of the mountain.

We had come for *dalo*. Of the three staple root crops it is the one with the most *mana*; these were for the Tui Levuka. Keli got four big roots from one garden, then went across the face of the hill to another plot to get four more. He picked some ripe paw paw, split them with his cane knife. We ate looking out over the Koro Sea. The view was superb. A toy boat rocked before Nairai Island, where the brig *Eliza* was wrecked. You could see Vanua Levu to the north and Viti Levu to the west. There was Tonga – the land where time stands still – off that way; we could not see Samoa, to the north-east, either, but we could make out the shadowy shapes of the Lau Islands, part of Fiji but lived in by the Tongan elite which has ruled the country for so long.

Afterwards Isikeli stood in the plantation looking seaward and swept his arm about to take in the whole view. *You see, we have here everything we need*, he said. *Everything we need* . . . There was an odd look on his face, compounded of pride, melancholy and yearning. It was as if land, sea and sky were simultaneously his and not his. He too, I thought, felt disinherited in the midst of plenty. He too desired what was before him, even though he already possessed it in the only way possible now: by being there.

On the way back down, we passed a party waiting for the truck to go to the wedding. Bright-coloured cloth, washed and scented bodies, soft strumming of guitars. They were drinking *yaqona* already, said Isikeli, a touch enviously. In the deserted village, the house was locked; Karoline had taken the key with her. Keli was only briefly discomposed. He broke in. Then we went down to the other end of the beach to photograph the resort built there on leased village land. Traditional-style *bure* houses, locked and empty, were scattered across green lawns under coconut palms. Isikeli had worked here and clearly felt uncomfortable trespassing on land that should have been his own. Back in the village, we searched for the *yaqona* pounder so he could powder our *sevu sevu*, or gift, for a friend of his who was the policeman at Somo Somo on Taveuni, but it seemed to have gone to the wedding too. We had a cup of tea, a swim and a shower, and then the truck arrived half an hour early to take all three of us to Levuka. I gave Keli my Welsh rugby jersey, which he accepted gravely: *Oooo, thank you*. We left $20 under the lamp.

The *dalo* we ferried by taxi to the Tui Levuka's house, an ordinary weatherboard dwelling that would not have been out of place in the suburbs of Auckland. Blackspot and I waited in the car while Keli took his tithe inside. At the Royal, he had his first drink in two years. Were we corrupting him? *One beer, two beer, then washdown!* he said and laughed. He tried to involve us in a plan for a business exporting *yaqona* to Australia; he knew it was popular among Aborigine in the Northern Territory.

Then, a confession. Our generosity made him feel bad. Especially the cloth. His wife was at the wedding wearing a dress made from material I had given her. We had been too kind; he had not been able to reciprocate. If we would only stay longer ... Blackspot was gazing fixedly at his drink, an almost smile on his lips. He'd wondered aloud when I bought the cloth if it was a good idea, but I'd ignored him. Now I was on my own. Unconvincingly, I told Keli that things he had given us were intangibles, which we could repay only with money. Not just food and hospitality but a gracious entry into his world. Which, culturally, was so much richer than ours. And . . . Keli looked even more perplexed than usual. I trailed off. There was a long, awkward silence before he laughed, raised his bottle and toasted: *You are like missionary,* he said. *You always say the opposite thing.* Opposite of what, I wondered? The truth? Or the opposite of what I meant? I was deeply hurt – me, a missionary?

The *Princess Ashika* had arrived by now; the sun had gone down. To avoid getting drunk, we went to the Old Capital Inn and ate chicken curry in a room full of edgy tourists. At the depot, we retrieved our bags. The ramp was down, the last stragglers were going aboard. Keli had been quiet since that moment in the Royal. Now he spoke.

There's just one thing I want to say to you . . . he began.

I bent forward expectantly. The boat sounded its horn.

It's going! said Blackspot.

He was right: the metal ramp that closed the stern was rising. There was no time for talk. We ran and leaped and waved goodbye from the edge of the ramp as it rose. As the little steamer strung with lights left the town behind in the gloom under the mountain, the last thing I saw was the massive rock outcrop up the back, like a great stone head, looking east.

The voyage to Taveuni took all that night and into the morning of the next day. A roll on/roll off ferry like the *Ovalau*, only larger, the *Princess Ashika* carried no vehicles, just masses of *taukei*. Raucous videos played the whole way: *Delta Force*, with Chuck Norris, Lee Marvin, Shelley Winters and Robert Vaughan, in which a TWA plane hijacked in Athens is rescued by a group of elite commandos; a strangely apposite 1950s movie about a revolt on a sugar plantation, full of cruelly moustached white men, crisply dressed, pointy bra-ed white women and sweaty black slaves; Sumo wrestling; Fijian hymns as we docked. During *Delta Force*, hearing a demand to *Show all passports*, I was already reaching for mine when I realised the instruction came from the video speakers, not the tannoy. I wasn't the only one; Blackspot did the same. Constant fear is basic to repression. As is boredom.

Mine was relieved when I heard a voice crying *Hey! Hey!* and woke from a doze to find a young Indian girl in a grubby white frock leaning over the back of the seat towards me, flashing her eyes, her red tongue darting between cracked black lips, her whole body humming. Her skin was a deep matte black; her teeth white as the imitation pearls round her neck, whiter than the lace of her dress. Vena couldn't believe her luck: here I was and all she needed to do was talk me into going with her. She was beautiful. Her father was rich. What more could I want? We could get off the boat at Savu Savu Bay on Vanua Levu and marry.

She could not have been more than twenty-five and was probably younger. Bright, funny and attractive, she was also deeply confused. Her plan to persuade me to come home with her required that she conceal what she had been doing in Suva the last few years, but it kept coming up: *I get drunk and fuck with men – that's my game!* she said savagely. She was troubled by a skin condition, an itchy rash all over her body which began, she said, after her second abortion. She hiked up her dress and raked painted nails along her thighs, crying out in despair: *I am cleanest girl in Suva. Why am I <u>scratch</u> all the time?* She was desperate to marry; despite her perplexity at our obsession with sun tans, she would only consider a European. *Fijians eat shoes,* she claimed, echoing a story Keli told us about a missionary cooked and eaten with his boots on because the cannibals had never seen shoes before and thought they were part of his body.

Ice cream dribbled down on her jacket but she didn't notice. She said she had $10,000 in the bank. Her father was eighty, her mother forty-seven; she ran away from home with a man when she was sixteen and hadn't been back since. Although she believed her father would know how to fix her skin condition, she was uneasy about the kind of reception she would get from him. When her pleas that I accompany her became too much, I showed her the ring on the third finger of my left hand and told her I was already married. This was, strictly speaking, true, although in other circumstances I would not have let on. Blackspot was, however, currently unattached. He was sitting nearby, reading, and when he looked up I got a rare glimpse of him through Vena's eyes. Thick-set, red-faced (high blood pressure), with slightly protuberant, wide-set eyes and a head of unruly black hair shot with grey, he looked, she said in horror, *like a devil*.

When she realised I would not, after all, be coming with her, a bleak coldness descended between us. Though we had spent most of the night together, as the moon set over Savu Savu Bay, and Orion, Taurus and the Pleiades faded among wind-swept cirrus from the dawn sky, she did not bother to say goodbye, but got off the boat with the other space travellers and walked away without a backward glance.

Savu Savu, on the south-eastern coast of Vanua Levu, has a good natural harbour which was, for those who believe in CIA involvement in the coup, a *raison d'être* for it. With the burgeoning movement for a nuclear-free Pacific and the loss of their bases in the Philippines imminent, the Americans needed an alternative and Savu Savu was on the list. That they have not yet used it is irrelevant: since the 2000 coup, it's been there for them if they want it.

Fiji was one of the lead countries in the original push to make the Pacific nuclear free, co-sponsoring with New Zealand the United Nations Resolution to this effect in 1975, and banning nuclear warships in its own waters even before New Zealand did. In 1983, the Reagan administration persuaded Prime Minister Ratu Mara to drop the ban; the founding of the Fiji Labour Party two years later was partly in response to this change of policy, and the Bavadra Government elected in 1987 was non-aligned and actively nuclear free. Meanwhile, since 1981, Ratu Mara's Alliance Party had been paying good money for advice on electoral strategy to Business International, exposed as a front for the CIA by the *New York Times* as early as 1977.

The most credible scenario for the coup probably involves US intelligence, the business community (European, Fijian and Indian), the governing elite, and sections of the army and police in an only perfunctorily clandestine plan to return power to the oligarchy which had ruled since independence. The incitement of racial hatred was a means of effecting this restoration, as it was in the 19 May 2000 coup by Ilikini Naitini, aka George Speight, against the Labour administration of Mahendra Chaudhry.

A year before his coup, Speight was sacked as chairman of the government-owned Fiji Hardwood Corporation, a position that gave him a key role in the negotiations over harvesting rights to the world's largest maturing mahogany plantation on Viti Levu; the wood is estimated to be worth up to half a billion Australian dollars. Speight lost his job because he accepted consultancy fees from one of the overseas firms bidding for the trees, an American company called Timber Resource Management; his personal resentment probably made him a target for recruitment. If he was, like Rabuka, a front man for the oligarchy, he was chosen with more care: there's no chance now that he will become a player in his own right while the oligarchy is firmly back in power.

After crossing the Somo Somo Strait, home of Dakuwaqa, the shark god who was and is brother to the local chief, the Tui Cakau, the *Princess Ashika* was shadowed into port by a pod of steel-grey dolphins taking turns to surf the bow wave. Somo Somo, the town, is split in two, with the village in the hollow and the shops on the hill; nothing stirred beneath the verandas as we checked into the Kaba Lodge and wondered what to do with the rest of the day.

I walked down the road towards the village, where a man standing alone on a platform was haranguing the empty town through a wildly distorting portable loudspeaker, sermonising about god knows what; his only audience, an old man sitting on a log in the vacant lot, had his back turned. This being a Saturday, I wondered if the preacher was Isikeli's friend, the Seventh Day Adventist policeman to whom we were supposed to be giving our *sevu sevu*, the small plastic bag full of powdered *yaqona* Keli had given us from his private stash. If so, I thought, he would not be getting it. Further on, I fell in with two girls, both called Maria, who wanted me to go home with them; but to their evident disappointment, I refused.

How was this? Here was not one but two dusky maidens leading me on. It seems inconceivable now that I could have been so gauche, so unadventurous, so callow as not to have gone. And I no longer recall exactly why I did not. With Vena it was obviously impossible, but these two . . . ? They were gorgeous. I'm reminded of my father who, on Nuku'alofa during the war, was taken, on the back of the barracks cook's motorbike, to an assignation with a Tongan girl in a hut in a nearby village. He at least went – though, as he put it, *nothing happened*. Which was perhaps wisdom: it turned out that the girl's family were closely monitoring the situation and that, if something had happened, my father, then a virgin, would probably have been forced to marry her.

Who knows? In my case, marriage was not a risk; my refusal probably had more to do with the fact that I didn't want our meeting contaminated by desire. Or was it a need to preserve my illusions: the legendary fleshpots of the South Seas might have lost their allure while we sat and chatted and ate fry bread, which is most likely all we would have done. The sadness of this does not escape me. Because I could not help but think of sex with these girls, faced with their brown, smiling, eager faces, I felt I had to say no. Their evident friendliness could not overcome my afflicted sense of myself as a sexual predator, albeit on a very tight rein. Perhaps this was, as Keli had said, the missionary position after all.

Blackspot wasn't there when I got back to the motel. I put on a load of washing and sat down to read Williams. One of David Cargill's successors, Thomas Williams was stationed at Somo Somo on Taveuni from 1843 until the Cakaudrove circuit was abandoned as hopeless in 1847. During that time he and his companion, the surgeon missionary Richard Lyth, began their book, which is in two volumes: the first (the one I had) is an ethnography, and the second a history of the mission. Williams, who was born into a strongly Wesleyan household in Horncastle, Lincolnshire, in 1815, and died at Ballarat in 1891, was the antithesis of Cargill: robust where the other was febrile, nearly impervious to doubt, energetic, clear-headed, smart and amused, he retained a capacity for sympathetic observation even when his sensibility was revolted. His book, the first comprehensive ethnology of the group, is a model of its kind, its only regrettable feature the excision from it by a third hand of material pertaining to Fijian sexuality.

In the absence of sex, it is the Fijian attitude to death which best exercises Williams's mind. The two customs of the land the missionaries found most objectionable were cannibalism and widow strangling, and Williams contributes to an understanding of both without ever quite gaining one himself. In his chapter on war he writes: *The return of a victorious party is celebrated with the wildest joy; and if they bring with them the bodies of the slain foes, the excitement of the women, who go out to welcome the returning warriors, is intense . . . the words of the women's song may not be translated; nor are the obscene gestures of their dance, in which the young virgins are compelled to take part, or the foul insults offered to the corpses of the slain, fit to be described . . . on these occasions, the ordinary social restrictions are destroyed, and the unbridled and indiscriminate indulgence of every evil lust and passion completes the scene of abomination.*

Without going into detail, then, the passage makes clear that Fijian warfare released people, as war everywhere does, from the tedium of the daily round, and allowed them to celebrate their own fertility in the face of the mortality which will certainly overtake them. These scenes were not different in kind from the orgiastic behaviour which follows victorious armies all over the world; but they were unusual: *Dead men or women are tied to the fore-part of the canoe, while on the main deck the murderers, like triumphant fiends, dance madly among the flourishing of clubs and sun shades and confused din . . . the corpses are dragged with frantic running and shouts to the temple, where they are offered to the god, before being cooked.* That death, even the death of others, could be approached festively is beyond Williams, as it is beyond any of the early missionaries; it is still difficult for us today to comprehend the mentality of two men from the Lovoni, the hill tribe on Ovalau who, encountering for the first time a European ship at Levuka, said: *After such a wonder, what is left for us to see? Let us go home and get our friends to strangle us.* Their friends apparently did.

In an extraordinary passage, Williams (if it was not Lyth) records his own attendance at a strangling. Learning that the old king, the

Tui Cakau, has died, Williams hurries to his house in the hope of preventing the strangling of the women but arrives too late: *The effect of that scene was overwhelming. Scores of deliberate murderers, in the very act, surrounded me: yet there was no confusion, and, except a word from him who presided, no noise, but only an unearthly, horrid silence . . . not a breath stirring in the air, and the half subdued light in that hall of death showed every object with unusual distinctness. All was motionless as sculpture, and a strange feeling came upon me, as though I was myself becoming a statue. To speak was impossible; I was unconscious that I breathed; and involuntarily, or, rather, against my will, I sank to the floor, assuming the cowering posture of those who were not actually engaged in murder . . . Occupying the centre of that large room were two groups . . . the middle figure of each group being held in a sitting posture by several females, and hidden by a large veil. On either side of each veiled figure was a company of eight or ten strong men, one company hauling against the other on a white cord, which was passed twice around the neck of the doomed one, who thus, in a few minutes, ceased to live.*

After the bodies of the two dead women – the Tui Cakau's wife and a servant – have been oiled and covered in flowers, their hair done, their faces painted vermilion, Williams is astonished to find that the old king is still alive. When his son and heir, very moved, embraces the missionary and says, *See! the father of us two is dead,* Williams demurs; but the son replies, *His spirit is gone. You see his body move, but that it does unconsciously.* It was in fact not uncommon for the dying to be dressed, painted and adorned, and placed in their graves while still breathing; if they cried out from under the earth, this was taken as a sign of the great strength of the departing spirit.

Later a lament is sung over the body of the serving woman: *Alas! Moalevu! there lies a woman truly wearied; not only in the day, but in the night also, the fire consumed the fuel gathered by her hands. If we woke in the still night, the sound of her feet reached our ears; and, if spoken to harshly, she continued to labour only. Moalevu! Alas! Moalevu! We used not to hear Moalevu called twice.* Then, as the bodies are carried from the house, water is poured inside and out, in obedience to the proverb: *For we must die, and are as water spilt on the ground, which cannot be gathered up again.*

Blackspot came back later and we watched a video so forgettable I cannot even remember what it was called. I woke several times in the night, troubled by nightmares of the sort that never quite cohere into even the surreal logic of dreams. From one of these – we were votaries of a new movement, the Recidivists, in white face paint and bowler hats like the bovver boys in *A Clockwork Orange* – I opened my eyes to see the wind lifting some T-shirts from the line in the tiny yard off the sitting room. As I went out to pick them up, the huge, shadowy, silent shape of a great white owl flew from the hurricane fence inches past my face and off into the night like a ghost of time.

Next morning we were woken by the sound of passionate hymn-singing from the Methodist church. The old corrugated-iron building was visibly reverberating with the fervour of the congregation; as we waited outside for the bus, I could see, through a gap left at the bottom of the walls to let air in, bare black feet pounding the earthen floor. We had decided, having nothing else to do – by decree, only church-going was allowed on Sunday – to catch, as we had on Ovalau, the bus that went around the island. There was also the question of that elusive white-sand beach to be answered; I had my camera ready.

The island was lush, rugged, almost pristine. Apart from tourism, its only other earner was copra. The coconut plantations ran down, acre upon acre, to the sea. Here and there were small grimy corrugated-iron sheds for drying the flesh of the nut. Red cattle grazed among the reddish-tinged trunks of palms making a criss-cross of lines before the blue water; the red was a lichen which grew only on the leeward side of the tree. The narrow coastal plain was scattered with villages, most of them featuring houses made traditionally of timber and thatch rather than the concrete block and corrugated-iron seen elsewhere. Brightly coloured washing hung on lines made of Number 8 wire. Little frond huts stood out on the tiny headlands of miniature bays; cooking fires smoked, broiling freshly caught fish. The reef was close in shore all the way. When the tide was out, the beaches, like those on Ovalau, looked grey and scungy. With the tide in, they were paradisiacal in that deceitful cinematic way . . . blue water, golden sand.

And people, people everywhere, a veritable field full of folk in bright lava-lava, or dresses, or a bizarre assortment of monogrammed or messaged T-shirts, carrying matches, biros, combs and cigarettes in their hair, their bodies oiled and scented, their ghetto-blasters playing reggae. Most of them, like us, were out looking for something to do on a Sunday. Their faces ranged from classic Polynesian, to Fijian, to more typically Melanesian, to Papuan. Among them, still wearing his HANG LOOSE T-shirt, was a man I'd made friends with on the *Princess Ashika*; he would not have looked out of place in Port Moresby. Although we hardly spoke, not having a language in common, there was a strange longing in the intensity with which we said goodbye to each other when he left the bus at Lavena.

That was the end of the road, a wide grassy common by the sea where the bus turned round and paused for a few minutes only. There I saw a man in a fine hand-printed T-shirt with ANTIOCH ASSOCIATION, LAVENA BRANCH on it: what could this mean? That spring in Fiji the hit song was New Zealand group Herbs' *Long Ago*, which you heard everywhere. It played in my head all the way back: *Close your eyes/imagine all those memories in your mind/realise/the downfall of that time has made you wise/long ago . . . it was so long ago.*

Bone-achingly weary from three hours sitting on the hard seats of the bus, we arrived back at the Kaba Lodge to find Porter and his friends from the Royal in the next-door unit. *You following us around?* I asked. He laughed, as affable and inscrutable as ever. We had a gin and tonic with him and John and Diane before setting off to walk to the Castaway Inn for dinner. Pink, lucid skies faded over the darkness of the road as the sun went down. Before going in to eat, we drank a beer by the sea, watching a little tanker moored at the end of a narrow jetty pumping diesel ashore in the last of the light.

What was going on between Blackspot and me? Why had the atmosphere turned so sour? Maybe it was just cabin fever; but I had come to suspect he was playing some kind of game with me. His treasure talk when pissed, I decided, was a bait I would not take. He was a cheery, not to say romantic drunk, but sober he was circumspect and dry. I did not yet realise it was my insufferable conviction of the superiority of my views that inflamed him most of all. Like two irascible old billy goats, we sparred as we ate, disagreeing as a matter of principle on every subject while remaining resolutely impersonal. I needled him about his ability, as producer, to raise the money for the film; he wondered aloud if our script was safe in my inexperienced hands – that sort of thing.

Afterwards, we walked silently back in the moonlight through a copra plantation replanted with coffee bushes. The headless trunks of the deliberately poisoned palms leaned across a post-apocalyptic landscape where cicadas rasped like generators among the starry white coffee flowers. Figures loomed up out of the dark, their voices soft, insinuating. No one ever said hello, but, after you passed, the girls would call out sweetly, sadly, *Bye-eee . . .* , irresistibly recalling Henry Adams's 1891 comment about Tahiti: *Even when I go swimming in the blue and purple light*, he wrote, *I never lose consciousness of a sort of restless melancholy that will not explain why it should want to haunt a spot that by rights should be as gay as a comic opera.*

I was already overcome with a piercing nostalgia for the Marias, but it was too late for that now. Instead, back at the motel, I told Blackspot, who controlled our finances, and had been trying to save money by booking us into twin shares, that I was sick of spending the best part of twenty-four hours of every day in his company.

What are you going to do about it? he said, as if asking me to step outside.

From now on, I said, *I want a room of my own.*

He shrugged. *Is that all?* he said. *Sure. Why not?*

We caught the plane out on Monday. The airstrip was a grassy paddock on a hilltop surrounded by palms. In the terminal, a sick Frenchman lay moaning across the seats, his face a vile yellow-green colour. Everyone avoided him as he was carried on board, in case whatever he had was contagious. The plane flew over ocean and islands, giving Landsat views of enormously complex reef systems under shallow waters. On the shores of Koro Island, clearly outlined, were the semi-circular shapes of ancient stone fish traps built on the reefs to harvest the tides.

At Nausori Airport the pervasive feeling of lassitude and threat returned. One of my bags, which I'd checked through, came back open. Whoever had searched it failed to snap back the lid on a bottle of hair shampoo, which had spilled over my books. Bruce Chatwin's *The Viceroy of Ouidah*, a slender, fey, lapidary homage to Marquez, and Umberto Eco's miscellany, *Travels in Hyperreality*, were sticky with goo. As the bus drove along Ratu Mara Drive towards Suva, I felt discouraged at the thought of another week of disorderly paranoia from military and police.

In town, Blackspot decided we could afford a night of (relative) luxury – or perhaps sanity – and we checked into separate rooms at the Grand Pacific Hotel down on the waterfront. Built by the Union Steamship Company in 1914 as a base for New Zealand and Canadian shipping services in the Pacific, its design mimics the first-class accommodation on Edwardian ships, with each bedroom opening onto wide decks on one side and on the other to a balcony overlooking the main lounge, where the ghosts of white-suited men and ladies veiled against the heat sat in wicker chairs under the potted palms. Its glamour had faded somewhat; our rooms were on the ground floor, giving out over a flat brown lawn to a row of lights and then the sea; but there was a pool and hot water, and the baths were as they had been before the war.

Blackspot said he needed a drink, and disappeared. I would have preferred a joint, but went instead to book us in for the rest of our time in Suva to the South Seas Private Hotel, which stood halfway up the hill behind the Government Buildings on the fringes of Suva's ritziest suburb, leafy Toorak. I ran into him later, quite by chance, outside the Garrick Hotel. He looked sly and amused as he suggested we check out the La Perouse Bar in the Star of India Hotel: it was closed. Then we tried Caesar's Palace, a sleazy, red-lit dive with a feeling of such dismal menace in the shadowy corners of its dim interior we didn't even go in. Upstairs in the Lounge Bar of the Garrick, I ordered two beers at the bar and, while they were being got, watched Blackspot take from his pocket a piece of paper, unfold it and then consult two men sitting nearby. They turned out to be cops who, when I returned with the beers, were insisting he put his map away in case it brought us to the attention of the Security Forces. More of his bullshit, I thought sourly.

The cops insisted on us joining them: Anaru, a dog-handler, was OK, but his mate *from the bush* was aggressively, incoherently and unpredictably drunk. As we sat and drank longneck after longneck of the inevitable Fiji Bitter, he became louder and crazier, and the place, which was a hang-out for hookers and crims, gradually emptied. Soon only the four or five girls who worked there remained, lined up timidly at the bar in the far corner of the room, while the lone gay barman was looking more worried by the minute. Ostensibly the cops were protecting us from pickpockets and other riff-raff but we all knew where the real threat lay: the boy from the bush might run amok at any moment.

I was feeling increasingly uneasy, and even Blackspot's habitual nonchalance was becoming a little forced. But, while it's true the law was in the hands of any rogue cop or soldier, burlesque was never far away either: an Indian photographer strayed in, and the cops demanded he take our picture. He was scared. As soon as he'd snapped us, he pulled the Polaroid from the camera and scarpered without his money; the nervous bar girls came over to look, and there was a moment of extreme tension as we waited for the greyish cloudy surface to resolve into an image.

Leaving the boy from the bush mesmerised by his own likeness, and Anaru rolling his eyes superstitiously in the barred light falling through venetian blinds, we eased out of our seats, said our goodbyes and faded away down the stairs.

What the fuck was that about, Freddy? I said to Blackspot, out in the street.

Just a tourist map, mate, he said, patting his pocket and grinning. *I was asking them about the best route to take around the island.*

The South Seas Private Hotel had an elegant glassed-in veranda running the length of the front of the white, weatherboard building. You could look out over the Botanical Gardens to Suva Bay. Here we met Mark, a journalist from 2SER, the radio station attached to the then Institute of Technology in Sydney. He had the edgy paranoia of a man determined to ferret out everything he could about the machinations behind the coup, and a crackling abrasiveness he (like so many Australians) was almost completely unaware of.

We rendezvoused with Mark that evening and walked down to the Garden Bar of the Grand Pacific for a drink, where he got into an altercation in the toilet, and was only saved from a beating by the intervention of a guy who happened to be in there as well. Tui was a tall, lean, bullet-headed man with fine features and straight hair, the same general build as Isikeli. In the aftermath of the toilet incident, he and his friend Tolo joined us. Tui was one of the detribalised street people of Suva, a kind of natural aristocrat of the sword-seller's desperate culture.

I believe in one – the root! he declared.

You are the Tui Suva, I joked.

He didn't laugh. *Every man a king*, he said.

He also knew where we could get some dope to smoke. Leaving Tolo behind, we took a taxi out past the docks, and in the rainy dark, drunk, stumbled after him up a hill. The small shack out the back of the deserted house was empty too, so we went down a slippery path, across a creek and up the other side to another house, where a girl of about fifteen joined us. We all walked back to the Queens Road and along to a hotel called the President's, where Blackspot and Tui and I drank the last three bottles of beer left in the fridge while Mark and the girl went off to score. In the interim, Tui told us how, after he left school, he went to New Zealand and worked for Fiesta Ice Cream in Auckland making chocolate bombs.

Mark came back without the girl but with a $10 deal wrapped in a page from the *Fiji Times*, and wanted to split immediately – he was hungry and had seen a Pizza Hut along the way. We talked him out of such an obvious breach of etiquette and called a cab instead. While we were waiting I showed Tui Cakobau's bullet, which, after learning what it was and where it came from, he pocketed: its mystery belonged to him, not me. The taxi arrived just as a group of drunken American men in suits entered the room.

More CIA men? I wondered aloud to Blackspot.

Nah, he said. *Businessmen.*

We were getting on better with every beer.

Tui's place was another little hut out the back of a house. It was tiny, bare, with hardly enough room for a tall man to lie down on his sleeping mat. A shelf with a lamp in the middle held his worldly goods. We sat in a circle on the floor while he went up to the house and came back with some food for Mark – tiny portions of fish cooked with greens, cassava, sweet potato. The dope looked lethal – brown and muddy, like some ganja from Vishnakaptnum I had once. No one had any papers, so I rolled up using some of the newsprint it was wrapped in. As I was about to lick it down, a fragment caught my eye: *Australia and New Zealand are out*, it read. *Indonesia, Malaysia, Singapore, Taiwan and Korea are in.*

It was a strong but not a paranoid stone, leaving us rooted to the spot, which was an old, dark, fragrant piece of beaten earth. *Another smoke, then we go listen to music*, said Tui. Walking down the gravel road to the main drag like ancient, ambulant stone gods, one of Johnny Bear's many works in progress, *Backroads to Nirvana*, came to mind: this had to be one of those roads. A gaggle of girls walked along the highway and turned up our way, rolling their eyes under the streetlights, smiling and calling out: *Bye-eee . . .*

Another taxi took us to a nightclub called the Bali Hai where, upstairs, a band was playing. We negotiated the security on the door and climbed past natty Polynesian boys in slacks and Hawaiian shirts contending on the stairs like denizens of a Pacific *Rebel Without A Cause*. It cost a dollar each to get in to the Sinai Room, where on a bench against the far wall we sat at a table with Tui, who had the knack of assuming he was the centre of any gathering. Bottles of beer arrived but I couldn't drink any more. Out of the smoke haze, improbably, Mrs Weeks from Tanoa House appeared wearing a tight-fitting orange knit dress, a single chain of pearls. With her big dark face and tall sculpted hair, she looked like a Tongan princess. *Call me Taka*, she said, and asked if I wanted to dance. It was a reggae band, and the floor full of people seemed hardly to be moving; not until part way through the song did I understand the rhythm for the subtle and very sexy thing it was . . . then suddenly it was over.

Mark had gone by now. Tui had been joined by friends; they were getting ready to make another joint, delicately separating the tissue from the foil on the gold lining of a Benson and Hedges packet to roll up in. Thinking to contribute, stupidly, I pulled out our packet of dope. Tui tried to stop me but one of the brothers had already noticed. He looked murderous. I don't know why; perhaps he thought I was trying to pre-empt him, or that I was saying our dope was better than his dope. Tui smoothed over what was clearly a much more serious breach of etiquette, and we left soon afterwards.

Walking back to the hotel, stopping in along the way at Traps, the bar where the intellectuals drank, Suva seemed as enticing as any city I knew. Blackspot had once again lapsed into pirate speech, but for once I didn't mind: it seemed to suit his battered personality and fallen cherub looks. Besides, though I never quite pinned down the resemblance, he reminded me of my father. As he tacked to his room, I heard him reciting his favourite verse, his namesake's Gnome: *Spend the years of learning squandering/Courage for the years of wandering/Through a world politely turning/From the loutishness of learning.*

Later, braving the curfew, dodging an army patrol cruising otherwise deserted streets, I went for a stroll in the gardens. I stood for a while beside what I thought of as the sacred stones outside the museum, unaware they were actually used to smash the heads of *bakolo* (men for cooking), then smoked a cigarette in the Band Rotunda. A police van passed on the road as I came back, and on the lawn of the hotel little brown frogs hopped away from my bare feet while another great white owl flew silently past my face.

At the Lebanese-owned mixed business round the corner from where I lived in Glebe, I'd become friendly with a young woman, Roshni Prasad, who sometimes worked behind the counter. When I told her we were going to Fiji, she gave me the phone number of her father, David Prasad, who lived just outside Suva. I rendezvoused with Blackspot at the Post Office – he'd just had another encounter with Porter, who seemed up to date with our movements – and called Mr Prasad.

Wait there, he said. *I'll come and get you.*

It was fifteen miles in his taxi to his place set back from the road on flats at the base of the hills. David Prasad was a nice man, humane, gentle, sane, and incredibly hard-working. As well as the taxi, he ran an automobile spare-parts business, a shop, a carrying operation and the seven-acre farm his house stood on. Since the coup, however, he had lost a lucrative contract and was having to cut his operations back.

His house was cool, dim and grimy, painted the same blue inside as Isikeli and Karoline's. There were cheap Fijian souvenirs in the sitting room – an imitation tortoise shell, a wooden lobster, a piece of *tapa* cloth. A covered altar stood in the corner next to the tape deck, and several stopped clocks hung on the wall. We drank fizzy orange cordial while pigeons cooed in the eaves above the door and his grandchildren ran around our feet. Outside in the blinding sunlight, a red and green Taveuni parrot squawked as it clawed up and down its cage.

Lunch was served in the kitchen. At a large table covered with bright plastic sheeting, we three men sat side by side eating rotis, chicken curry, dahl, lemon pickle and drinking sweet tea, while chooks climbed up onto the hearth of the open fire and pecked at the covered pots. The women who had cooked us this meal – David's wife, a large, sad-faced woman in her forties; the wives of his two sons – huddled in the doorway, giggling and watching us eat. Later they were joined by a Fijian woman, babe in arms, the wife of a tenant on the farm. This casual mixing of races, in the midst of incessant talk about racial tension, though a candid refutation of the politics of division, was also threatened by them. David Prasad remarked upon the restlessness of *the natives* and wondered aloud how best to liquefy his assets and emigrate.

Out the back was a converted garage where, David said, we could have stayed in comfort – and slightly crazed style: a kind of kaleidoscopic 1950s mufti. As we left, the women waved and called to us through the bars of the locked security door leading onto the porch at the front of the house: *When you come back . . . ?* they sang as we scuffed through red dust to the car.

That afternoon I bought the spices Roshni had asked for – curry, turmeric, garlic powder – at a supermarket on Renwick Street. Back in Glebe she told me her mother had cancer. I saw Mrs Prasad one more time, out the back of the vegetable shop next door to the mixed business where Roshni worked. Grey and ill, she had come to Sydney to die.

On Friday, after we had picked up a rental car, Blackspot said he had someone to meet at the Travelodge. Resisting the urge to ask who, and relishing the opportunity for some time alone, I smoked a joint, took off my shoes and went for a walk in the gardens. I had developed an itchy rash between my toes, and thought a stroll in the cool wet grass might give me some relief. Besides, I loved the museum in the half dark, with its enigmatic, unbloodied standing stones on the forecourt outside, like transmitters of intelligence of the lost and the gone. Here, more than on Ovalau, more than on Taveuni, I was able to feel myself in touch with the ancient past.

Solemn meditations upon the otherness of the other are as much a staple of the European fantasy of the Pacific primitive as dusky maidens. No doubt I thought I was communing with spirits somehow abroad there or perhaps domiciled in the stones themselves – never mind that I was unaware of their real purpose, though I did know they had been uplifted elsewhere and brought down here when the gardens were established. To me they were as resonant as the fragment of a tree trunk inside the museum, in which two branches had grown around a parcel of human bones placed in the fork between them. And the marijuana helped. Soon I was in that half-tranced state in which we believe the gods are beginning to talk through us. So it was that I drifted from there down into the arms of a truly scary other.

From the museum, I was going to cut diagonally across the gardens to the highway and then go down to the sea on the other side of the road. What I had forgotten, or never known, was that adjacent to the corner of the gardens to which I was headed are the gates to Government House. I hit the fenceline some way up from the road, and was following it down in the misty half dark, stoned, minding my own business, when a sudden voice growled out of the night: *Who's there?* With a lurch in my gut, I realised I'd blundered right into the arms of soldiers guarding the gate to the Governor-General's residence.

There were two of them. The one who had challenged me was a huge guy, a good six inches taller than my six feet, with a bulk to match. He had a semi-automatic rifle slung over one shoulder which he fingered throughout our conversation. The other, similarly armed, was a sixteen-year-old kid in a uniform several sizes too big for him, who stood a couple of metres back in the door of the guard house, his eyes enormous, and did not say a word. Meanwhile, on the concrete apron outside the locked gates, in the white glare of a street light lined with faint rain, the big guy interrogated me.

What you doing here? he asked.

Just going for a walk, I said.

Can't believe you, he said. *Where your shoes?* He was eyeballing me from about six inches away.

I've got this rash on my feet . . . I began.

Can't believe you, he said, and said again to every attempt at an explanation I made: how to convince this man I was doing what I said I was? I stuck to my story . . . I was just going for a walk; I was barefoot because of the rash between my toes; I was a tourist. *Can't believe you.* He asked for my passport. I said it was back at the hotel. Which hotel? I told him. *Can't believe you*, he said. *I think you after something, I can see it in your face . . .*

This was, in a way, true, and despite the pressure I was under, and the fear I felt, I had the sense not to say anything about the film. If I had, I'm quite sure he would have done what at one point he threatened: *You know what we going to do now? We going to get the van, put you in it, take you down to the jail, sit you in a cell, then lock the door and throw away the key!* To my shame, I pleaded with him, my voice cracked and insincere. That didn't work either. Feeling disgusted at this abject behaviour, steadying myself, summoning what authority

I could, I said: *Look, I'm a tourist. I was just going for a walk. That's all there is to it.*

There was a very long pause. The kid soldier's eyes were huge as dinner plates now. The big guy grinned, took his hand off his gun and offered it to me to shake.

Had you scared then, eh? he said, and roared with laughter.

It didn't seem that funny to me. When he invited me up to the barracks for a drink, I said I was meeting a friend.

Bring him too. You can meet the boys.

Before I left to go stumbling back up the hill to the hotel to get my shoes, he, like so many others we met, wrote down his name and address on a bit of paper and gave it to me: *Filimone Milamoce, R.F.M.F., Box 102, Suva, Fiji.*

Feeling shaky, I went down to the Travelodge to meet Blackspot. He was, as usual, sitting on a high stool at the bar deep in conversation with the barman; he made a point of breaking it off as soon as he saw me, but I didn't say anything. My story delighted him: he beamed, put his arm round my shoulders, patted me on the back and congratulated me, whether because of my narrow escape or because I had got my comeuppance, I'm still not sure. I know he had a genuine affection for me, but perhaps he was also anticipating a waning of my naive belief in the natural goodness of all Fijians. And an end to my campaign to turn our film into some kind of exploration of white guilt in the face of the corruption Europeans bring with them like a plague.

It was our last night in Suva. Leaving the Travelodge, we went up to Traps again and there fell into a conversation with a drunken Tongan who was looking for an Indian girl to fuck. He had, he said, fucked every other kind of girl, but never an Indian. Defensive and aggressive, he muttered incoherent tales of rugby-playing days in New Zealand and said he would be happy if the King of Tonga did sell Ferdinand Marcos a passport, as he was then proposing to do. And this: *The Fijians fight the Indians, the Indians fight the Fijians – the Tongans don't give a fuck!*

The ruling oligarchy in Fiji has long had a preponderance of people from the Lau Islands to the east, where Ratu Mara, the oligarch Rabuka eventually restored, came from. They are classically Polynesian, with strong cultural links to Tonga. By contrast, most Fijians are ethnically Melanesian, culturally Polynesian. However, this becomes less true the further west you go. Broadly speaking, the east is Polynesian, the centre Polynesian/Melanesian, the west Melanesian. The political situation can be described as the government by a Polynesian-dominated elite of a peasantry made up largely of Fijians and Indians.

When the first Europeans came to Fiji, they came via Tonga, and absorbed a Tongan view of the Fijians before actually meeting any. At that time, in the late eighteenth century, there was extensive contact between Tonga and Fiji, as well as with Samoa to the north and east. The Tongans were the premier long-distance ocean sailors in the central Pacific, but the Fijians had better timber and made better canoes. Tongans intending to build canoes used to sail to Fiji and do it there, a task which might take as long as five years. During that time they might also hire themselves out as mercenaries to this chief or that in the wars and raids which were a constant of the life then. Fiji was thus a kind of finishing school for young Tongan men.

Tongans also came to Fiji, to Taveuni, to gather or buy the red feathers of the parrot that lives there. The feathers were taken up to Samoa, there to be exchanged for women or fine mats. Men were also exchanged: when the intricate calibration of genealogy and succession threw up a woman of such high status no Tongan man had the *mana* to marry her, she was typically offered to a Fijian 'prince', who would then make the voyage to Tonga to live with his wife. In this way, the chiefly lines of Fiji and Tonga became entwined in a complex web of blood relations.

The Wesleyans, like the explorers, merchants and beachcombers before them, came into Fiji from the east. They had already involved themselves in the civil wars fought in the Tongan islands in the 1830s. When the Christian party among the Tongans announced their intention to smite the heathen, the missionaries abandoned the New Testament and began preaching blood and thunder from

Old Testament books like Isaiah, Samuel and Joshua, and some of the gorier psalms – to such effect that the teeth of the enemy were in fact broken as advised in the psalm: *Thou hast broken the teeth of the ungodly*.

It was an extension then, not a change of policy, when the Wesleyans next gave their active support to Ma'afua'tuitoga, the self-proclaimed Tui Lau, and his Tongan Christian soldiers as they made war in various parts of eastern and central Fiji during the middle years of the nineteenth century. These incursions had a major effect in diminishing the power of the key confederation of Fijian tribes ruled by Cakobau of Bau, and were a decisive factor in Cakobau's eventual decision to embrace the *lotu*, the Christian way: had he not done so, his kingdom would have been lost and Ma'afua become ruler of all the lands about the Koro Sea.

Fiji's calamity is that the tribal configuration arrived at in 1874 still largely pertains. A lasting consequence has been neglect of the western lands. The west was less visited, less studied and less known than the east; less consideration of its needs was given when power-sharing arrangements were made around the time of cession. Most of the western chiefs did not even sign the Deed of Cession, and some revolted against it afterwards: they were put down by the combined forces of Bau and the British. This neglect of the west has continued until the present day, and was a factor in the rise of Bavadra and the Fijian Labour Party; it is exacerbated by the fact that most of the sugar cane is grown in the west, and most of the tourist resorts are there too. The final irony is that it is in the west that Fijian/Indian marriages are commonest: here, the two cultures have mixed most successfully.

After Traps, we kicked on to a club called Scruples to hear a reggae band. There I met a Fijian woman called Lily, whose last night in town this was: the next day she was booked to fly to Hamburg to marry a German she had slept with once in 1983. Was this the right thing to do? she asked. Should she go or should she stay? As we talked, in distress or anxiety, she twined her big, warm hands in mine, then bent her head until our temples met and our necks rubbed together. This intimate, emotional, utterly un-sexual touching went on for some time; it reminded me of footage I once saw of couples from one of the hill tribes in Papua New Guinea on the eve of marriage: the intended spent the whole night sitting side by side, heads together, as if synchronising brain waves. As we disengaged at last, I knew Lily would indeed go to Germany.

Back at the South Seas Private Hotel, we smoked another joint with Mark, who was edgy and paranoid after his attempt to interview an army officer had been thwarted, apparently by Military Intelligence. He had been driven, in darkness, to some derelict, spooky part of Suva where he was met, not by the officer, but by armed men in balaclavas. His driver, a local journalist, was menaced and he himself told that he should get on a plane in the morning and go straight back home.

He was right to be scared: this was the local face of a murderous politics. Just as the threat by members of the Taukei Movement to make *bakolo* of Richard Naida, Bavadra's press secretary, had to be taken seriously, so the fate of the Red Cross man, John Scott, who helped negotiate the release of the hostage Parliament after Speight's coup, shocked but did not surprise Fiji-watchers: along with his partner, Greg Scrivener, he was dismembered in his Suva apartment and the crime passed off as sex and/or drug related.

Probably the joint wasn't a good idea: about five minutes after Mark went to his room I heard a blood-curdling cry, and he arrived back at my door pale and literally shaking all over: someone was outside his room staring in the window. I had a look. Dark hedges loured over the moonlit lawn, which looked sinister but empty. Whoever it was, they weren't around any more. Blackspot was awake now as well, but he couldn't see anything out there either.

Mark was adamant, and determined not to spend another night in the hotel. It was 3 a.m., and there was the curfew, but I agreed to drive him to the Travelodge where all the other journalists were staying. He calmed down a bit, threw his things into his bag, and we crept down the hill in the little white car, pausing only to let an army patrol in one of the ubiquitous Toyota utes go by. I watched him skedaddle into the bright orange light of Reception, then drove up the hill feeling like I'd strayed inadvertently into a Graham Greene novel. We didn't see Mark again until we were back in Sydney.

Saturday was another rainy day in Suva. Soft grey drifts of fine mist were blowing in from the sea as we took the slick wet road around the foreshore as far as Laucala Bay, where my father had been stationed in the war; he'd gone from there for his year in Tonga before being sent west to Guadalcanal, Espiritu Santo and Rabaul. Dad had always spoken of Tonga as a kind of paradise lost. As a busy school teacher in a small mountain village, married to a woman of a temper precisely opposite to his, and with a rapidly growing family to provide for, he used to fantasise sometimes about returning to the simple life he had lived at Fu'uamotu in 1943, where he had been offered the Tongan girl to marry.

I don't think he was ever entirely serious about this; on the other hand, serious intent is not required to nourish fantasy. Later, after his first breakdown, and indeed for the rest of his life, he recognised that this dream would never come true, or at least not for him. What about me? I don't know. It's still not clear how much of my idealism was personal and how much cultural: as the dominant trend in the nineteenth and early twentieth centuries was to disparage, destroy or assimilate indigenous cultures in the Pacific, so since World War II (though with strong historical roots in the earlier period, particularly among the missionaries) white middle-class Europeans have tended to over-privilege these same cultures, often to an absurd degree: I remember a friend telling me once how, driving past a sacred mountain in the Bay of Plenty, one of those in the car with her insisted they turn the music on the radio down as a mark of respect.

Awareness of a weakness like this was a start I had yet to make, but awareness doesn't cure it: you tend to keep on behaving in accordance with a prejudice even after you reject it intellectually. I didn't understand why my attitude filled Blackspot with derision, just as I didn't appreciate the freedom of action which is possible once you start seeing things more clearly. For the moment, I was locked into the state of mind which ascribes to other cultures, and particularly the presumed original versions of those cultures, the virtues of nobility, simplicity, honesty and grace so conspicuously lacking in our own. Yet it is obvious, as Blackspot might have said, that such qualities belong only to individuals and these individuals can come from any culture, or any time, at all.

Leaving Laucala Bay and its anonymous barracks behind, we looped back north onto the Kings Road, which is what the highway circling Viti Levu is called from Suva north and west to Nadi, where, on its way back south and east to the capital, it becomes the Queens Road. The seal lasted only a few kilometres past the airport, and we were soon slipping and sliding along a muddy red rock track like something you would expect to find in the outback.

After an hour or so, a tall dark figure dressed in white loomed up on the side of the road, waving frantically. We stopped. He was an Indian from Lautoka, stranded. *I am a Christian man*, he sobbed, unzipping a little vinyl holder to show us the Book of Common Prayer inside. He had come all the way from the other side of the island on the promise of a job, only to be told it had already gone to a Fijian. Blackspot gave him $8.50, the bus fare back to Lautoka, and we left him still tearful, this time with gratitude, waving like a tall ghost in blackface as we pulled away.

Somewhere past there along the rocky road a stone flew up and smashed the petrol filter on the car's fuel line. Driving conditions were so bad we did not even notice, but when we stopped in Korovou an Indian passing in the street saw the leak. He went to a nearby shop, bought a replacement filter and then put it on for nothing, grovelling in the thick red mud to do so. We lost half a tank of gas; had he not alerted us, we would have lost the rest as well and been stranded ourselves somewhere in the wilds up ahead. I thought it was instant karma: if we hadn't helped that guy from Lautoka . . . *Bullshit*, said Blackspot, sardonically.

Learning by stages how to keep some purchase on the greasy road, we drove on by fat brown rivers, through lush green valleys, past ragged bush-covered hills. The parrot trees were a riot of orange against the dark green of their leaves. Whole villages sheltered among the clean, straight trunks, the *bure* like shaggy earth mounds between the trees, where brightly dressed people passing to and fro in the deep shadows appeared suddenly radiant in tall diagonals of falling sunlight.

The rich wet greens and vivid orange and chocolate earth browns ended suddenly as we came through a cutting, over a hill and into the land of Ra: wide, dry, yellow-brown, with mysterious black stones standing before fields of silvery cane; low, conical, hills; upland meadows of golden grass sweeping on to the mass of the Kauvadra Range in the distance. We soon found a lovely broad bay with little grass huts lined up against a white-sand beach at high tide, the blue shapes of islands offshore. Halfway along, standing between the road and the sea, was a round field ringed with trees. As we pulled in, a big youth with a shambling gait came across the green. One eye was turned, the other cloudy, and he seemed to look right past us as in broken English he explained there was a tariff to pay for the privilege of parking. We gave him a dollar and then went for a swim, picking our way over sharp grey coral until it was deep enough to dive into the warm shallow water.

When we came out, a whole tribe of kids was waiting. They surrounded us, chattering and laughing. One of them shimmied up a nearby coconut palm and picked us a green nut each, and one for the road as well. With his cane knife he expertly trimmed the nuts, then sliced off the tops so we could drink the sweet, cool, ineffably refreshing liquid within. I gave him fifty cents, whereupon the rest of the kids crowded hysterically round, clamouring for more. An older man chased them off.

He turned out to be the father of the young man with the turned and cloudy eye, and custodian of the land, which he called 'The Meeting Place', explaining it was exactly halfway between Suva and Lautoka. While we were chatting, a truck full of men on their way back from a day's work cutting cane pulled up and half a dozen people got down. A man in a blue boiler suit produced a bottle of the local gin, made from sugar cane, and two glasses, and we all sat down in a circle in the centre of The Meeting Place and drank it with beer or water chasers. The routine was the same as for *yaqona*, without the handclaps: you took the glass by turns, drank the gin in a swallow, then handed it back to the man with the bottle, who then poured for the next person. The beer, while it lasted, and the water which followed, was passed more casually hand to hand around the circle.

When the gin was gone, which it soon was, another bottle was sent for and then another truck stopped on the road. This, we were told, contained the chief who, with much ribald ceremony, was invited to join us. Those sitting called, and he refused; they called again, with an exaggerated respect verging on outright mockery, saying, *Haere, haere*, or a something very like it; and in due course he yielded and came over. Even so, he had to run the gauntlet of his own men trying, not very hard, to grab his genitals. The boiler-suited man was his brother, and the alert handsome boy I was sitting next to – Gabriel John Koro – his son.

Gabriel's friend, a dark boy with bad skin and curly hair, picked flowers – spider lilies, which grew in great scented clumps around The Meeting Place – and placed them behind our ears. The talk turned to cash crops, specifically the marijuana they had recently started to grow in plantations up on the hills: could we help them sell it into Australia? This easy talk of commerce made way at times for philosophical interludes, as when Gabriel pointed to the mouth and eyes the three shallow depressions on the end of a coconut make, and said: *Look, the monkey face*.

But we are men, I replied, and he happily took up the cry.

We are men! we said.

Gabriel's father, the chief, had fought in World War II, and after a few gins stood up and improvised for us a *haka*, during which he saluted, presented (imaginary) arms and sang a version of *God Save The Queen*, all with the same exaggerated respect bordering on mockery with which his people had called him from the truck. And Gabriel told me something I have been unable, through all my many attempts to quit cigarettes, to forget: *If you want to smoke*, he said, seriously, *you should smoke*.

It was getting on for dusk by the time we finished the second bottle of gin. Light faded on the sea, erasing the horizon and turning the offshore islands to pale shadows of themselves: there the dead went down into the underworld. A cool wind sprang up and rattled in the leaves. We got up to go, not so much drunk as high on good humour and bonhomie. Blackspot fetched Isikeli's bag of *yaqona* from the car and we gave it to the chief as a *sevu sevu*, then said our goodbyes and drove on to the Raki Raki Hotel, where we had a few more beers with a couple of lads in the carpark. Later, I smoked a joint in the orchard out the back of the hotel, looking across the fence at more of the strange conical hills you find in Ra, while ripe lemons squished underfoot and the aroma of rotten citrus rose, with the sandflies, in clouds around my ankles.

It is in the hinterland of this part of the country that Degei, in Thomas Williams's words, *the god most generally known in Fiji*, lives. *He is*, the missionary continues, *the subject of no emotion or sensation, nor of any appetite, except hunger. The serpent . . . is his adopted shrine. Some traditions represent him with the head and part of the body of that reptile, the rest of his form being stone . . . he passes a monotonous existence in a gloomy cavern – the hollow of an inland rock near the N.E. end of Viti Levu – evincing no interest in anyone but his attendant, Uto, and giving no signs of life beyond eating, answering his priest, and changing his position from one side to the other.*

Williams also mentions songs the people of Rakiraki, where Uto attends every feast, compose about the god and his priest: the example he quotes is a grumbling dialogue in which the two lament the poor portions (in this case of turtle) laid aside for them: *Indeed, Uto! This is very bad. How is it? We made them men, placed them on the earth, gave them food, and yet they share with us only the under-shell. Uto, how is this?* Uto's reply is not recorded, but the fragment thereby loses none of its grim, Beckettian flavour.

Degei was known all over the archipelago, and snakes were revered even on islands where they do not naturally occur; where they do, they guarded sacred groves, places where fertility rites were held, and caves where the dead were buried; in some parts, when a snake was found it was picked up, anointed with oil, laid on a soft cloth and taken to the local temple. Nevertheless, each locality also had its own tutelary god or gods, about whose sexual adventures obscene tales were told. He or she it was who spoke directly to the priest, coming down, during the *yaqona* trance, into the temple via a strip of *tapa* tied to one of the back corner posts.

As there were many local gods, so the path by which the dead left this world was usually via some local landmark, often by way of a plunge into the sea, as at Raki Raki Ra. But the ultimate road was the same for all, though not all would arrive safely at Bulu, the land of the dead. Whatever gate it took, the spirit came first to a solitary outcrop of hard reddish clay spotted with black boulders, to the right of which was a grove of trees and on the left cheerless hills. Here the spirit had to throw the sperm whale tooth given it on burial at a pandanus tree; if he hit it, he could then ascend the hill to await the spirits of his strangled wife or wives. If he missed, he was doomed to remain alone and forever in that place. And if he hit it, but his friends and relatives neglected to strangle his wife or wives, he had, like an unmarried man, to go on alone. The spirit of a bachelor was unlucky, needing to avoid the clutches of the Great Woman. Even if it did, it still had to confront Naqanaqa, a bitter hater of unwedded men, whose vigilance and enmity was so great it was said that no single man had ever actually got past him: they were dashed to pieces like rotten firewood on a great black stone. No wonder, then, that marriage, even though it could land you in jail, was preferred to bachelorhood.

The married men, along with the spirits of their wives, proceeded by canoe to a town called Nabaqatai, in which lived both real people and the unreal examiners of the dead. Because spirits only travel in straight lines, the doors of the houses of Nabaqatai were always opposite each other. A parrot called twice to announce each arrival of a spirit canoe, alerting Samu and his brothers, the examiners of the dead, aka the Destroyers of Souls. They hid themselves in mangroves on the other side of the town and placed a *tabu* on the path; if the spirit was brave, it would defy the *tabu*, but it would still have to face Samu. Liars and boasters were destroyed; truth-tellers had to beat Samu in a fight before they could pass on to meet Degei. Those Samu killed, he and his brothers ate; those he wounded wandered forever in limbo.

Even then their trials were not over. On top of Degei's mountain was a precipice where a steering oar was set up. The spirit was questioned again and directed to sit either upon the end of the oar, which extended out over an abyss at whose bottom was a lake, or on its base on the land. The oar was then tipped up, throwing those sitting out on it down into the lake, through whose waters they swam to the land of the dead below. The others, the elect, Degei returned to the land of the living as gods.

In Bulu itself, spirits lived as they do on earth, only in better, larger bodies. The most favoured inhabited Burotu, an Elysium of scented groves and cloudless skies; but the cowardly and the profane suffered arcane punishments, the worst of which was to be condemned forever to beat a heap of filth with a club. Clearly, not many attained even this fallen heaven, especially considering that the souls of men killed by other men were held to have been utterly extinguished, and those whose bodies had been eaten had their souls simultaneously consumed by the gods.

Next morning, we drove on through the Land of Ra. Fields of sugar cane, Asian cattle, Indian peasants, Fijian villages, black rocks and brown dry grass, the yellowy green of mangroves, blue sea and islands offshore a paler blue. When we came to a turnoff, Blackspot, who was driving, took it, heading inland towards Mt Victoria.

What're you doing? I asked. He was looking particularly Irish this morning; I suspected him of drinking in his room.

Don't you remember, he grinned. *There's gold in them thar hills.*

I knew the Australian giant Western Mining had their gold-producing Emperor Mine up here somewhere – along with Degei's cave – but that didn't seem to be what Blackspot was talking about. *What do you mean?* I said, with more asperity.

The brig Eliza, he said. *You've read all the books. Don't you know the story?*

Oh for fuck's sake, I said, *it's that buried treasure again, isn't it?* and stopped talking to him.

He didn't seem fazed, not even when a flat tyre then an over-heating engine turned us back. He was smiling to himself as we bumped down the mountain again and went on along the coast road through the nondescript towns of Ba and Lautoka to a resort called the Anchorage at Vuda Point, where Fijians are said to have landed when they first came out of the west to these islands. A hurricane had ravaged the resort two years before and they were only now rebuilding. We thought it might do as a location for the Retreat our heroes were employed to construct, and on that basis approached the Kiwi owner. *Why not?* Jack Ferguson said.

The beach at Vuda was immense. You could imagine the unsung from any of the islands of the western Pacific washing up here. I picked my way past a litter of plastic and went for a swim while a pair of white herons drove off a pair of blue herons; when I returned to the car, an Indian fisherman, Abdul Hafiz, had taken Blackspot in hand. He showed us his two boats and also that of his second cousin, Amzad Ali, the man who tried to hijack an Air New Zealand jet at Nadi in an attempt to force the reinstatement of the Bavadra Government; Ali, a Moslem, was thwarted when the co-pilot knocked him out with a full bottle of whisky. His boat was a smart white and aquamarine speedster moored out in the wide blue river.

Cattle pulling a load of firewood crossed the tidal river mouth as the sun set in the western ocean. A man walked along one of the miniature railway lines that serve the cane fields, nonchalantly driving two cattle, two goats in his train. We went up to Abdul's house to have a cup of tea in the pastel-green sitting room with his three brothers, his sister, their mother and a part-Melanesian pregnant sister-in-law. Everyone gathered around as we were shown photos of lads already in other lands, part of a sustained attempt to persuade us to sponsor one of the brothers into Australia. They would give us half the family lands – river flats, cane fields, gardens, orchards – if we would do it. It was hard explaining we did not have the means to employ anyone, and that without a job no one would be allowed to immigrate.

Along with the photos were two newspaper clippings. One of the brothers, Abdul Samat, had caught a five-metre white pointer shark:

here was the photograph to prove it. He had also, spectacularly, rescued four men from a burning boat, then, even more impressively, gone back and secured the engine. A thin, quiet, shy young man with the reddened, sleepy eyes and greyish scurfy skin of an habitual *yaqona* drinker, he smiled and took our admiration as his due. I exchanged addresses with Abdul Hafiz before we left, and a brief correspondence ensued: *My family talks with clean heart and what we say we do it*, wrote Hafiz.

We drove to Nadi, checked in at a malodorous guest house and ate goat curry for dinner. Over the meal, Blackspot finally came clean – or as clean as he could get. He said there was a tradition in his family of knowledge of the whereabouts of some of the 34,000 Spanish dollars in gold coins the American brig *Eliza* was carrying when, on her way from Sydney to Sandalwood Bay on Vanua Levu in 1808, she was wrecked on Mocea Reef, south of Nairai Island. A renegade Swede named Charlie Savage is said to have buried a portion of the lost treasure on Viti Levu, where it still lies, along with the bones of many of those who coveted it. Armed with his family tradition and a few contacts, Blackspot said he'd researched the matter in Suva and thought he had a good idea where to start looking. When I said that was absurd, he protested: *You can't deny me a recce, can you?* And, mockingly: *Anyway, you've got your treasure hunt, why can't I have mine?*

What do you mean? I asked coldly.

That fucking lost continent of Mu or whatever it is you're looking for, he said.

I was furious with him. I lay awake in my bed for hours, dissecting his personality, hating him for his joke on me, hating myself for getting sucked in by it. Trying to deny the point of the spoof, I refused even to see that it was hilarious. Throughout my broken, vengeful sleep, the hysterical barking of dogs did not once stop; in the early pre-dawn grey, the crowing of roosters began. It was our last day, and we intended to check out the resort hotels before going to the airport. Putting aside my baleful resolutions of the night before, I decided to behave as if nothing had happened. Or was I saving my revenge for later?

There was an exhibition of primitive art in the echoing glass and steel lobby of the Regent, mostly sculptures from New Guinea, along with some lovely naïve paintings of village life by a woman simply called Grace. The art sat oddly amongst the outré flower arrangements, and was largely ignored by the well-heeled, mostly Japanese and American guests passing to and fro. Nothing for us to do there, so we took a turn around the pool, then went to go. As we passed through the lobby a lift hissed open and half a dozen men in suits and sunglasses emerged.

Is that Porter? I said to Blackspot.

He looked; but the man was already walking away in the other direction and, since we had only ever seen Porter in shorts and a T-shirt, it was hard to say.

The Fijian Resort was full of Kiwis and Aussies instead of Yanks and Japs. We drank several cups of coffee with a couple of aging Tauranga lasses, Sue and Pat, who were holidaying there together. All their food was flown in with them; they were bussed from the airport to the hotel, never needing to leave their capsule for more than an instant: an advantage, they thought, given the uncertain times. The resort was on a small offshore island reached by a causeway. Sacred Point, on the south or seaward side, had been built over with ersatz *bure* and beyond was one of the few reefless white-sand beaches we had seen. *Artificial*, the waiter said. *They trucked it in.* I asked him why they were so hard to find. *Simple*, he said. *The best ones already have resorts on them.* Nevertheless, there was one place: Natadola, aka Ten Dollar Beach. The turn-off was on our way back to Nadi.

It was one of the loveliest beaches I have seen: a brilliant stretch of golden sand, perhaps two kilometres long, between truncated bluffs; a high, glassy green swell breaking into white foam, blue water beyond and nothing but scrubby sandhills behind. We crossed a single-lane wooden bridge and bumped along the track for a while, then stopped in amongst the brush, there to roll the last of our dope into a joint. We scattered the seeds in the sandhills and went to the beach to smoke it.

As we lit up, a swarm of black dots came down onto the sand at the opposite end, growing larger as it made its way towards us, and turning out to be made up of a dozen or so kids from the local village. There was hardly enough time to finish the smoke before they arrived. Without any preliminaries, they sat down in a semi-circle around us, unwrapped from handkerchiefs or pulled from their pockets collections of sea shells, and a solemn convocation began. The rules of trade were precise: one shell at least to be purchased from each vendor, to be paid for at the nominated price, but in a lump sum at the end, the money to be divided up later. The shells, each gathered personally by the vendor on the reef at low tide, were of the highest quality, and the exchange proceeded in the best possible humour. Among the goods were items of manufacture, including a necklace of tiny spiral shells and a kind of round black seed strung on nylon fishing line which I bought off a shy dark girl called Emma. When we said we had been in Raki Raki, they yelled as one: *Raki Raki Ra!* as if it were indeed a place of wonders. We totalled up our purchases: we spent ten dollars on shells at Natadola.

We took a teenage girl back to town with us. Toraki wore white, and had several of her front teeth missing. I could see her frowning to herself in the rear-vision mirror most of the way, nervous to be alone in a car with two white boys; but if you caught her eye, she smiled. Outside, red earth showed through the tilting hills of silver-tasselled cane, where old women in white saris flicked with bendy sticks at the flanks of slow oxen, and men with straw hats rode blue tractors. When the wind came the fields shimmered. Tiny pink, yellow, green, blue, white-domed antique mosques graced the landscape. Pine trees were burning on the hills up the back, the smoke making a sepia haze in the air and turning the clouds prismatic. The plantations, said Toraki, had been set alight by young unemployed men who wanted the land for growing cane.

On the strip in Nadi, I bought a red shirt with pineapples on it, and Blackspot a yellow one with purple guitars. Outside a music shop we stopped to listen to a reggae version of the old Don Gibson song *Sea of Heartbreak*, recorded by artists as diverse as Johnny Cash, The Searchers and Poco: *The light in the harbour/Don't shine for me/I'm like a lost ship/Adrift on the sea/A sea of heartbreak.* Two schoolboys told us it was by local hero Marika Gata, and found us a copy of the tape. I tried to spend my last few coins in an Indian souvenir shop. *Everything I have for this miniature kava bowl,* I said, showing the man the money. He refused. He did not believe me. He was convinced I must have more than that.

Our last day seemed blessed: we had discovered both a major location and a theme song for the movie. At the airport I ate some raw fish in coconut milk, followed by pieces of pineapple. I did not learn until later about the fish, a delicacy, which feeds in the waters below the ubiquitous seaside latrines. Blackspot ceremoniously tore up his map and, as a peace offering, bought two litre bottles of Frigate Rum duty free, one for each of us. A dark-eyed girl smiling and waving from the terminal was the last thing I saw. It was raining when we stopped over in Brisbane, raining on the grey Sydney streets we had left behind only two weeks before, as if even perpetual inundation could not wash away their sadness and their grime.

Next day I had lunch with a friend at a café in Glebe. When the waitress put down on the table the warm duck salad with raspberry dressing I had ordered, I realised something was badly wrong: I had contracted hepatitis A. The following months were blurred with nausea, persistent diarrhoea and a dragging sense of foreboding, during which the bottle of black rum sat on the bookcase like a visible sign of the doom my ailing liver was telegraphing to my brain. Hardly the best state of mind in which to write the first draft of a screenplay, but I soldiered on, a yellowish, big-bellied, hollow-eyed spectre with stick-like arms and legs, while Blackspot wavered between exaggerated concern for my health and helpless frustration at my intransigence.

I can't blame him or the illness for the demise of the film; it had more to do with my insistence that the treatment's female lead, Anne, become in the draft a Fijian woman, so as to allow us to explore the political and cultural predicament in the islands. Her name was to be, of course, Maria. Blackspot did everything he could, short of firing me, to head me off, and even so the Film Commission bore with us for a while, giving us more money for a rewrite and only cutting us loose when that, too, failed to conform to the original treatment.

This reverse, and the rather more protracted failure of *Ghosts of Empire* to become a film, taught me one lesson: unless you set out to tell a life story, the autobiographical has no place in screenplay writing. Especially if, as in my case, you are trying to dramatise unresolved or problematic elements. You can no more smuggle bits of your life into the design of a film than you can express personal angst in the plan for a building. If the finished work bears some relation to your own self and its preoccupations, well and good; but that is never the place to start. You start with a character, or characters, and a story, and everything you do afterwards is at the service of these.

A worse casualty was the friendship: Blackspot and I didn't speak to each other for years after the wreck of *Running to Paradise*, and, although we sorted it out before he died, not long ago, of heart failure, we both carried the burden of that missed opportunity for a decade or more. Nevertheless, one of the consequences of my meeting Keli, Karoline, Vena, the Marias, Tui, Lily, Taka and others, along with Blackspot's relentless satire on my search and the prolonged wrangles I had with him, was that I became able to make a clearer distinction between fantasy and reality. It was like learning the difference between loving sex and sexual love. I also knew, finally, who we were: Blackspot was the piratical hell-raiser and burnout, and I the steady-rolling man who betrayed him.

4

Home

O N A WEDNESDAY MORNING I CAUGHT THE SCHOOL BUS OUT of the village and, as we laboured up the Old Bog Road, saw Sophie in amongst the kids in their blue and maroon uniforms going over the hill for the second day of the first week of the new year.

Where are you off to? she asked, seeing the leather hold-all I carried.

New Zealand, I said. *I'm going to the Centennial of my old primary school.*

How interesting, she said. *I hope you have a great time.*

What was it made me, at that very instant, with the blue bay below flickering past the grey trunks of the gums, doubt it? *I hope so too,* I said. *Hope I don't turn out to be the ghost at the feast.*

The words, no sooner out of my mouth, sounded ungrateful and forlorn, and if there had been a way I would have taken them back. The ghost at the feast: Macbeth, surely? Why did I feel so burdened, rather than blithe, happy and free?

Sophie got off at Umina and I went on to Woy Woy to catch a train to Central, a bus to the airport and a budget flight on Kiwi Airlines to Hamilton. With the hours spent travelling, the unforeseen delays and time lost across the Tasman, it was night before the plane lumbered down in slanting rain towards what appeared to be a cow paddock on the flat rich grasslands south of the town. The shadowy black and white Friesians grazing through the perimeter fence raised their heads in mild alarm as the wheels thumped onto the concrete strip. We disemplaned and hurried across the open field to a corrugated-iron shed to stand, like cattle ourselves, in single file between zig-zag chain barriers while rain rattled on the roof and the questionable among us were hauled off to have their bags examined. I was lucky, passed with only a searching glance, and soon found my friend and her partner among the small crowd waiting in the terminal apparently still being built around them.

They had to get up early next morning to drive to New Plymouth, so they dropped me off in town at about eight o'clock. I made a booking at the bus terminal, then sat down at a café to await the opening of the museum, where a small exhibition of Philip Clairmont's work was hung. Nothing I had not seen before, but everything I wanted to see again. At midday, with a head full of jagged colour, tipping space and a yawing sense of the provisional nature of identity, I made my way back to the terminal. The bus to Auckland picked up and set down in every small town along the way to the metropolitan area, then wound slowly among the outer suburbs, stopping in places I had not seen since adolescence, or had never seen. At Papakura, a Polynesian drag queen who spent the trip rolling two gleaming steel balls between her fingers got out and went into a shop called Mystic Junction, while at the newsagency, a nondescript middle-aged man who reminded me of my father put down his cardboard suitcase and thankfully, tearfully embraced a nondescript middle-aged woman who looked nothing like my mother.

Down by the wharves in the city I caught another bus to Avon-dale. My sister's plain weatherboard house had been opened up and added on to; new wood on the deck gleamed under a luxuriant bougainvillea. It was about four on a steamy afternoon. She was at the kitchen bar preparing food. *Look at me!* she said. I looked. She seemed much the same. *No, look at me*, she said again. I still did not notice the scar above her lip where a skin cancer had been removed, and felt vaguely derelict of my responsibilities when it had to be pointed out. She is two years older than me, and sometimes treated me as you do something of no great value which nevertheless is unquestionably yours. Out of inertia I usually went along with this, while keeping my own counsel as to what the real state of affairs was.

With her partner and their three children, we had a picnic tea in a small park on the northern shores of the Manukau, sitting on a rug spread out over the green grass while the flat greyish water extended from our feet to the hazy other shore. I felt again the confusion of returning to my country of birth: everything looked at once familiar and strange, instantly recognisable yet lacking in detail, like a world seen through the cloudy veils of anaesthesia. Avoiding the fetid pile of someone's clothing abandoned on a slope beside a dripping tap, I changed in the toilet block and went with my niece for a swim out in the warm sandy-bottomed sea. Later, in the dusk, as the crickets began, we toiled up the hill to the car and drove back to Avondale, hoping for an early start next morning.

I remember hardly anything of our trip down the island next day. I know my sister and I stopped at Madonna Falls to sip the miraculous water sliding down the slatey rock into a slippery pool, and again at Raurimu, where we climbed an old tower made of splintery timber and rusty iron and looked out over that marvel of railway engineering, the spiral. And at Horopito, I saw a house I imagined could have been ours had we continued to live in that part of the country: a wooden villa with a green corrugated-iron roof and white weatherboard walls, standing alone down a back road on the western slopes of the mountain. There was a bay window on one side at the front and a veranda on the other; twin corrugated-iron water tanks stood on the tankstand outside the kitchen; a straggly plum tree leaned over the roof at the side, and out the front was a row of hydrangea bushes and a macrocarpa hedge. A thick plume of wood smoke rose from the chimney, for inside, perhaps, they were burning black matai or maire logs from the felled forest, so durable one might last a whole evening in the grate. In the fields of knee-high grass round about, the bright cones of lupins rose up yellow, purple, red, blue; while the rain, breaking like long stems of glass on the hulks of cars rusting in the paddocks, on the unpainted falling-down sheds and abandoned houses, and on the white distance of the unseen mountain, persisted.

We met our elder sister among the throngs of pleased, self-conscious adults at the school and went in together to sign up. There was a hitch: my registration had gone astray. There was no identity tag for me, nor was I listed on any of the sheets of names. The woman at the desk went red-faced with embarrassment, or was it irritation? *We're booked out*, she said. *There aren't any places left.* I could see past the gate-keeper a room full of photographs, and felt again that piercing childhood fear of exclusion.

I've come all the way from Australia, I said. *I rang . . .*

The woman sighed.

My elder sister intervened. *Surely*, she said, *one more won't make that much difference?*

Suddenly the woman smiled and relaxed. *Of course*, she said. *You're right. One more won't matter.* As my sisters moved through to look at the photos, she took my thirty dollars, wrote out a name tag and gave me the small gifts everybody got: a notepad; an inscribed blue Bic biro; two cloudy plastic bottles with blue lids, one containing volcanic sand, the other mountain air.

The photographs were of all the many classes there had been over the last hundred years – or at least, all that had come before a camera. Like everyone else, I gravitated to the ones in which I might find my own freckled, toothy, tousled image and a gratifying sense of remembrance of the barefoot ordinariness of my childhood. I had then, for the only time in my life, gone by a nickname, Eddie, which I still mourned, since it did not travel with me when, aged ten, I left that place.

Most of the class photos in my era, the 1950s and early 1960s, were taken by my mother's brother, whose business it was to travel from school to school photographing classes then selling the prints back to the parents and the schools. Though usually a rather stiff and awkward man, he had a manner of dealing with kids which was anything but, calling us indiscriminately, hilariously, *Snow* and *Curly* and *Freckles* and *Ginger* and *Blackie* as he sent us off to stand in our lines. I still recall the tremulous mingling of pleasure and dread in these occasions: pleasure that he was my uncle and dread that he would embarrass me by alluding to the fact. He never did, beyond a slight squeeze of the arm or extra pat on the head as I took my place, as one of the smaller boys, towards the end of one of the back rows, where we stood side by side on plain wooden benches.

I had not been thinking of our dead sister, but now, having confirmed that Eddie was alive and well back then, I realised she would be here too and went looking for her. It was a shock when, having identified a year and a class in which she should have appeared, I found her missing: as if her absence from us now were somehow prefigured by this absence back then. There must have been a simple reason for it: she was away sick that day, perhaps. Nevertheless, as I moved quickly on to other years and found her sitting round-faced and optimistic with the other girls along the front, I felt a pricking behind my eyes, the choke of unshed tears in my throat, a tipping sense of grief. The Centennial was nothing to her; she had left all the yearning and nostalgia behind long ago.

The dream I had that night might have been provoked by this stumble into unexpected sorrow; then again, it is one I have had before. We were staying at the Junction in a ski lodge to which our elder sister belonged, and after a buffet meal in the company of familiar strangers in the enormous marquee, it was there we went to sleep. Once we had chosen our bunks and found our sheets and blankets, I went to bed and drifted, down, down and out into a confusion of images, stumbling half blind in the debris of the underside. Here were days like stones bumping together in a roiling river. Here were houses in which the absences were more palpable, more resonant, than any living presence had been. Here were skies the colour of rage, of silence, of tears.

Out of the phantasmagoria, I saw myself walking. It was the path through the bush that led from Burns Street to the town baths. Midway along I stopped before a pile of litter on the forest floor, a mound I raked open, bird-like, with my foot: glittering within was a lizard, the skin iridescent, the body undulant, the eye bright and empty. Then, suddenly, in the way of dreams, I was on the mountainside, toiling upward on a track zig-zagging through snow drifts towards the clouds that loured about the hidden peak. A shadowy form was beside me, holding my hand, walking with me as we made our attempt upon the summit: our dead sister.

At once I began to feel afraid. The enormous slope of the mountain loomed above us, an enigma I could not comprehend. It was white and hidden as death. I slowed, stopped; felt my sister's hand slip loose from mine, and watched her slight, bent figure climb staunchly on until the clouds reached down to enfold her. I was left alone on the mountainside, like a carriage of bones from which the soul has departed. And then, instead of turning and going back, I laid myself down among the hieroglyphs of snow drifted across red volcanic rock, black soil, to wait for the fall that would cover me, the oblivion of my own end.

When I woke into the rain of Saturday morning, head aching, body stiff and sore, dragging myself to consciousness, I could still see, just for a moment, that shrouded form going on and up into the nether world, without a backward glance, a goodbye or a regret, like one whose mission was over. I heard my sisters talking in the next room, one sitting on the other's bed, just as they used to do when we were growing up. It was comforting to listen to their voices without quite being able or even wanting to hear what they were saying. I lay there, going over the dream, fixing it in my mind, for, although it recurs, the details are always slightly different: what is common to all versions is the parting on the mountainside and the aching sadness – whether for her leaving or for myself being left, I am never sure – with which I lie down in the snow.

Or was it the sadness of the place? Ohakune began as a surveyors' camp in a natural clearing in the middle of Te Rangakaika, a forest of enormous trees on the south-west slopes of Ruapehu. Not long before John Rochfort, the government surveyor who cut the path that would be followed by the Main Trunk Line, pitched his tent near the junction of the Mangawhero and Mangateitei rivers, a professional gentleman explorer, Englishman J. H. Kerry-Nicholls, passed through the area on his way to cross the southern border of Te

Rohe Potae, the forbidden land of the King Country. He described *a perfect network of broken, rugged ranges, which in many places appeared to have been hurled about by the terrific throes of an earthquake. The soil everywhere was of the richest description and many of the colossal trees averaged from thirty to forty feet in circumference at the base, and towered above us to the height of considerably over 100 feet, forming a grand canopy* ... He also mentions that, out of this canopy, even when the sky above was clear and blue, a constant, drenching rain fell from the saturated foliage of the giant trees.

Kerry-Nicholls and his companion and interpreter, J. A. Turner, camped for the night at the place known to us as kids as Lake's Reserve, where two ancient volcanic craters have filled with fresh water. *A little before dusk we came suddenly out of the forest into a small, circular, open flat, fringed with toe toe and covered with a luxuriant growth of native grass. On our left, a grassy ridge rose in a semicircle, and all around the open space the trees rose one above the other in the most attractive way, while a variety of shrubs dispersed about in the most picturesque order, made the place appear like a perfect garden. Right in the very centre of the natural parterre was Rangatauaiti, a beautiful lake of a completely circular form, and the water of which, looking like a polished mirror, was of the deepest blue. Beyond this flat, the native name of which was Rangitanua, and separated only by a low ridge crowned by a luxuriant growth of vegetation, was another open space, in the centre of which was Rangatauanui, an oval-shaped lake larger than the former, but in which the water was the same limpid blue. The trees on the further side rose in a dense forest growth, and as they came close down to the water, they were reflected in the depths below with grand and beautiful effect. In fact, the whole surroundings of these lakes appeared so attractive after our long journey through the forest that we seemed to have got into a quiet corner of paradise.*

Kerry-Nicholls's account is predicated upon the fact that he is the first to see these sights, and his book, with its wearying superlatives, its boyish enthusiasms and its unconscious brutalities, never once questions this assumption of primacy. In fact, he was not the first but the last to see most of what he saw, for within a few years of his journey an orgy of destruction began all along the path he took, beginning, perhaps, with the unaccountable ruin of the Pink and White Terraces in the 1886 eruption of Tarawera and continuing, further south, with the cutting of the railway and the consequent desolation of the forests.

For with the railway came the sawmillers. It seems incredible now that Ohakune was once part of a forest stretching miles in every direction. Its eradication was so complete it might never had been. Trees hundreds of years old were felled with axes and saws, dragged away by teams of bullocks to the mills to be cut up, taken from thence to the station and railed away who knows where. Perhaps some of them ended up on the shores of Blackwattle Bay. What could not be milled was burnt, and the stumps, grey and fire-blackened, in my childhood still lay out in the green fields like the bones of prehistoric beasts. They were the origin of most of the firewood we burned on cold winter nights and remain a resource for locals even today.

When I was a child, and enamoured of Greek mythology, I used to wonder if these trees, like the trees of Greece, had souls which could sometimes be glimpsed dancing in the form of young girls in forest clearings. And then it seemed to me that the wailing I heard sometimes in the clear, still mountain air, the rushing of a wind that did not move the leaves in the beech trees, the agony of silent screams that beat about the windows of the house, was caused by the souls of trees dying but not yet dead.

The ancient forest was destroyed in a paroxysm of rage or greed and, by the 1950s, what was left behind was not some bright shining brave new world but a dump, a sadness, a dereliction. Houses, grey as the stumps in the paddocks, sagged on their weedy sections. Grass grew down the middle of gravelly roads. Nameless bits of machinery rusted in the shadow of empty buildings. Even the fields where carrots and potatoes grew fat in the red volcanic earth enriched with ash from the burnt bush straggled hopelessly away into stagnant puddles and choked ditches. The place looked not so much new as abandoned.

On a trip back here in 1980 with a photographer friend, we found an image of this sadness: out on the Rangataua Road was a forsaken four-room cottage, whose twin windows and gaping door from the road resembled the face of some gaunt survivor of catastrophe. We stopped the car, got out, climbed the fence and walked over to it through the knee-high dripping grass. It was full of ghosts. On a wall next to the fireplace, and again on the wall by the doorway leading into the hall, someone had scratched the word HELP in tall, trembly letters. Across the floors lay a scatter of barbed wire, broken glass, rotted wood. In the tiny kitchen, as if built for dwarfs, was the red rust and debris of a shattered coal range. And on the bedroom wall, torn from newspapers and pasted up, were a dozen or more images of brides on their wedding days, their grooms absent, their white dresses gone dusty and brown with the years.

Perhaps it is absurd to seek the sources of personal melancholy in a sense of place. Nostalgia for the previous state of the landscape is anyway based on a misconception: had change not occurred, the town itself would not have existed and there would be no one here to recall what used to be. Nevertheless, emotional truths exist beyond the facts of history; the mistake may be to seek to validate or explain them with reference to historical processes, when they are more likely rooted in personal or familial experience. It is probable that my notion of the place as some kind of paradise lost is really because my childhood here was happy; our family, during the thirteen years we spent here, a seemingly happy family; and it was only after we left that the stresses and strains which broke us apart from each other and, in some cases, broke us apart in ourselves as well, manifested. And yet . . . could not a landscape and a history stand as images for that encroaching disarray, that violent sundering? My father thought so.

In his Masters thesis, *Community and School in Ohakune (a descriptive, participant-observer study)*, he wrote: . . . *the scattered haphazard quality of its settlement, its untidy appearance, have contributed towards the defensive and yet disparaging attitude that has been observed in so many of its inhabitants. Unsolved economic difficulties reinforce this view and generate a conviction that things will never be any different. This conviction in turn gives rise to a dubious outlook on change which hardens into resistance. Though not satisfied with conditions as they are, 'Kune' folk are wary of anything that is different.*

Saturday was a hubbub and a blur, a day at the school spent threading in and out of rooms full of people themselves threading past and present together to make – what? A dress to wear to the dance that night, perhaps. I had never been to an event like this before and was unprepared for the way in which people anxiously or hopefully scanned the faces they met, then, inevitably, let their eyes drop to the name tag below for confirmation or a disappointment. What was it we expected from our shared past, if not the intelligence that our futures had taken us away from each other? What did I want? Like everyone else, I wanted to meet those who would say, *Yes, I remember you, you're . . .* and then would I know any better who I was?

It was in the History Room, where a black and white National Film Unit documentary shot at the school in the 1950s was playing, that I met my first teacher. I was one of those children who took to school for a while as a novelty and a diversion; when I realised it was a permanent commitment, I refused to go and had to be dragged screaming and kicking down the cavernous corridor of the infant block, off which all the classrooms opened, to the Head Mistress's office. I no longer remember if the hand that gripped me tightly by the upper arm belonged to my father or my mother, nor what happened when we got to the end of that corridor: just my stubborn feet bumping along the wooden boards of the floor and the monstrous sound of my own wailing bouncing off the walls. Like other recalcitrant children, I solved the problem of compulsory attendance by falling in love with my teacher, Miss Reddington.

This infatuation survived her troubling name change part way through the year – she married and became Mrs Hancock – and now, in the History Room, when a small round woman in her fifties with laughing eyes tapped me on the shoulder, I fell into her arms as if I was still that teary five-year-old. She hugged me to her as tightly as she probably did back then, and in her embrace I felt the past forty years fall away. When we drew back and looked at each other, I thought she did not seem much older than I was then, and she explained she'd started teaching when she was very young, a girl, really, only just out of her teens. What else did we talk about? I forget. One of the frustrations of these occasions is that no conversation goes uninterrupted, and soon she was drawn away to prove the memory of some other overgrown infant; but the feeling of that embrace still has not left me, as if true nurture, once given, can never be lost again.

It was also in the History Room that I met the older sister of my first girlfriend. I already knew that Florence Moule was dead; my mother had told me how she had died a few years before, of leukemia, leaving a husband and three children. Florence was a skinny girl with glossy chestnut hair and bony knees, who could run as fast and fight as well as any boy. Our love affair was a thing of kicks and blows. Sitting opposite each other in Primer Four, we showed our affection by belting each other over the knuckles with our rulers or kicking each other's shins under the desks. At lunchtime, we played chase, contriving to end up as often as possible in a giggling heap on the soft carpet of needles under the pines which grew along one side of the playgrounds. Once, after school, we were almost caught by a teacher kissing behind the concrete steps on the shadowy side of the infant block. And when her parents visited mine one day, and I was asked to show her round the section, we made a nest in the long grass up the back and did there whatever six- or seven-year-old girls and boys do with each other. Florence once scratched the top off a wart on her knee and, where the blood ran down the inside of her calf, a hundred other warts grew up. As kids, we found this impressive; but when I learned what she died of, I wondered if it was an early sign of disorder in her blood.

Her sister, Merrilyn George, is the author of *Ohakune: Opening to a New World*, subtitled *A District History*. I have my father's copy, with his name written in his own hand on the flyleaf along with the date, 1990: the year both of its publication and his death. Merrilyn had the same wide-set, deep eyes, straight nose and bowed, generous mouth Florence had. She was, as my father had been, a teacher at Ruapehu College. Her history of the district is a vast compendium of information into which many disparate accounts are subsumed; like all good local histories, it is a finite assembly made out of the infinite store of the unsung: one of those books which, if you're interested, open at any page to reveal wonders. But when it came to her sister's death, her eyes filled with tears and she could not go on.

There were photographs in the afternoon, and more informal socialising; then the labours of the local volunteers resumed, as they transformed the marquee from assembly hall back to vast buffet restaurant, and the rest of us milled around uncertainly for a while then drifted off to change for dinner and the dance which was to follow. I was feeling a bit disconsolate. While both my sisters had found old friends to catch up with, I had not: where were the boys who called me Eddie, the ones whose farms I had stayed over at, going round the sheep on the tractor, or feeding out hay to the cattle, or helping night and morning in the milking shed?

I found them that evening, standing round just outside the entrance to the bar, which was another, smaller tent opening off the marquee: Bobby Hammond and his brother John, Barry Wallace, Alan Proud, various others I had known less well. Ken Summerhays, John Trigell and Andrew Weir seemed not to have come, and Brian Culpan, who now lived in Taihape, was too ill, laid low by the cancer which would take him off not long afterwards. Bobby Hammond had been my best friend. He was often at our place and even came away with us on holiday once. The back paddocks of the Hammonds' farm out on the Raetihi Road adjoined the hilly slope opposite our house on Burns Street which we leased as grazing for my sisters' horses, and I spent many happy weekends with them. Bobby had been one of the tallest and I among the smallest boys in our class, so it was a surprise to find that, as a man, while thickset, he was a few inches shorter than me.

I bowled up to him and shook his hand, expecting – I don't know. I suppose I thought we would pick up from where we had left off, and talk perhaps about the way we hunted pukeko with willow bows and bracken arrows. He did not seem particularly pleased to see me; in fact, he was clearly uneasy in my company. We exchanged a few pieces of information, then fell silent. With the others it was the same: every time I tried to start a conversation, their eyes would glaze over and shift; they would shuffle and glance sideways at each other, waiting for me to go away so they could resume their easy talk amongst themselves. Most of them still lived locally – Bobby was farming in the Rangitikei – and saw each other now and again. I was evidently some kind of risky interloper. I hung around for a while listening to them, then drifted off.

What about the girls? I found only one, Jenny Gilbert, married with children and living in Wellington. We had a nice talk as we ate our buffet meal. Her parents had been friends of my parents, and they also knew Stan Frost, my godfather. Stan, the art teacher, a cockney and a bachelor, had not come to the Centennial. He'd retired some years ago to a small bay on the southern shores of Lake Taupo, and was now a recluse, neither seeking nor welcoming company, spending his days fishing and his nights alone in a house which had, Jenny said, filled up with the clutter of years until all that was left were the solitary tracks from room to room among the piled-up newspapers and other junk. He had always seemed so urbane, with his crinkled grey-black hair and kindly eyes, his excellent cooking, his fondness for liqueurs. How had he become so isolated? Stan had a special feeling for our sister and, in a terrible oversight, after her death no one in the family thought to tell him: he heard about it later from a stranger.

When Jenny went to find her husband, I looked around for my sisters. The elder was having the time of her life. She looked regal, exalted, beautiful, surrounded by old girlfriends and old admirers, picking up, it seemed, where she had left off aged fourteen. Perhaps those few extra years made all the difference. My other sister, while she did not move so effortlessly amongst the throng, nevertheless has the social skills to make the most of any situation, however she might actually be feeling. There were enough of her contemporaries to ease her passage into the dance hall, which was where the evening was now going.

Along with so much else, the geography of the old school eluded me, and I did not recall the hall opening off the big marquee to the south: perhaps it had been built after we left. To get there you had to pass through a canvas tunnel which, once the rain started again, turned rapidly into a mud bath. The hall itself was a big oblong wooden building with a stage at one end, chairs round the walls and two rows of bright lights suspended on metal shafts from the high ceiling. Even though the band was already tuning up to play, these lights stayed on, as they did throughout the dance: there would be no skulking in the corners tonight, nowhere for anyone to hide in the shadows.

The band was a local combo, drums, bass, guitar, keyboards, and all, along with the two female backing vocalists, sang. They were good: both self-effacing and dynamic, they knew exactly what their audience wanted. They could charm, flatter, embarrass or cajole dancers onto the floor and, once there, keep them hopping, playing medleys of songs everyone knew: as soon as that frisson of recognition ran through the crowd, coaxing even the shyest out, they'd change the tune for another, just as familiar or beloved, keeping everyone afloat on a wave of nostalgia. Pretty soon the floor was packed, at first with couples who waltzed or fox-trotted elegantly around the room, as the adults used to do at school dances in the 1960s, later with the more usual, indiscriminate flail of bodies in motion.

I was now in an agony of self-consciousness. I hung around the door for a while, amongst the press of people coming and going to and from the marquee and the bar, and, when that thinned out, tried to find a corner down the back where no one could see me: a futile hope in the brilliance of that room. Sometimes I went out to the marquee or the bar, but there were only those intent on conversation with their friends or serious drinking. I had no appetite for the thin weak beer, nor for whisky either. I would happily have walked the couple of kilometres back to the ski lodge, but I had no coat, a cold wind had blown up in the afternoon, and now a sleety, slanting rain was rattling on the canvas. I stood for a while at the north entrance to the marquee, looking out at the mist hissing through the macrocarpas, then went back to the dance hall.

I don't mean to sound self-pitying. Everyone knows what it's like to be alone on the fringes of a dancing room, the one without a partner, the one lonely and alone. Even if it's never happened to you, you know. There's a ghost at every feast and this time it happened to be me. Perhaps I was still mourning the loss of Eddie; perhaps I was just blue; or was I an embodiment of that *defensive and yet disparaging attitude* my father had identified? I've always been an observer, relishing the view from the edge, the outsider's peculiar perspective; but I prefer seeing to being seen. I hated the way my baleful presence took away, however minutely, from the pleasure of others, but could find no way to prevent it. Various kind souls saw my predicament and came to ask if I was all right. *Yes*, I lied, *I'm fine*. And thought, but did not say: *Leave me alone*.

Now the dancers spontaneously made two lines along the floor, facing one another; those at the end furthest from the band joined and made a couple and danced madly up between the lines to the head, then rejoined and laughed and cheered as the next pair made their hilarious way up the avenue of dancers. It was wonderful fun, one of the best dances I haven't been in. I can't remember how it ended, though I recall my sisters coming flushed and sweating from the floor, their eyes lit with delight. I guess it got too late for the kids, the band called it a night, and everybody straggled away into the rainy dark.

One thing sticks in my mind. A member of a First Fifteen rugby team my father had coached in the 1950s came up to me on the fringes of the dance and told me a story about one of Dad's coaching innovations. Lacking members for the chorus of the Gilbert and Sullivan opera he was producing (*The Pirates of Penzance*), he announced that only those players willing to audition would be selected for the next match, and then made the practice of dancing a means of finessing the ball-playing skills of his team. This man, whose name I forget, at one point looked hard at me and said, as if quoting a line from one of those comic operas: *You can't grow old without regrets, as I'm sure you will agree*.

But I did not agree. *What happens, happens*, I said. *You have to see things as they are and just go on*.

At the Sunday morning church service we sat, like kids again, in rows in the big marquee, while various people came and went on the stage up the front. One was a hundred-year-old woman, the oldest surviving pupil of the school, who must have enrolled around the time the twentieth century began. Another was the local Member of

Parliament, the then Prime Minister, Jim Bolger. He made a clumsy attempt at electioneering, spruiking his government's loathed education policy to an audience which included many teachers and seemed aggrieved when he was heckled from the stalls. And then, after one last feast, more speeches and goodbyes, along with promises to meet again, it was over.

This was early afternoon. We'd agreed that, afterwards, we'd go out into the landscape for a picnic. I'd learned on my last visit to Ohakune that there were two other lakes nearby, so secret we did not even know about them when we lived there. I thought perhaps this was where we might go, but my sister refused. I never found out exactly why, only that something had passed between her and our mother there on a previous visit. In fact she wanted to go straight back to Auckland, and by the time we talked her out of that there wasn't much time left for picnicking. Instead, we decided just to drive up the mountain.

The rain of the night before had blown away and it was a lovely, late-summer day. As we climbed through a remnant of Te Rangakaika, the forest of vast trees, tawai, rimu and matai, started to shrink, change, thin out, until the bush was mostly just mountain beech and mingi mingi. It took on a more formal cast, like a Japanese garden. The rough ridges of the volcano, which look so smooth at a distance, loomed raw and red above us until erased by the snowline. We came to a lay-by where a few cars were parked. *Here*, I said and we pulled off the road, stopped and got out.

The air was icy cold, fresh as time. I walked out onto a bluff, below which flowed the beginnings of the Mangawhero, the river which, lower down, runs behind our old house in Burns Street. A rough path led down through the bonsai forest to the stream. Picking my way over tumbled boulders, I went down into the creek bed and, leaving my sisters and the gaggle of other sightseers behind, walked upstream. When I was far enough away, hidden from sight, and the voices of the day trippers had faded, I chose a deep pool between two boulders, took off my clothes and lay down naked in the freezing water. After a while I turned over, put my head under, and opened my eyes to the dazzle and speckle of pebbles below; and

194

beneath the trickle of water heard the vast silence of the mountain opening my ears.

Afterwards I felt chilled, cleansed, back in touch with some substratum of personality or history which is always there, like a reflection in a dark pool which cannot be seen while the sun is out but rises slowly to the surface at the crepuscular hour. Coming down naked with my clothes in my hand, I met my elder sister walking up the creek to find me. I dressed and went back with her to the cars. Our other sister had not come down to the river. We parted there on the mountain road and drove away in opposite directions, our elder sister back to Wellington, I and my other sister to Auckland.

Over the thirty or so years since the family left Ohakune, I had been back and back and back, searching for something so lost I did not even know what it was. Some of these visits 'home' were attended by bad luck, like the time I left my wallet, with all I had in it – a hundred dollars – in the phone box outside the Post Office after an unsuccessful attempt to ring Stan Frost. Without spending money, I had to cut short my stay and in the middle of a cold and rainy night walk the couple of kilometres to the Junction to catch the train.

On the visit with the photographer, he'd shot off a couple of rolls of black and white film as we traversed the map of my childhood memories. The prints were intended to illustrate an account of the state of this map at that time, Christmas 1980, but although I did write something, it was never finished, and joined all the other incomplete or unpublished pieces I wrote over the years about this place and my relation to it. Most of these were poems rather than prose, and while they sometimes evoked the physical setting and emotional climate prevailing there, they never arrived at a lucid account of their own subject matter.

How could they? Although it may once have done so, a *where* can no longer answer the question *who?* They were dissimulations of an inchoate identity, doomed attempts to define a self through a survey of its origins, as if the essence of personality could be expressed through a sense of place. Landscape as a reflection, or manifestation, of self was the ostensible subject – and especially the landscape of childhood. Or rather, it was not the landscape, but the self which regarded the landscape which was the real subject of this poetry; or not even that, but the self regarding the self who wrote the poetry of landscape. But there were no poems after this latest visit; in the fallout, as if it were some kind of addiction, I decided to give up altogether the writing of poetry.

I wrote my first poem when I was fourteen, in response to a request from a Mr Heather for something for the school magazine. This lumbering anapaestic contraption was inspired by a photograph of a wildebeest stampede from a book called *Serengeti Shall Not Die* (1960) by Bernard and Michael Grzimek; I was mortified when Mr Heather changed my *wildebeest* into *wild beasts*, but I didn't say anything. What I got out of it was a sense of my own power as a person who could write a poem: self-ascribed power remained a core attribute of the delusional self I would inhabit for the rest of my poetry-writing life, along with an association between that power and a kind of virtue. As if only the good wrote well.

It's not unusual for an adolescent to write a bad poem and publish it in the school magazine; what is perhaps unusual is for the adolescent to continue writing bad poems into young adulthood and beyond. Poetry had value in our home. My father had written when he was younger, although he never mentioned it until much later, when he was an old man and I asked him about his small, battered collection of poetry books from the 1940s. My mother, however, was given to mysterious pronouncements on the subject. Once when I was going on a trip by myself that involved some dead time spent on a railway platform waiting for a connection, I asked her what I was to do. *I don't know*, she said in her impatient voice. Then, reflectively: *Why don't you write a poem?* I pondered the advice for years. Was that what you did when you had nothing else to do?

Other things she said suggested that the writing of poetry was a higher calling. I didn't realise my mother wrote poetry herself; if I had, I might have taken more notice of what she was saying. Or less. As it was, I think I internalised the values she found in poetry: mystery; authority; wisdom; insight; power; virtue. I didn't realise, and perhaps she didn't either, that those values can be in the poetry without being in the poet; or in the poet without being in the poetry. I think she thought, as I came to, that they could be assumed as attributes of the self, and were worth assuming, because poetry was the key to the soul and only poets had that key. Under her largely unsuspected influence, I decided to become one myself.

So the activity was always secondary to the role. I assumed the identity of an Exalted Being, thinking that poetry would flow from it the way water flows from a spring. It didn't. It was hard to find a place to begin, and even harder to end; I don't think I ever finished a poem, I only abandoned them. I don't mean fashionably abandoned in that cool modernist way, I mean abandoned in frustration, like a botched piece of carpentry. This hell of indecision on a technical level was one of the things that made it a relief to quit the practice.

It's weird how my ideal of the poet as Exalted Being survived all those misbegotten attempts. I thought the poems were true in conception and flawed only in the execution; that work could overcome these flaws and the original would shine forth in all its glory. Not so. My problem is simply put: I made the unwarranted assumption that the experiences I wrote about were significant because they happened to me. My observations were valuable because I was an Exalted Being; and those other, unexalted beings, the meat and potato readers of poetry, would yearn to be like me and could, perhaps, through the poem in which I used landscape and childhood to evoke my own derelict emotions, for a moment even become me.

This is where addiction comes in; this is the schizophrenic plot I was mired in. I use the word advisedly: in R. D. Laing's currently unfashionable existential description of schizophrenia, a false self is constructed in order to protect the real self from exposure to inadequacies which may be revealed through interaction with the world. But preventing the 'real' self from interacting with the world causes it to wither and fade, while the false self, always a fabrication, becomes increasingly dissociated from both world and 'real' self. That was my position: my 'real' self, the Exalted Being, had to be protected from knowledge of the badness of the poetry it wrote by the duplicity of a false self which, increasingly, as at the Centennial dance, was exposed as a ramshackle, barely credible fiction made out of nostalgia and yearning.

The contradiction between the self-regarding self and the false face the world sees can be resolved by a lopping of self or world. Lopping the world is what the Laingian schizophrenic in extremity does, and it is usually calamitous: the illusion of self-sufficiency can be nourished for a time, but ultimately you diminish to the point of nullity. Lopping of the self – radical surgery to cut out the Exalted Being – with a mixture of desperation and tough-mindeness can be done. My addiction was to a self-image sustained by illusions I generated in the poetry I wrote: if I stopped doing that, maybe I could learn to live as an ordinary person in the world.

The exemplar of ex-poets is Rimbaud. One of the more embarrassing memories of my twenties is the way I used to pretend it was no use writing because Rimbaud had said it all already. It's no comfort knowing I wasn't the only drug-addled hipster who thought that way. What did we think we were doing, imitating the doom-obsessed cadences of Robert Lowell's *Imitations*? Nobody knows why Rimbaud, who didn't ever give up drugs, stopped writing poetry, because he never said another word about it. Well, he did say one: *rinçures*. It was to a business colleague in Aden who, on a boat back from France, learned that the taciturn, perhaps embittered coffee merchant and trader in general goods he knew on a day-to-day basis was famous in Paris for his poetry. *Rinçures*, the trader gnarled, when Bardey asked about it. Slops. Dishwater. Rinsings. Rimbaud may have been a *poète maudit*, but he was never a bad poet; he was immaculate. And he knew – or had known – it. Perhaps all the answers, along with his Abyssinian book, are in that trunk of his writings the British Army found and then lost again at the railhead near Harar in 1942.

Surely there is a question going begging here? I mean, what's the difference? I doubt if Bobby Hammond and my other ex-school friends would see any distinction between what I'm doing now

– literary non-fiction – and poetry. It's the same thing, isn't it? Who cares if the lines reach the edge of the page or not? Fernando Pessoa, in the person of his semi-heteronym, prose writer Bernardo Soares, insisted there is a difference: *In prose we speak freely. We can incorporate musical rhythms, and still think. We can incorporate poetic rhythms, and yet remain outside them. An occasional poetic rhythm won't disturb prose, but an occasional prose rhythm makes poetry fall down. Prose encompasses all art, in part because words contain the whole world, and in part because the untrammeled word contains every possibility for saying and thinking.*

The other reason Soares preferred prose to poetry is my own: *I have no choice, because I'm incapable of writing in verse.* This is un-questionable, but the contention that prose is the higher form can be argued: perhaps Pessoa, who was not one but at least four different poets, and felt compelled to see things from every possible point of view, was being mischievous when he put those words in Soares' mouth. Perhaps, too, his idea of poetry, *circa* 1931, was more traditional than those now prevalent. On the other hand, no one would dispute that there are among us some who are incapable of doing the things they most want to do, and this leaves them with a psychological problem which is peculiarly resistant to resolution. How do we come to have ambitions beyond our abilities?

I never told my mother I gave up writing poetry. In the mistaken belief that I was an Exalted Being, she encouraged me to the last – just before she died, she asked to include previously published poems of mine in two anthologies she had a hand in editing. I refused, but did not say why; she did not ask. We no longer talked literature, had not done so for a long time: it was a way of avoiding arguments. From the first real conversations we had, when I was in the Seventh Form at college and she was my English teacher, we differed. I still remember our earliest literary quarrel. The class was doing Yeats and I hesitated over one of his short lyrics, *The Choice*:

> The intellect of man is forced to choose
> Perfection of the life, or of the work

And if it take the second must refuse
A heavenly mansion, raging in the dark.

I didn't see why you couldn't have the perfect work and the heavenly mansion; I still don't. My mother thought the choice was valid and had to be made. Looking back, I can see that, in the mid 1960s, with literary ambitions her husband and six children did not even know she had, of course she felt that way. She had postponed her work for so long it must have seemed like something gone forever. All she had was our unheavenly home.

Another Yeatsian remark she liked to quote derives ultimately from the French writer Villiers de l'Isle-Adam, whose play, *Axel*, Yeats saw in Paris in 1894: *As for living, our servants will do that for us*. The smug elitism incensed the seventeen-year-old socialist in me but, again, as our unpaid servant, she must have found a secret irony there which was probably a comfort to her as she did the housework. We do have to do our own living. The choice she made, which was to dedicate her life to poetry, left her lonely. Although she was successful, both in the sense of becoming a popular poet and, at times, a good one too, and although she was surrounded by family and friends, at the close of almost every day no one was there with her, and she felt this lack grievously. Nowadays, when I look in the copy of Yeats's *Collected Poems* she gave me, it's the second quatrain of *The Choice* I linger over:

When all that story's finished what's the news?
In luck or out the toil has left its mark:
That old perplexity an empty purse
Or the day's vanity, the night's remorse.

In the literary arguments we had later, in the 1970s, I vehemently contested her neo-romantic views without ever clarifying my own arduous radicalism, probably because what I said and what I did were so at odds with one another: what is more neo-romantic than a poetry of landscape written in the voice of the lyric I? It took me a long time to admit that rhetoric contradicted practice; longer to abandon the practice. After that, I avoided talking poetry with her so as not to say I did not like my own verse because it reminded me of hers. Or that I did not like hers because it resembled mine. We were poetic kin but, even at seventeen, I was rejecting the affinity.

Is there an unwillingness to look at mother–son relationships in our culture? Amidst the plethora of recent books on family – mothers and daughters, fathers and sons, fathers and daughters, siblings and grandparents of all descriptions – I can't think of one about mothers and sons. There are a lot of unanswered questions. Are we still a culture in which some married men after a certain age start calling their wives *Mum*? What are the implications of this startling usage? Do we marry our mothers or just never outgrow them? Why is the sacredness of motherhood almost always evoked when sons are spoken of, hardly ever for daughters? Why is it so difficult to talk about this?

I've always assumed that men call their wives *Mum* because their kids do, or at least started doing it when their kids did: *Ask Mum*. Probably for the same reason, you do come across wives who call their husbands *Dad*, though it's less common. What about mothers' love for sons? There are cases in the literature of women violently in love with their sons, and plenty of anecdotal material about the kinds of sons this love can breed: recklessly depraved, cruelly repressed, startlingly flamboyant, dromomaniacal, weirdly accomplished. Why has no one gone into this in any detail?

My mother loved me but I was always suspicious of her love. I felt it was the adolescent in me that she loved – the promise, the clever boy who shared clever jokes with her. When I told her once I thought her preferred age for me was about twelve, she laughed and looked away; it was her veiled laugh, concealing surprise, vexation, denial. Was it because she loved the pre-sexual me, or for some other reason? In the days when we did get on, she used to flirt with me and I'd flirt back. Nothing unusual there: she was of a generation which used flirting as a way of gaining access to power otherwise denied them. After a while I found the flirting we did awkward and false, and ceased to indulge; oddly, nothing ever replaced it. If we couldn't flirt, we couldn't relate, it seemed, except coldly, across a gulf, like disappointed lovers.

Our flirting carried the implication that we were better than other people. We were superior types: clever, sensitive, accomplished, educated and so on. She would flatter and I would preen. A presumption of superiority which must constantly be reinforced using a certain kind of banter is not conviction, however; it is insecurity. The coruscating doubt which wore away my confidence in the poetry I wrote was also part of my inheritance from my mother. Yet she always encouraged me. And if my role, in her mind, especially in later years, was somehow to support her in the face of the same doubt, then my refusal to do so was probably another cause of the coldness between us. Her response to my refusal was always simply to ask again. And again. And again. Until she died. And this too is characteristic of mothers with their sons: however disappointing the man, they never quite lose hope in the boy.

Overwhelming desire has sinister applications. The compulsion to shape a child can warp growth: generating hopeful monsters fated never to prevail, pallid clones, the agonies of the self-destructor. There is steel in the manipulations of sons by mothers denied a direct lever on the world. I never quite believed my poetic ambition was my own; I thought it was my mother's displaced onto me when it looked as though she would not get her chance. When she did, it was open to me to feel abandoned like a poor draft or a bad poem, discarded once, then picked up again and again over the years in search of that elusive twist which would make everything fall into place. I resisted the idea as strenuously as I tried to turn myself into a poet; it was a long time before I realised self as poem and self as poet were twin answers to the same demand. You will not be happy / successful / admired / fulfilled / loved unless you are a good person/poem. You will face misery/failure/obloquy/frustration/hatred if you don't produce them yourself. That's more or less how it went.

The constant iteration of the I – implied or stated – in lyric poetry seems to me now a symptom of sickness. The clamour of I's, each with their need, their view and their say-so, is tiresome beyond words. To add your own I to the others is to obscure signals with static. The planet is going up while you are listening for the unique accent of your own voice. But the reiteration of the I in my head was more painful: while someone was being born, loving, living or dying before me, 'I' was looking to put this 'experience' into 'poetry'. That was the sickness in me; that was what made me wild to get out of the maze. It meant letting go of my mother, and leaving her to the labyrinth; but that was where she wanted to be, and anyway, such was the cacophony in my own head, I had no choice but to go.

For the Exalted Being has a shadow, a monster bred of high hopes and their disappointment, allied with an excoriating self-consciousness. Call him the Lacerator, who can be turned either against the world or against the self. Since I have the more robust soul, mine has been turned mostly against the world; I suspect that to the degree I have done so, our dead sister was prey to self-laceration. In her diaries she is specific about her voices: the one that told her she was better than other people – in a word, exalted; and the other, *low down and to the side*, the relentless Self Lacerator, endlessly vicious, endlessly hating, who said she was so worthless she must die.

Most of the time she did not credit her special voice, calling it delusional and resisting its blandishments; the other, while no less delusional, she could not withstand. It attacked her in bursts, or waves, which she learned to see coming. These were of fearful intensity, and included visual hallucinations: the loathsome face of her tormentor mutating out of walls or houses. Her decision to end her life was not taken in the throes of one of these attacks, but during the aura, when she felt it coming on. She could neither prevent nor endure what was approaching and made the only escape left to her.

She was diagnosed as schizophrenic, a modern disease, first described medically in 1896. *A peculiar destruction of the inner cohesiveness of the psychic personality with predominant damage to the emotional life and the will*, wrote Emil Kraepelin of the disorder he called *dementia praecox*. The word schizophrenia was coined a few years later, in 1908, by Eugen Bleuler, who called it *a specific type of alteration of thinking, feeling, and relation to the external world which appears nowhere else* . . . What the condition was called before these early definitions is unclear. *Possession*, perhaps; or *second sight*; or simply *madness*. (One of our forebears – it was either my mother's father's mother or his grandmother – had second sight, which perhaps explains the schizophrenia running in the family; on the other hand, our paternal line is also afflicted with poetry and mental illness.) Whatever diagnostic tools have been used in the last century, and whatever causes adduced – heredity, chemical imbalance, familial warps, sexual abuse in childhood – the existential fact of schizophrenia remains, an irreducible, almost indescribable experience a small percentage of people all over the globe suffer with torment, and, occasionally, exultation.

It is a characteristic of schizophrenia that people with it commonly have no insight into their condition. My sister did not believe she was schizophrenic, and it was her decision to stop taking the pills prescribed for the condition which brought on the final crisis: she did not want her experience reduced to formulae, nor her psyche to be described in terms of a pathology. However wrong-headed that may be, and however much we who are left wonder if she would still be with us had she accepted diagnosis and treatment, her courage and willingness to act according to her beliefs cannot be denied. She who had such a fragile hold on things nevertheless did not doubt her psyche was more complex than any exterior description of it and had to be lived on its own terms. That the struggle exhausted her is no surprise. Despite her fierce determination to comprehend, there was a black hole, passing all understanding, in the centre of her being.

In the way of our family, we were twinned: our elder sisters; myself and her; our two younger sisters. We were also, as a family, competitive with one another, and the cruelty of rivalry impacted damagingly on the younger sibling of the pair my sister and I made as I handed the punishment for failure on. Was the natural fellow-feeling of sister and brother always mastered by the desire to out-do one another? No, not always, but often. Competitiveness was nursed into us, not for the sake of misery or strife, but as a means of *forcing*

– my sister's term. *Comparative thinking* is another. For the sake of excellence, in other words. To better our poor post-colonial selves.

We were secular Methodists: our father grew up in a Methodist household, and our mother, the child of free-thinking, spiritualist Douglas Social Creditors, nevertheless subscribed to a version of the ideology which gave the Methodists their name. The Holy Club, of which John Wesley was a member at Lincoln College, Oxford, in the late 1720s, organised every hour of every day, with specific times to pray, read, eat and exercise, and adhered strictly to religious precepts and practices, among them the visiting of prisons and comforting of the sick: it was because of this systematic routine that its members were derisively called *methodists* by their fellows. We were enjoined to follow a similar regime in the cultivation of our intellectual skills, and in the process learned to converse not with god but ourselves. Yet the subject of this discourse was the same as that of the religious: our own merit. And the Pentecost? That was to be the solitary ecstasy of creation, in which the one would speak for the many.

This method now has the approbation of the whole culture behind it. However destructive it is within families, we, as a people, still believe in it as a motor for achievement in all the larger social groups. Its accent is everywhere, along with the fear, the scorn, the anger, the pain and the overwhelming need for revenge it breeds. Most of all it is with us in the base need to assert oneself by the torture or destruction of others. Competitiveness within the family is worse, enshrining the meanest qualities of our polity in the individual psyche, there to flourish in the practice of self-aggrandisement, not towards the world at large but against someone close: the closer the better. For when all others have fallen back or away, this is the hell of exalted and unexalted alike: negativity visited on the self – that is to say, no one.

In one of her last letters to me, my sister quoted what Lear says of Cordelia: *Her voice was ever soft,/Gentle and low, an excellent thing in a woman.* She meant to question the enforced passivity of women, especially good women. I can still hear the lucid, high, light quality of her questioning, utterly clear-sighted. She must have known she was herself an exemplar of Cordelia and, like Cordelia, loved according to her bond and died from taking the hatred of the world into her soul. Her empathy was such that everything penetrated; she saw people as they were, in all their beauty and terror; and her constant striving was to give back only what was uncontaminated with fear or loathing. Her tragedy was that despite her desperate search for a role, her very gifts meant there was none; no way to express her voices for the common good. Rather die than witness the death of love is something she might have said.

Or was it that she knew her insight was failing? Her clarity of perception, as intense as it sometimes was, deserted her absolutely when she was in the throes of an attack and increasingly became diminished or occluded at other times as well. So perhaps it is fanciful to say that in another place and time she might have been called to an oracle. Divinity is our first monoculture: from gods to god to none, with the fanaticism of true believers everywhere a last revenge of the One. It is 1,650 years since the water of speech was quenched at Delphi, a long time to be without the guidance of voices within; the miracle is they're still with us, now irredeemably our own. How are they to be spoken?

The wilful stilling of my poetic voice did not end the cacophony in my head. Nor did I expect that it would. Rather, its absence initiated a long diminuendo towards a calm I may never attain but will always seek. I located the source of this now departed voice in the landscape of my childhood, but the location was never precise. It was somewhere abroad, haunting the ramshackle houses of Waimarino County, wending away into weedy paddocks like the Mangawhero, lost in the wild bush on the other side of Dreadnought Road or frozen with the snows of Ruapehu.

Has it gone home for good? I have not been back to Ohakune since the Centennial, but one day I will. In the interim, when I think of that place, it is the two lakes, unvisited on that trip, to which I return. What passed there between my sister and mother? They are the two in the family who most resembled each other, and this resemblance has only strengthened since our mother's death. Was this the burden of their conflict there, the unappeasable demand to distinguish self from other, daughter from mother? Or was it just another of those power struggles our family was addicted to? Or are they the same thing?

The time I went there we got out of the car to walk the rest of the way just as a goods train came rattling and swaying down the railway line. I stood as close as I could to the rolling stock, as I did when I was a kid, ionising my aura and feeling the negativities strip away in the rush of the slipstream. On the other side, a dirt road and then a bush track led to the first of the lakes, called, inscrutably, the Dry Lake. It was a round of black water fringed with pale green raupo, where black shags perched on the black stumps of sunken trees, hanging out their wings to dry. The track skirts this smaller lake on the way to the second, the Mirror Lake, so called because on a clear day you can see in it a perfect reflection of the mountain.

On the path that circles the Mirror Lake there are places where you can undress, go down to the quaking marshy edge and slip into the cold water to swim and watch your pale body trail above the unknown depths of the crater. This we did, turning the bush to a ripple of yellow-green around us. The day was still, but not so still that afterwards we could not see the reformed image of the mountain tremble when the merest breath of wind came down off the snow, as if that obdurate mass of ice and stone was, in reflection, no more than a thought.

Now the Mirror Lake, with its ghostly, unclimbable mountain, seems like the eye of that pure landscape I could not enter into, could not make over into 'poetry' – something existing apart from the self or the self's quest for oblivion; and needfully apart: renunciation as the only possible form of possession. The skull in the window is nothing to this other mirror, which endures even when no one is there to see. Lake, mountain, mountain, lake, doubling and redoubling, make a truer picture of the self: as mirror, as ruin, as other, as home; home, finally, for all the others.